Our Families
Our Neighborhoods
Our Communities
Our Country Today
Our Country's History
Our World Today

OUR COUNTRY'S HISTORY

Senior Author

Stanley Klein,
Professor of Education,
Western Connecticut State College

Program Consultants

E. Gene Barr, Elementary Social Studies Resource
Teacher, East Lansing, Michigan, Public Schools

Dr. Marlowe Berg, Professor of Education,
College of Education, San Diego State University,
San Diego, California

Dr. Marilee Bradbury, Former Resource Specialist,
Social Studies Department,
Jefferson County, Colorado, Schools

Dr. Claudia Crump, Professor of Education,
Indiana University Southeast, New Albany, Indiana

Jeanne Freeze, Elementary Social Studies
Supervisor, Pinellas County, Florida, Schools

Dr. Cara Garcia, Assistant Professor of Education,
Graduate School of Education,
Pepperdine University, Los Angeles, California

Deanna Gordon, Elementary Supervisor
of Health, Science, and Social Studies,
Roanoke County, Virginia, Schools

Dr. Richard Haynes, Coordinator of Social Studies,
Durham County, North Carolina, Schools

Dr. David Hill, Associate Professor of Education,
University of Mississippi

Ida Hunt, Assistant Principal,
Austin, Texas, Independent School District

Dr. Harold Karbal, Curriculum Administrator,
Region 6, Detroit, Michigan, Schools

Jimmie Martinez, Former Resource Teacher,
Social Studies, San Diego, California, City Schools

Dr. Alma Swiers, Director of Curriculum Services,
Kern County, California, Schools

Carlee Whipple, Instructional Consultant,
North Area, Memphis, Tennessee, City Schools

STECK-VAUGHN COMPANY

Austin, Texas

SOCIAL STUDIES CURRICULUM SPECIALISTS

Dr. Lois Wolf
Former Director of Special Education
Bank Street College of Education
New York, New York

Dr. Nancy Wyner
Assistant Professor of Education
Wheelock College
Boston, Massachusetts

READABILITY CONSULTANTS

Dr. Joseph C. Cillizza
Professor of Education
Western Connecticut State College

John M. Devine
Assistant Professor of Education
Western Connecticut State College

CLASSROOM READERS FOR THIS LEVEL

Simon Alvarez, Longfellow Elementary School, Albuquerque, New Mexico
Sigmund A. Boloz, Ganado Intermediate School, Ganado, Arizona
Barbara Capron, Roger Wellington Elementary School, Belmont, Massachusetts
Dolores Coards, Public School 125, New York, New York
Winifred Doan, Gertrude Case Elementary School, Knoxville, Pennsylvania
Carol Hutson, Fall-Hamilton Elementary School, Nashville, Tennessee
Virginia Jasontek, Parham Elementary School, Cincinnati, Ohio
Diane Kostick, Arnett C. Lines Elementary School, Barrington, Illinois
Sister Mary Patricia, Principal, St. Augustine/Our Lady of Mt. Carmel School,
    Bridgeport, Pennsylvania
Ron Sima, Coordinating Training Teacher, Los Angeles Unified School District,
    Los Angeles, California
Judy Wooster, Green Acres Elementary School, Tonawanda, New York

CONSULTANTS FOR SOCIAL STUDIES DISCIPLINES

History
Dr. Burton F. Beers
Professor of History
North Carolina State University
Raleigh, North Carolina

Government/Citizenship
Dr. F. Chris Garcia
Professor of Political Science
University of New Mexico
Albuquerque, New Mexico

Geography
Dr. James Kracht
Chairman, Department of
Curriculum Instruction
Illinois State University
Normal, Illinois

Economics
Dr. William A. Luker
Director, Center for Economic Education
North Texas State University
Denton, Texas

Sociology
Dr. Susan Rosenholtz
Research Associate
Department of Sociology
Stanford University
Palo Alto, California

CONTENTS

GLOBES AND MAPS

CHARTS, GRAPHS, AND DIAGRAMS

STAFF

Project Editor: Stephen M. Lewin
Editor: Malcolm C. Jensen
Editorial Director: William F. Goodykoontz
Curriculum Editor: Richard Ravich
Editorial Developer: Claudia Cohl
Revision Editor: Katherine Randall
Project Coordinator:
    Susan Washburn Buckley
Writers: Linda Beech, Daniel Rosen
Contributors: Burton Albert, Elaine Israel,
    Janet McHugh, Anita Soucie, Cindy Thames
Research: Glen Davis, Diana Reische,
    Anita Soucie

Production Editor: Nancy J. Smith

Senior Art Director: Mary Mars
Art Director: Carol Steinberg
Revision Art Editor: Dorothy Irwin
Designer: Kirchoff/Wohlberg,
    Mary Anne Asciutto
Editorial Assistant: Rosemary Moran
Cover Design: Skip Sorvino, Jack G. Tauss
Cover Illustration: Guy Billout

Coordinator, Field-Testing:
    Patricia M. Conniffe

CHAPTER

1 We, the American People

The book you are about to read is a story—an exciting adventure-filled story about our country. It is a **history** of the United States.

What is history?

History is the story of everything that happened before today. It is everything that happened in the past. You have a history. Your family has a history. The United States has a history.

You are not very old, so you have a short history. Your parents are older, so they have a longer history. The United States is even older. So its history is longer than your history and your parents'.

A HISTORY OF PEOPLE

Your history is a history of people. First of all, of course, there is you. Then there are your parents and your other relatives. There are also your neighbors, your teachers, and your friends. All of these different people have played an important role in your life. Their thoughts and their actions have helped make you the person you are today.

The history of the United States is also a history of people. This is because it is people who make up a country. Their thoughts and their actions—past and present—help make a country what it is today. Look at the Americans pictured on pages 12–13. What do their pictures tell you about the people of the United States?

A few quick answers probably pop into your head right away. Americans differ in sex and age. They also differ in looks. But *how* are they different in looks? The answer to this question can tell you a lot about the kinds of people who have been part of American history.

The faces of Americans show that many different kinds of people created our history. Americans have their roots in

On page 10: Americans are all ages, sizes, shapes, and colors. About 230 million people live in the United States.

many different parts of the world. They have a wide variety of religions, languages, foods, and holidays.

The United States has often been called "a nation of immigrants." An **immigrant** (IM-*uh-grunt*) is someone who moves to a country from some other country. Perhaps you are an immigrant. Perhaps your parents, grandparents, or great-grandparents—your **ancestors** (AN-*sess-terz*)—were immigrants. Every American is either an immigrant or the **descendant** (*dee*-SEND-*unt*) of people who were immigrants. Long ago or recently, someone in your family came to the U.S. from another country.

Who Are the Americans?

Look at the person in picture 1. She is an American Indian. She is the descendant of the first people to come to the Americas. Her ancestors came here many thousands of years ago. Look at the person in picture 2. He is a Mexican American. His grandparents came here from Mexico about 40 years ago. The language his family speaks at home is Spanish because this is the language of Mexico. People from Mexico first came to settle our land more than 400 years ago.

Many Americans have come from Spanish-speaking places other than Mexico. They have come from islands such as Puerto Rico (PWAIR-*toe* REE-*koe*) and Cuba. They have also come from mainland countries in Central and South America. Today Spanish-speaking Americans, or Hispanics (*hi*-SPAN-*iks*), are the fastest-growing group in the United States.

The people in pictures 3, 4, and 5 all come from European backgrounds. Today in the United States, there are more people with European ancestors than there are people from any other region of the world. More than 35 million people have come as immigrants to the U.S. from the countries of Europe. The number is still growing. The great-great-grandparents of the girl in picture 3 came here from Britain about 150 years ago. The grandparents of the man in picture 4 came here from Italy about 60 years ago. The woman in picture 5 came here from the Soviet Union a few years ago.

Can you tell the backgrounds of the other people on this page? Perhaps the following information will help.

There are millions of Asian Americans in our country today. The first big group of Asian immigrants to the U.S.

came from China about 150 years ago. Today there are many Chinese Americans and Japanese Americans in the U.S. Many of these people live in the western part of our country.

Most immigrants came here because they wanted to. The ancestors of one group of Americans, however, were forced to come. Hundreds of years ago, many black people were taken from their homes in Africa and brought to the Americas as slaves. More than 100 years ago, slavery was outlawed in the U.S. But black Americans have had to fight long and hard to win full rights as American citizens.

The history of the United States is the history of all these people—and many more. It is the story of what made people come here. It is the story of what they found when they arrived and how they built a new life. It is the story of how their new land changed them and how they changed their new land. It is a story of people of many different languages, beliefs, and customs, and how these people built a strong and a free country.

A HISTORY OF FREEDOM

An important part of our history is how Americans have searched for freedom. "Freedom from what?" you might ask. "Freedom to do what?"

You will see as you read this book that these questions have many answers. We can say, though, that they all boil down to one answer—the freedom to make choices about one's own life.

Some of the first people to come here from Europe came to make their own choices about religion. Many of them were not allowed to practice their religion in their old countries. So they came here to be free to worship as they chose.

Some people came here to be free to find new land. They could not own land in the countries where they had been born. Sometimes this was because there was no land available. Sometimes there was land, but poor people could not afford its high price. Sometimes governments did not allow certain people to own land. So people came here, where they had their choice of land.

Still other people came here to be free to choose new lives for themselves. Maybe they had been poor in their home countries. There may not have been any jobs for them there. Here in the United States, workers were needed. Here people could choose new kinds of work. Here they had a chance to improve their lives.

Perhaps the most basic freedom people sought in America was the freedom to choose their own government. Two hundred years ago, Americans fought a war for this freedom. As a result of this war, the American Revolution, a new nation called the United States came into being.

The government of the United States is based on the idea of **democracy.** In a democracy, the power to govern comes from the people. They elect people to represent them in government. Then these **representatives** make or carry out the laws of the land. This kind of democracy is called a **republic.**

These eighteen-year-olds register to vote. Voting is the right of every citizen.

LEARNING ABOUT HISTORY

Suppose that you wanted to put together a history of yourself. You could start with the things you remember. Perhaps you remember the first day you went to school. There are some things, though, that you do not remember—the day you were born or the first time you walked. How would you find out about the parts of your history you don't remember?

One way is to ask people who may remember—your parents, or an older brother or sister, for example. Another way of learning about the past is by using old photographs.

There are other ways to search too. You may be able to find **documents** (DOCK-*yuh-ments*) about yourself. (A document is a written record.) Your birth certificate (*sur-*TIFF-*i-kit*) tells you when and where you were born. Even an old letter or diary written by a relative might tell you something more about yourself. Each bit of information is another piece of your history. What do the things on page 17 tell you about Sarah Davidson?

Finding Historical Sources

Putting together the history of the United States is like piecing together your own past. The way you learn about yourself is the way **historians** (*hi-*STOR-*ee-unz*), people who study the past, learn about our country's history.

Like you, historians sometimes use **primary sources.** Primary sources can be people who were at an event that happened long ago. These people can tell the historian what they remember about the event.

A primary source can also be a document that was written at the time and tells what happened. These documents might be letters, diaries, or government papers. They might be a few years old or hundreds of years old. Each one of them tells a little about the past.

Pictures can also be primary sources. Photographs have been taken of people and events for more than 125

Dear Aunt Alicia,

Thank you so much for
of congratulations on the birth
Sarah Alicia. We very much
little baby to have the name of
love so much. Sarah Alicia i
strong, and a joy to behold.
slept through the night for the
is now nine pounds 11 ounces an
She's also got quite a temp

219 West 81 St.

THE CITY OF NEW YORK—DEPARTMENT OF HEALTH
BUREAU OF VITAL RECORDS
CERTIFICATE OF BIRTH REGISTRATION

CERTIFICATE OF BIRTH

DEPARTMENT OF HEALTH

DATE FILED OCT 23 '72 1:19

Birth No. 156-72-115442

CHILD	FULL NAME	First Name	Middle Name	Last Name
		SARAH	ALICIA	DAVIDSON
	Female	NUMBER OF CHILDREN born	ODC	DATE (Month)(Day)(Year) June 20 1972	Hour 4:26 PM

Place of Birth: New York, Manhattan
Name of Hospital or Institution: Roosevelt Hospital

MOTHER'S FULL MAIDEN NAME: Joan Rebecca Lipson
MOTHER'S AGE at time: 31
MOTHER'S BIRTHPLACE, City and State: New York

Residence: NY — NY — New York
Street and house number: 219 West 81 Street

FATHER'S FULL NAME: Michael Frederick Sabin Davidson
FATHER'S AGE at time: 31
FATHER'S BIRTHPLACE: New York

Date of Report: June 20 1972

Signed: H. L. Luschinsky, M.D., F.A.C.O.G.
Name of Signer
120 CENTRAL PARK SOUTH
NEW YORK, N.Y. 10019
Address

BUREAU OF RECORDS AND STATISTICS — DEPARTMENT OF HEALTH — THE CITY OF NEW YORK

Print here the mailing address of mother. Copy of this certificate will be mailed to her when it is filed with the Department of Health.

Name: Mrs. Joan Davidson
Address: 219 West 81 St   Apt 5 K
City: New York   State: NY   Zip Code: 10024

ABOVE IS AN EXACT COPY OF A CERTIFICATE OF BIRTH REGISTERED FOR YOUR CHILD. IT IS SENT WITHOUT CHARGE. IF THE CERTIFICATE CONTAINS ANY ERRORS, RETURN THIS COPY WITH THE CORRECT INFORMATION TO THE BUREAU OF VITAL RECORDS, 125 NORTH STREET, NEW YORK, N.Y., 10013. YOU WILL BE ADVISED HOW TO HAVE THE RECORD CORRECTED. IT IS IMPORTANT TO DO THIS AT ONCE.

WARNING: DO NOT ACCEPT THIS TRANSCRIPT UNLESS THE RAISED SEAL OF THE DEPARTMENT OF HEALTH IS AFFIXED THEREON. THE REPRODUCTION OR ALTERATION OF THIS TRANSCRIPT IS PROHIBITED BY SECTION 3.21 OF THE NEW YORK CITY HEALTH CODE.

NOTICE: IN ISSUING THIS TRANSCRIPT OF THE RECORD, THE DEPARTMENT OF HEALTH OF THE CITY OF NEW YORK DOES NOT CERTIFY TO THE TRUTH OF THE STATEMENTS MADE THEREON, AS NO INQUIRY AS TO THE FACTS HAS BEEN PROVIDED BY LAW.

John V. Lindsay, MAYOR
Joseph A. Cimino, M.D., COMMISSIONER OF HEALTH
Paul E. Stern, CITY REGISTRAR

My folks told me that
we are going to be mov
-ing to Chicago in a
few months. My Dad
has a new job there
and he has to be close
to his work. I really
don't want to leave
all my friends here,
but Chicago sounds
great too. I told my
parents this and they
understood, but still
we must go.

April 14, 1980

Well, diary, the move
is only three weeks away.
Am I excited? Well, yes
and no. My folks have
bought a new house,
and I'm going to have
my own room there, as
well as a place to

years. Historians can see what certain people looked like, how they dressed, and what they were doing. Even before photography was invented, artists painted pictures of what they saw. Photos and pictures are helpful to historians.

Sometimes historians use **secondary sources.** Secondary sources may be people who were not present at an event but remember people telling them about it. Your great-grandparents may have told your grandparents about something that happened to them a long time ago. Your grandparents may have passed the story on to your parents. Your parents may have told you. Although you were not born when the event happened, you still know about it. Stories like these are important secondary sources of information. Any book written by someone who did not take part in an event is also a secondary source.

Digging for Proof

Sometimes, though, the search for information goes back so far that no one remembers what really happened. There may be clues, but there is no real proof. Sometimes the historian must depend on the work of **archaeologists** (*ahr-kee-*AHL-*uh-jistz*). These are scientists who search for evidence of people and places that may have disappeared thousands of years ago. By digging in the ground, they may uncover **artifacts** (AHR-*ti-faktz*), pieces of pottery, tools, or art made by people who lived in a place long since buried by time. These artifacts help archaeologists and historians to piece together the story of a people almost forgotten.

Why Study the Past?

The search for the past is important. For without knowing about what happened yesterday, it is hard to understand what is happening today. If we don't know the past, it is hard to build ideas and hopes for the future. This is why we study history. History tells us where we came from and how we got here.

CHAPTER 1 REVIEW

Words to Know

Choose eight words from the list below. Use each word in a sentence.

ancestor   historian/history
archaeologist   immigrant
artifact   primary source
democracy   representative
descendant   republic
document   secondary source

Facts to Review

1. What is history? Do you have a history?
2. Who were the first people to settle in America?
3. What is the main difference between the ways most Africans and most Europeans came to America?
4. What is democracy? Why do we say that our country, the United States, is a democracy?
5. What are some of the ways Americans differ from each other? What are some of the things Americans share?

Things to Think About

1. Pretend you have a pen pal in another country. Write a short letter to this pen pal describing the different backgrounds that Americans have.
2. Pretend you are coming to the United States today as an immigrant. You are going to live in the community you really do live in. Write a paragraph describing your reactions upon first seeing the "new" community that will be your home.

2 Our Land, the United States

The United States is the world's fourth largest country in size. Only the Soviet Union, Canada, and China are larger. The land the U.S. covers is one of the richest on Earth. It has climates that are good for growing things. Its many different areas give it a variety of "faces," many of them very beautiful.

Look at the pictures on pages 23–24. What do they tell you about the types of land the U.S. covers? What do they tell you about the use people make of the land?

AMERICA'S MANY FACES

The 50 states in the U.S. stretch from Maine in the east to Alaska and Hawaii in the west. Forty-eight of these states lie between Canada in the north and Mexico in the south. The other two states are Alaska and Hawaii. Can you find them on page 22? Puerto Rico is a special part of the U.S. It is an island in the Caribbean (*ka-ruh-*BEE-*un*) Sea. Although Puerto Rico is not a state, it is part of the U.S., and the people of Puerto Rico are American citizens.

Let's take a look at our big country. Imagine that you are in a spaceship flying across the U.S. from east to west. You will be looking at the **landforms** (the shape of the land) that make up our United States.

Our spaceship first flies over the *Coastal Plain*. Below we see a large, flat strip of land stretching from Maine to Florida and curving along the Gulf of Mexico. **Agriculture** (growing crops) is very important here. The main crops are vegetables, fruits, rice, cotton, sugar, and tobacco.

Many rivers cut through this area. These rivers provide water for both agriculture and **industry** (making goods). They also provide a way to move goods and crops from one place to another.

On page 20: The United States is a land of beautiful scenery. The rock cliff called El Capitan rises more than 600 feet *(183 meters)* from the floor of California's Yosemite Valley.

Our spaceship now passes over a long chain of mountains known as the *Appalachian Highlands*. The Appalachians (*ap-uh-*LAY-*chuns*) are a fairly low mountain range. Among them are fertile river valleys and **plateaus** (*pla-*TOZE), high flatlands. People here use the rivers for both shipping and water power. Industry has done well here.

West of the Highlands, the land flattens out as we pass over the *Interior* (*in-*TEER-*ee-er*) *Plains*. (*Interior* means "inside" or "within.") Actually it is two sets of plains. The Central Plains are to the east and the Great Plains are to the west. In the Central Plains, there is plenty of rain and the soil is fertile. The land itself is gently rolling. So farming is at its best here. There is less rain in the Great Plains. This land is used more for raising sheep and cattle.

Great rivers like the Mississippi and the Missouri cut through this region. Many smaller rivers flow into these big rivers. They help both agriculture and industry. It is from the Interior Plains that the U.S. gets much of its grain,

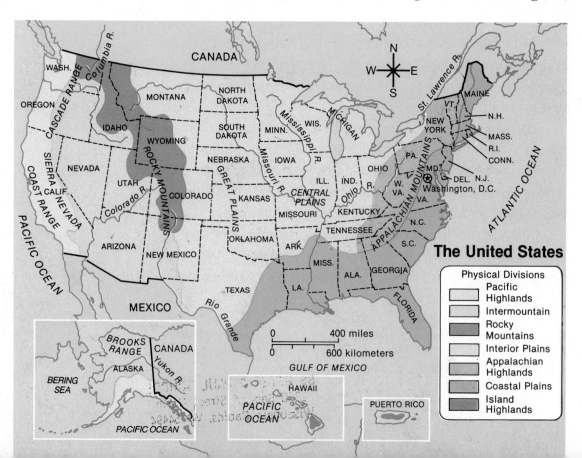

The United States

The scenery of the American land is full of variety. People bale hay on a Midwestern farm (top left). A disabled mountain climber enjoys the challenge of the Rockies (above right). On the Mississippi River, the Gateway Arch soars above St. Louis (right). The Golden Gate Bridge spans the entrance to San Francisco Bay in California (below).

Alaska borders on two oceans. Fishing is an important industry in many of its small coastal towns (right). Alaska's Mt. McKinley is the tallest mountain peak in North America (below).

meat, and dairy products. Many of the biggest industries in the U.S. are also located here.

You have crossed the Interior Plains. Suddenly rising in front of you are nature's skyscrapers—the *Rocky Mountains*. The Rockies are one of the biggest mountain ranges in the world. They are more than 300 miles *(483 kilometers)* wide. They stretch from Alaska through Canada and the U.S. into Mexico. The Rockies have some of the most rugged and most beautiful land in the United States.

Beyond the Rockies, you pass over more rugged and beautiful land. This land is the *Intermountain Area*. (*Inter* means "between.") This is a region of plateaus and **canyons** (deep, narrow valleys with steep sides).

As we continue to travel westward, we come to a series of mountain ranges known as the *Pacific Highlands*. In most areas, the Highlands of the Pacific Coast are quite close to the sea.

Far north is Alaska, the largest state in the U.S. More than 2,000 miles *(3,218 kilometers)* farther west is Hawaii, our only island state. It is made up of islands in the Pacific Ocean, formed over the years by the action of volcanoes.

Now you know something about the important landforms of the United States. You know that our large country looks different from one region to another. You have made an important step in learning about the land that all Americans share.

AMERICA'S MANY RESOURCES

The United States is lucky to have an enormous supply of **natural resources.** (Remember, resources are things we use. Natural resources are things we use that come from nature, like air, coal, or cattle.) The U.S. has fertile farmland and good climate for growing crops. It has seacoasts which give us food and shipping routes. The U.S. has rivers, lakes, and water power. It also has great forests which

Lumbering is an important industry in parts of the U.S. with rich forests.

give us wood for homes, ships, and tools. Finally, there are mineral resources. Coal, iron ore, oil, copper, gold, and silver all lie under the surface of the United States. Without all these resources, the U.S. could not have become the rich industrial country it is.

When people from Europe first arrived in America, they could see its vast resources. Half the land was covered with trees. So it seemed the wood supply would be endless. Rivers were many and pure. Surely they too could provide all the water a growing nation would ever need. Later Americans found great pockets of oil lying underground. Surely there would always be enough oil too.

For hundreds of years, Americans lived as though their resources were endless. As Americans grew in numbers, so did their use of resources. Unfortunately, Americans failed to look ahead. They pumped wastes into the rivers. They did not understand that they were poisoning the water. They stripped mineral resources from Earth in large amounts. They did not know that these resources could not be replaced and could run out one day.

Today we know how valuable our resources are. We have learned that we must treat them like a treasured gift. When we use them, we must treat them with care.

Reviewing Globes and Maps

One way to get a good picture of the U.S. is to use many different kinds of maps, such as political maps, relief maps, and climate maps. Each map will show you something different or new about our history. In this section, we will review some basic map and globe skills. If you master these skills, you will be able to get the most out of the maps and globes you find in this book.

Using Maps

Maps are drawings of Earth. A map can show all of Earth or just a part of it. The smaller the piece of land shown on a map, the more detail a map can show.

The two maps below are the same size. However, one is a map of California and the other is a map of one city in California—San Francisco. You can see that many more details are shown on the map of San Francisco.

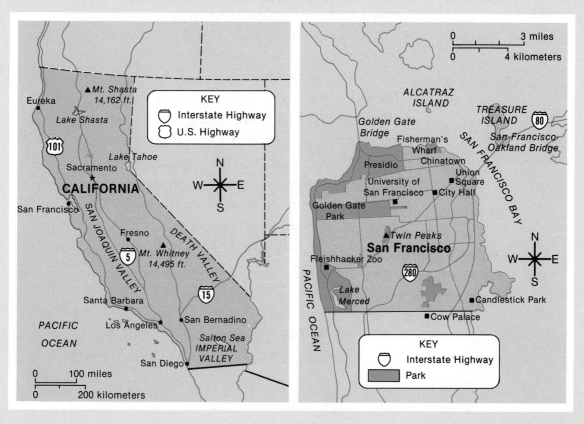

A map can show you how big a place is and how far one place is from another. Suppose you wanted to figure the distance from one side of California to the other. The **scale** tells you the distances on the map that equal 100 miles and 200 kilometers. How would you figure the distance across California? Which map would you use to figure the distance from San Francisco's City Hall to Fisherman's Wharf? What distances are shown on the scale of the city map?

Maps can show you where things are located. Many maps have a **compass rose** to help you tell directions. The compass rose on each of the maps on page 27 shows the four main **directions:** north, south, east, and west. You can see that San Francisco is north of Los Angeles and it is south of Eureka (*yuh-REE-kuh*).

This compass rose shows the halfway, or intermediate, directions as well. One of the halfway directions is southeast. Can you name the other three halfway directions?

On some maps, you might see only this: **N.** How can you tell where the other directions are?

Using Globes

Flat maps are easy to use, but a **globe** gives a more accurate picture of Earth. A globe, like Earth, is shaped like a sphere *(sfeer)*, or ball. A globe shows the true shapes and sizes of land. It also gives you a better understanding of direction—what it means to say that one place is to the north, south, east, or west of another place.

An imaginary line, called the **axis,** goes through the center of Earth. One end of the axis is called the South Pole, the other, the North Pole. Earth is always spinning around its axis. The direction it turns is always the same—east.

The equator is an imaginary line that runs east and west around the middle of Earth. The equator divides Earth into a Northern Hemisphere (HEM-*us-feer*) and a Southern Hemisphere. (*Hemi* means "half.")

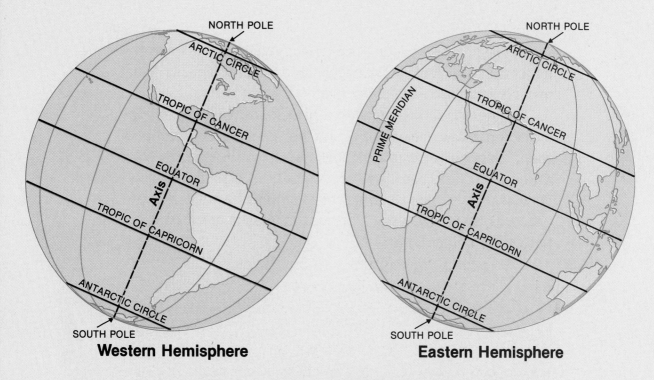

Western Hemisphere   **Eastern Hemisphere**

Other imaginary east-west lines circle Earth north and south of the equator. These lines are called **parallels** (PA-*ruh-lellz*). Parallel lines are lines that stay the same distance from each other and never meet. Can you name some other parallels circling Earth besides the equator?

You can use the parallels to help locate places on Earth. For instance, you can see that the tip of Florida lies just north of the Tropic of Cancer. Through what state does the Arctic Circle run? Does the equator run through the U.S.?

Other imaginary lines, called **meridians** (*muh*-RID-*ee-unz*), run from the North Pole to the South Pole. The Prime Meridian divides Earth into the Eastern Hemisphere and the Western Hemisphere. Which continents are located entirely in the Western Hemisphere? Which are in the Eastern Hemisphere?

Many Kinds of Maps

There are many kinds of maps. Each kind gives special information about Earth. Most use **symbols** to give this information. Often a **key** (legend) is used to show what the symbols stand for.

A star (★) might stand for a capital city. A large dot might stand for a major city. A small dot might stand for a smaller city. What might a solid black line stand for?

A map that shows boundaries of states or countries and the location of cities, major rivers, and the like is called a **political map.** The map below is a political map of North America. What do the solid black lines stand for? Notice that color has an important use on this map. All areas colored the same are part of one nation. This map shows at a glance that Alaska and Hawaii are part of the United States.

Find these cities on the political map: Seattle, San Francisco, Santa Fe, New Orleans, Chicago, Boston, Atlanta. Which are major cities? How can you tell? Which of these cities is nearest the area where you live?

Suppose you wanted to locate the highest point of an area. You would look at a **relief map.** A relief map shows the land's **elevation** (how high the land is above sea level). Colors stand for different elevations. Look at the relief map of North America (below). What is the highest area of the eastern United States? Where is there a long chain of mountains in North America?

KEY
- Mountains
- Highlands
- Plateaus
- Plains

Another useful kind of map is a **climate map** (below). It shows what the weather is like over long periods of time. This map shows the average rainfall in North America during the course of a year. Like the relief map, the colors used are very important. Each color stands for a different amount of rainfall. Use the map key to find out how much rain your area has in a year.

Two or more maps used together can give you even more information than one map used alone. For example, compare the relief map and the climate map. What do these two maps show you about the rain that high and low places receive?

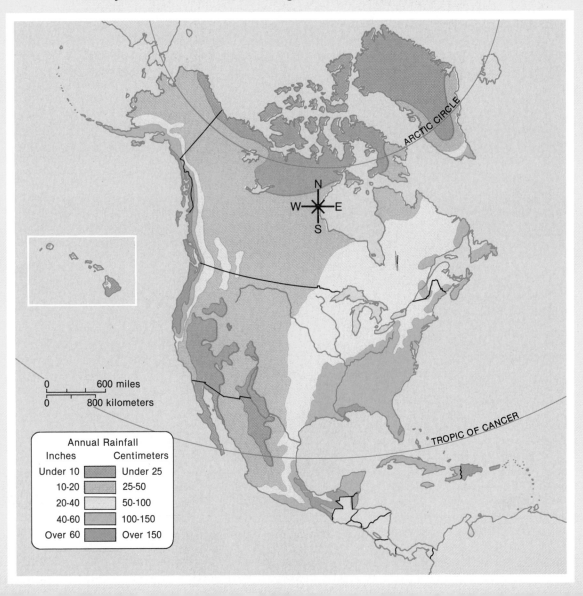

Do you know where in the United States there are large stretches of forest land? Do you know where there are grasslands? Do you know where there is tundra? This **resource map** shows you. Plants and trees are natural resources. Other resource maps might show where there is fertile soil or where there are major oil deposits. These are all natural resources. Resource maps also can show things like factories or industrial centers. In what way are these resources?

Resource maps can be used with other maps, too. Compare the map below with the climate map. What does this comparison tell you about how rainfall affects plant life?

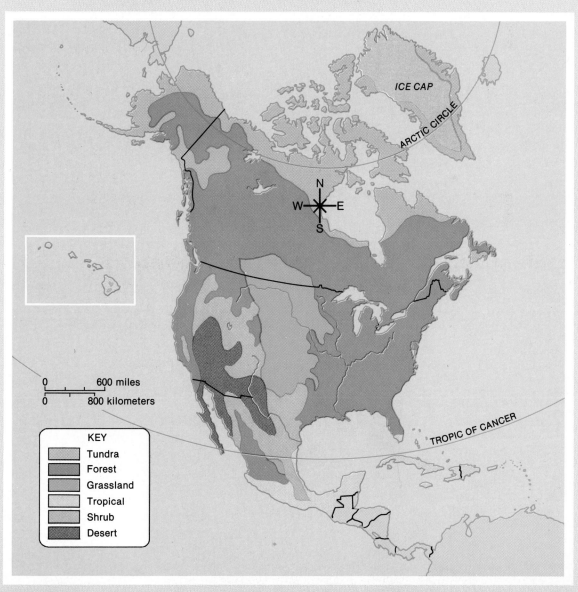

ICE CAP

ARCTIC CIRCLE

N
W—E
S

0   600 miles
0   800 kilometers

TROPIC OF CANCER

KEY
Tundra
Forest
Grassland
Tropical
Shrub
Desert

A **road map** is a special kind of map that can be used when you travel by car. Main roads are shown with thick lines. Smaller roads are usually shown with thinner lines.

Numbers on the highways and roads are the route numbers. The route numbers on the map match route markers you can see along roads and highways.

Here is a road map of the St. Louis, Missouri, area. What road runs north-south along western St. Louis? What route would you take to go from Brentwood to the airport?

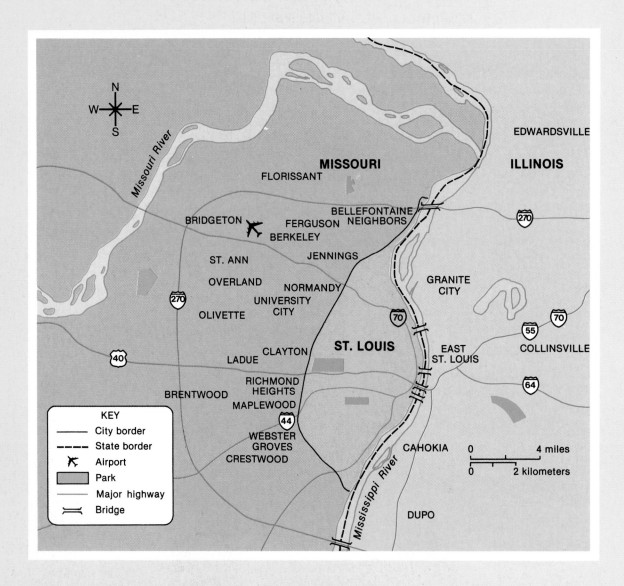

Words to Know

Choose 10 words from the list below. Use each word in a sentence.

agriculture	industry	plateau
axis	key	political map
canyon	landform	relief map
climate map	map	resource map
compass rose	meridian	road map
direction	natural resource	scale
elevation	parallel	symbol
globe		

Facts to Review

1. Which coast of the U.S., the Atlantic or the Pacific, has a flat coastal plain bordering the ocean?
2. In which part of the country are the Mississippi and Missouri rivers?
3. Which U.S. state is made up of a number of islands formed by the action of volcanoes?
4. What are some of the natural resources that the U.S. has in abundance?
5. Why must we treat our resources like a treasured gift?

Things to Think About

In Question 4 above, you were asked to list some of the most abundant resources in the U.S. Pick one of these resources from your list. Write a short report on what your life might be like if the U.S. didn't have any of this resource.

Unit One
Discovering Our Land

3 The First Americans

A man on horseback rode across the dry range country of New Mexico. As he rode, a great trail of dust followed him. George McJunkin, a black cowboy, was on the lookout for stray cattle. It was the spring of 1926.

Suddenly something caught McJunkin's eye. In a ditch he saw a pile of large bones. McJunkin was puzzled by these bones. They didn't look like the bones of cattle.

McJunkin was curious. He got off his horse and climbed down into the ditch for a better look. The bones were indeed much larger and whiter than the bones of modern-day cattle. Nearby were pieces of flint (a hard rock). Someone had hammered the flint into sharp points. "That's funny," McJunkin thought. "These don't look like the Indian arrowheads we usually find around here."

Back at the ranch, he told other cowhands about his findings. The tale spread. Finally, a scientist, J.D. Figgins, heard the story. He studied the strange bones and sharp flint pieces. After much study, Figgins made his report. The bones were those of ancient bison (BYE-*son*), a kind of buffalo. The pieces of flint were the points of spears 10,000 years old. Said Figgins: "Hunters must have roamed these lands at least 10,000 years ago. They killed the bison with spear points made of flint."

McJunkin's discovery gave scientists some important information. It showed that people lived on this continent at a very early date. Since McJunkin's discovery, more finds have been made. Today scientists believe that people have lived on our continent for at least 25,000 years.

How did these first Americans reach the Americas? There are no written records to tell the story. But scientists have found enough evidence to give us a pretty good idea of how the Americas were first settled.

On page 38: This painting is by a modern Navajo artist. It shows two Navajo women weaving a rug on a loom. Navajo women have been famous for their skilled weaving for hundreds of years.

ICE MAKES A BRIDGE

Imagine a climate so cold that ice seemed to swallow Earth itself. The time was thousands of years ago in the Ice Age. Great sheets of ice, called **glaciers** (GLAY-*sherz*), covered much of Earth. These glaciers grew larger each winter. They did not melt much in the summers because it was cold then too.

As the ice sheets grew, they sucked up water from the oceans. So the oceans shrank. Some land that had been under water was now above it. One place where there was new land was between Alaska and Asia. A "land bridge" now linked the edge of Asia to Alaska. Plants grew in the rich new soil from the ocean floor.

Soon animals from Asia began eating their way across this land bridge. One such animal was the mammoth (MAM-*uth*). This huge, hairy animal had a trunk and tusks. It looked a bit like a modern-day elephant, except it was much larger. Behind the grazing animals came small groups of hunters. They carried spears tipped with stone points. The hunters were following these ancient animals, which were their main source of food.

For hundreds of years, these hunters came over the land bridge. They were the first humans to reach the Americas. These Native Americans were the ancestors of the American Indians of today.

PEOPLE OF THE AMERICAS

Many thousands of years passed. By now the great sheets of ice had melted. The water level rose once more. Once again, the land bridge was covered by the sea. No longer could humans walk across from Asia. But small bands of people had already wandered to every part of North and South America.

As they scattered, each group had to work out ways of getting food. Those who lived on rivers, lakes, or along the

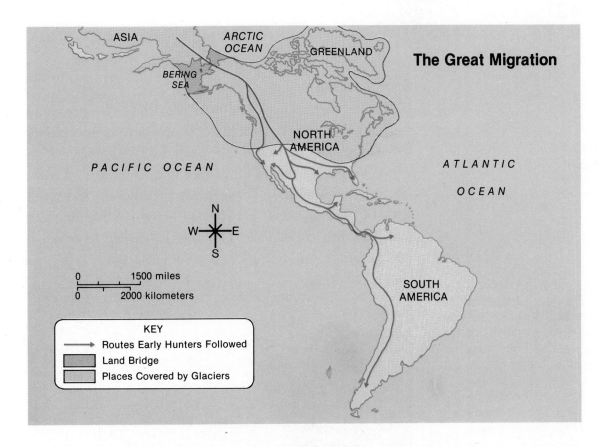

The Great Migration

coasts mainly fished for their food. In other places, people still hunted as their chief way of getting food. Still other groups had begun to gather plants to eat. They also learned to plant seeds and grow things.

These different groups often lived far apart. They began to use new words to describe things. Over the years, more than 200 different languages came to be spoken in the Americas!

The American Indians had many different **cultures** (ways of living). Each group had its own customs, language, and religious beliefs. Some groups continued to live in small communities of a few families. Others lived in larger villages of hundreds of people. There were Indian groups who became very powerful and built great cities.

All American Indians, however, were similar in some ways. All had great respect and love for the land and its plant and animal life. All depended on the land to meet their needs.

Growing Up

All Indian parents expected their children to be quiet and well-behaved and to work hard. There were always plenty of relatives around to see that a child did just that.

A young girl would be surrounded by aunts and cousins and grandmothers. These family members would teach her. In many groups, a girl was thought old enough to marry by the age of 13 or 14. So girls learned to cook, to make clothes, and to find food at an early age.

A modern artist of the Pawnee tribe painted this scene. It shows the way Pawnee women used to preserve corn. They roasted ears of corn over a fire (left). Then they scraped the kernels off the ears (right) to be dried and stored for winter.

Every girl learned how to make thread out of tough animal tissue. Needles were made from animal bone. Girls watched their mothers and aunts work deerskin and buffalo hides into soft leather for clothes.

An Indian boy knew that his main job as a man would be to catch game for food and hides. Nearly every boy learned to make weapons and to use them well. From his father and uncles, a boy learned to hunt deer or rabbit or to fish for the fish in the nearby rivers or sea. To be a good hunter, said the elders, one must first learn to think like the animal. Indian boys practiced this skill.

A young Indian expected to live very much as his or her parents and grandparents did. These elders would pass on all that the young people needed to know.

CUSTOMS THAT FIT THE LAND

Think how large the United States is. Think how different the land and climate of Minnesota are from the land and climate of Oklahoma or Alabama. Indians lived all over what is now the U.S. They had to work out ways of living that suited the land and the climate of their own place. Knowing how to build canoes was important in the lake regions, but not in the desert. There it was most important to know how to save water.

In one part of the country, there might have been many different groups. Often their ways of life were similar. Usually this way of life depended on where the Indians settled. It depended on the landforms, the climate, and the **vegetation** (the plants) of the area. The map on this page shows where groups with similar ways of life lived. Next we will learn about these different groups of Indians.

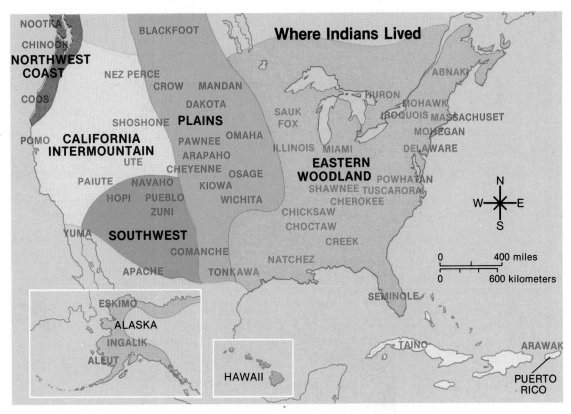

The Northwest

A light rain is falling on the village when someone yells with excitement, "The salmon are coming!" As many as six or seven times a year, the big fish leave the Pacific Ocean to swim back up the river to where they were born. Men hurry to spear the silvery fish. Nets are thrown into the water. Hundreds of salmon can be gathered in these nets in a day's work.

The women go to work drying the fish. They place wooden frames over low fires. The women split the salmon. Then they put them on the frames where the fish will dry very slowly. As the fish dry, their oil drips into carved wooden bowls.

There are plenty of other foods from which to choose. The ocean and the bays are alive with life. Sometimes the men take their big canoes into the ocean. There they hunt

Indians fished for salmon
in the Columbia River.

seals and sea lions. On other days, the villagers go to the shore and dig for clams. They also hunt game in the nearby forests. The Indians can get so much from the land and sea that they do not need to farm.

Girls and women collect many kinds of berries, nuts, and other plants. They also make fancy clothing. Their cloth is made from tree roots that are pounded into pulp.

Between Mountain and Coast

Farther south, along California's coast, the Indians also fish with great skill. The ocean provides food, so these Indians also have no need to farm.

But less rain falls here. Sometimes in dry years there are hungry days. To protect the group against such times, the women gather acorns each fall. They pound these into flour which will be made into bread or mush.

These Indians also make beautiful baskets decorated with patterns of beads and feathers. The baskets are used to collect and store wild berries, roots, and nuts.

Life in the Southwest

This is a land of sunlight and shadow, canyon and cactus. Here the Indians live differently. Many of them belong to the Pueblo (*poo-*EBB*-loe*) people. (*Pueblo* is a Spanish word that means "village" or "town.")

A village here looks something like a modern apartment house. It is a series of rooms stacked up against a cliff. The walls are made of *adobe* (*uh-*DOE*-bay*). This is a mixture of clay, straw, and water. One Pueblo village is five stories high and has 800 rooms. To reach their rooms, the Indians use ladders which lean against the outside walls.

Many cliffs in this part of the country are flat on top, like the top of a table. They are called *mesas* (MAY*-suhz*). (*Mesa* is the Spanish word for "table.") The Indians use the wild plants that grow here. From the yucca (YUCK*-uh*) cactus, for instance, they weave headbands, aprons, sandals,

Indians of the Northwest carved totem poles with the shapes of animals.

and baskets. Mint and wild onions are used to season rabbit stew. Sap from milkweed is dried into chewing gum.

The Pueblo raise their own crops on the mesa as well. These include beans, squash, and pumpkins. The Indians spin cotton into thread which they weave into cloth.

The most plentiful crop is corn. This corn grows only three feet high. But what colors! Yellow, black, red, white, blue . . . and speckled corn too! The Indians are the first people to grow corn. At this time, people in Europe had never even heard of corn.

Since there is little rainfall in the Southwest, the Indians learn to plant their corn near rivers. In some places, ditches are dug to control the flow of water to the crops (see page 49). Do you know what this practice is called?

Hunters of the Plains

A person can walk for days on the Great Plains without seeing another person. Then, near a river, the traveler might notice planted fields of corn, squash, and beans.

Nearby are the houses of a village. Smoke rises from holes in the roofs. The houses have wood frames, and walls and roofs made of sod (topsoil held together by the roots of grass). Inside, women bend over a cooking fire. The meat of a buffalo is roasting on the fire. Tonight the meat will feed the three or four families who share each house.

Once a year, part of this village moves out into the group's hunting grounds. Dogs are used to haul some of the supplies. Women carry the rest. While on the hunt, the Indians live in tepees (TEE-*peez*) made of buffalo hides.

There are no horses in the Americas at this time. So the Indians must hunt on foot. Buffalo herds are a source of food, hides, tools, even fuel for the Plains Indians. The hunters try to drive the buffalo into a trap. Sometimes the big beasts can be driven into a mudhole, or over a cliff. The men on foot have become excellent hunters.

Buffalo were a central part of Plains Indian life. In the picture above, women work to preserve buffalo hides in a Comanche village. Two hunters wear wolf disguises as they sneak up on a buffalo herd (below left). Mandan women load firewood into boats made from buffalo hides stretched over willow rods (below right).

The Woodlanders of the East

An Indian moves silently through the forest. He is a member of the Iroquois (IR-*uh-kwoi*) group, one of the largest in the Northeast. November days are cool, so the scout wears clothes made of buckskin, the skin of a deer, and ankle-high moccasins. His shirt is decorated with porcupine quills.

The Iroquois stops to peel pieces of bark from some birch trees. Carefully he seals these strips together with roots and gum from a spruce tree. He is making a canoe. He covers the frame with strips of bark. When finished, the canoe will be strong enough to carry him on the next part of his journey.

To these Indians of the Eastern Woodlands, trees are an important natural resource. In the spring, the Eastern Indians gather sap from the sugar maples to make sweet syrup. They also use wood to make ladles, bowls, and other tools. Sheets of bark provide the walls for their homes, called longhouses. Their villages are protected by tall wooden stakes that form fences. The forests also are home to many animals which the Indians hunt for food.

Many Woodland tribes are farmers also. Corn is their most important crop. The women plant the seeds in the spring, "when the oak leaves are the size of a mouse's ear." They also grow squash, beans, potatoes, and tobacco.

Learning New Ways

When people from Europe first came to North America, they met Indians for the first time. The Europeans brought many new things to the Indians. They brought horses and other tame animals that would do work or could be raised for food. Can you think of any other things the Europeans brought to North America?

The Indians taught the white settlers many things too. Can you name any? You will read about some in the next chapters. Most of all, the Indians taught Europeans how to survive in the beautiful wilderness that was their home.

THE SACRED EARTH

To the Indians of North America, Earth was sacred ground. The Indians believed that Earth was a living thing to be carefully protected. The Pueblo Indians always wore soft moccasins to guard against hurting Earth's surface with sharp heels. They also used their farm tools with great care. They did not want to make any cuts in Earth that were not needed.

The Pueblo, like other Indians, thought of themselves as part of nature. To them, humans were just one of the many living creatures on Earth.

Indians used their ideas about nature in how they lived. They were clever farmers. The Zuni (ZOO-nee) Indians lived in a desert in the American Southwest. Yet they were able to grow corn. They planted their corn in dry ditches, called gullies. Then they built little dams at the ends of the gullies. When it rained, the water had to run through their corn rows. The dams kept the water from flowing away. In this way, the Zuni were able to grow corn with just a little rainfall.

When settlers from Europe came to the New World, they had different ideas about nature. They thought of nature as something that had to be conquered. The land was so large that few people worried about wasting resources. Life in the New World was hard. Survival always came first.

As the United States grew, people saw that the resources of Earth would not last forever. Today more Americans are remembering the lesson of the Indians. We are trying to save our resources. Living in harmony with nature appeals to more and more Americans.

Indians of the Southwest planting their crops.

SKILL BUILDER

Thinking About Dates

Your teacher asks you when Christopher Columbus made his first voyage to America. You say, "1492." Think a moment. What does 1492 mean? How are our years counted? When was the year one? Weren't there years before this?

All the years on our calendar are measured from the date set as the birth of Jesus Christ. Years that follow this date are labeled A.D. These letters stand for the Latin words *Anno Domini* (AN-*oe* DOM-*uh-nee*), which mean "in the year of our Lord." Years that come before Jesus' birthdate are labeled B.C., meaning "before Christ."

The year following Jesus' birthdate is called 1 A.D. The next year is called 2 A.D. Columbus made his first voyage to America in 1492 A.D. or 1,492 years after Jesus' birthdate.

The year before Jesus' birthdate is called 1 B.C. The year before this is 2 B.C. The first Olympic Games were in 776 B.C. How many years was this before Jesus' birth?

We also measure time in groups of 100 years called **centuries.** Centuries are measured from Jesus' birthdate too. The years from Jesus' birthdate to 100 A.D. are called the first century A.D. The years from 100 to 200 A.D. are the second century A.D. In what century were you born?

The centuries before Jesus' birthdate are figured in the opposite way. The years from Jesus' birthdate back to 100 B.C. are the first century B.C. The years from 100 to 200 B.C. are called the second century B.C. In what century B.C. were the first Olympic games held?

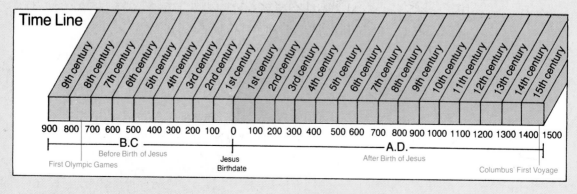

Time Line

9th century 8th century 7th century 6th century 5th century 4th century 3rd century 2nd century 1st century 1st century 2nd century 3rd century 4th century 5th century 6th century 7th century 8th century 9th century 10th century 11th century 12th century 13th century 14th century 15th century

900 800 700 600 500 400 300 200 100 0 100 200 300 400 500 600 700 800 900 1000 1100 1200 1300 1400 1500

B.C — A.D.
Before Birth of Jesus   Jesus Birthdate   After Birth of Jesus

First Olympic Games   Columbus' First Voyage

Words to Know

Use each of the words listed below in a sentence.

A.D. culture

B.C. glaciers

century vegetation

Facts to Review

1. What are some clues scientists study to learn when early people first came to North America?
2. Why did people follow animals across the land bridge between Asia and Alaska?
3. Why did the land bridge disappear?
4. Name three ways early people got their food.
5. Why didn't Indians along the Pacific Northwest Coast need to farm?
6. How did the Zuni and other Southwest Indians manage to farm in a land with so little water?
7. Name four things that the buffalo provided for the Plains Indians.
8. How did Indian girls and boys learn about their people's way of life?
9. Why did Indians in different parts of North America develop different ways of life?
10. How did the Indians view Earth?

Things to Think About

1. Reread the story of George McJunkin's discovery, told on page 39. Using clues from the story, try to picture the scene in your mind. What might the ditch filled with bones look like? What might be the expression on George McJunkin's face? Draw a picture of the scene as you imagine it.
2. Compare the ways American Indians looked at nature and the land with the ways European settlers looked at them. Write a paragraph telling which view you think was kinder to the land in the long run. Give your reasons.

CHAPTER

4 Europe Reaches Our Shores

A great golden dragon sailed on the sea. On its sides, giant paws paddled through the water. When the creature neared land, those watching onshore could see that it wasn't really a dragon. It was a large, colorful ship with 10 long oars on each side.

Inside were fierce-looking men. Their hair was long, and blond beards hid their faces. They wore pointed helmets, knee-high boots, and coats made of iron rings.

These sailors were the Norse, or Vikings (VIKE-*ingz*). They came from what are now Sweden, Denmark, and Norway. The Norse were skilled sailors. They left their homelands and rode the high seas to raid other countries. They landed in secret, then quickly stormed villages and towns. They fought, burned buildings, looted, and killed. Sometimes they captured young people as slaves. Then, as quickly as they had come, the sailors from North Europe left. They headed out to sea, back to their own shores.

Between the years 900 and 1100, the Norse raided much of Europe. They settled Iceland and discovered Greenland. They also were the first Europeans to reach North America.

How do we know? What proof do we have?

For many years, the Norse told their adventures in story poems, called **sagas** (SAH-*guhz*). The authors of these tales had great imaginations. So we can't believe everything that is in them. Yet these sagas do contain much that was true.

Norse coins, tools, and traces of old buildings have been dug up by archaeologists in Canada. (Remember, archaeologists are scientists who study the buried remains of the past.) These things also give us clues to Norse life.

From the sagas and studies, we are now able to tell the story of the voyages that led the Norse to our shores.

On page 52: A Norse ship sails the high seas. To people in coastal villages, these ships and warriors were a terrifying sight.

ERIC AND LEIF

In the year 982, a man known as Eric the Red set out to find an island mentioned in an old story. He left Iceland and sailed west.

Freezing winds rocked the little ship. Chunks of floating ice came close to tearing into it. Then at last, Eric and his men sighted land.

It was a rugged, mountainous land. Eric landed there. Then he stayed for three years to explore it. He sailed in and out of the many bays along the coast. He walked up and down the valleys. He was sure that people could farm and live there.

Eric chose a name for the land. He called it Greenland. Greenland really wasn't very green. But Eric was thinking of bringing people to settle in the new land. "Many would want to go there if it had so promising a name," said Eric.

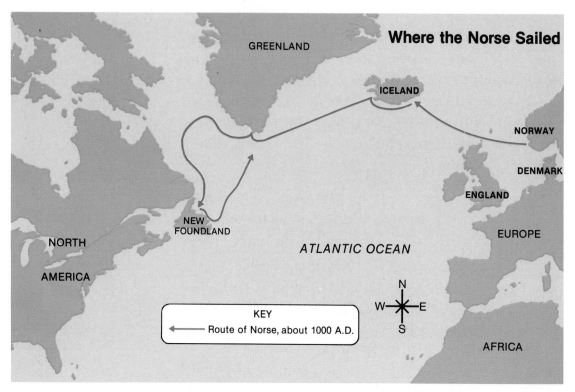

Eric's Colony

Eric returned to Iceland. In a few years, however, he returned to Greenland, leading a fleet of 25 sailing ships. Aboard were about 400 men, women, and children.

The Norse settlers founded two settlements, or **colonies,** on the coast. Norse hunters found plenty of wild game for food and trade. Before long, Norse ships sailed from Greenland loaded with furs, walrus tusks, and dried fish. They sold these goods in Norway.

Eric's son, Leif *(leef)*, was also an **explorer** (a person who travels to little-known lands). He sailed west from Greenland to find new lands that he had heard about. Leif and his fellow Vikings sighted land. Today many scientists think that this land was North America. The Norse named this country Vinland (VIN-*lund*) and started a settlement there. Scientists think the word *Vinland* means "grass" or "grazing lands." Later other Norse founded settlements in Vinland.

The Norse did not stay long in Vinland. They were greatly outnumbered by the Indians living there. Perhaps they fought with the Indians. In any event, they decided to return to Greenland. In time, only the sagas of these Norse remained to tell of the settlement in Vinland.

CHRISTOPHER COLUMBUS

Tales of the Norse trips to lands to the west reached other parts of Europe. No one paid much attention to them, however. So they were soon forgotten. Then, in the 1400's, Europe became interested in exploring once again.

The people of Europe had built up a trade with India, China, and other Asian countries. There was a great market for Asian goods—spices, silk, and gold. But the early routes to Asia went over land, through mountains and deserts. These routes were long and dangerous. So traders began to look for routes that used both sea and land. Such

In European cities, women bought silks from far-off Asia. Merchants sold the silks and other goods in street stalls.

coastal cities as Genoa (JEN-*oe-uh*) and Venice in Italy became important links in the trade between Asia and Europe. Italian merchants sold goods from Asia all over Europe. By the middle of the 1400's, Italy controlled much of Europe's trade with Asia.

Rulers of other European countries grew jealous. They began to look for other ways to get to Asia. One thought was to find an all-water route. The race to find one began. A man named Christopher Columbus joined the race.

Columbus' Dream

Christopher Columbus was born in 1451 in Genoa, Italy. Genoa was one of the busiest and most exciting cities of its time. It was filled with sailors, ships, and the promise of adventure. It's no wonder that the young Columbus grew interested in a life at sea.

By the time he was a teenager, Columbus had made several sea journeys. At the age of 25, he went on a journey that almost led to his death.

Columbus went to sea on a ship carrying goods to northern Europe. Suddenly the ship was attacked by pirates. The battle raged all day. Hundreds drowned and Columbus was wounded. At last the ship sank in flames. Columbus splashed into the sea and nearly went under.

Luckily an oar floated by. Columbus grabbed it and held tight. Then, resting on the oar, Columbus swam through the darkness for six miles. Finally he reached the town of Lagos (LAH-*goosh*) in Portugal.

The boat-filled harbor of Genoa, Italy, was a busy place in Columbus' time. Trade between Europe and Asia was booming.

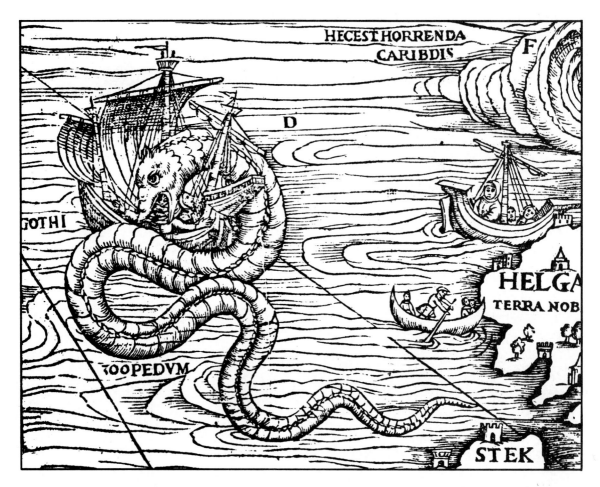

HECEST HORRENDA
CARIBDIS

F

D

GOTHI

HELGA
TERRA NOB

ZOOPEDVM

STEK

Sailors in Columbus' time did not know much about the sea. Some thought that sea monsters like this one were always ready to swallow up passing ships.

From Lagos, Columbus went to find his brother Bartholomew (bahr-THAHL-uh-myoo), who had a shop in nearby Lisbon. For the next few years, Columbus helped Bartholomew run his shop. He also sailed on Portuguese ships. He studied math, astronomy, and drawing. He learned to speak Latin, Portuguese, and Spanish. Then Columbus married a wealthy woman. She introduced him to important people in the court of the king of Portugal.

During this time, Columbus read widely. His favorite book was by Marco Polo. Polo had visited China about 200 years earlier. He had returned to Europe and written a book about the great riches of China. One part of the book that Columbus really liked told of a palace. "The floors of its rooms," wrote Polo, "are entirely of gold, in plates like slabs of stone, a good two fingers thick."

The more Columbus read and studied, the more he believed he knew the nearest route to the East. It lay to the west—across the Atlantic Ocean.

Like most educated people of the time, Columbus knew Earth was round. But he believed that it was smaller than most people of the time thought. Columbus thought that China lay only 2,600 miles (*about 4,000 kilometers*) to the west. He was wrong. It was really more than 10,000 miles (*about 16,000 kilometers*).

On one important point, however, Columbus was right. He knew his dreams of discovery and glory couldn't come true without help. He needed ships, sailors, and supplies. He needed money. Columbus needed to get the support of one of Europe's kings or queens.

The Long Wait

In 1484 Columbus turned to the king of Portugal for help. The king said no. Downcast, Columbus traveled to Spain. There he approached Spain's King Ferdinand and Queen Isabella. It took six years to get their answer. Once again it was no.

Still Columbus clung to his dream. One day he shared this dream with a monk named Juan Perez (*hwahn* PAIR-*ezz*). Perez told Columbus not to give up. The monk said he knew Queen Isabella and would write to her.

Once again Columbus saw the queen, but once again he was turned down. His demands were too high. If he reached the East, Columbus said, he wanted gold, gems, spices, land, and more.

Columbus had waited and struggled for years. He was very angry and would not budge. So Columbus saddled his mule and rode away.

Meanwhile, one of King Ferdinand's advisers spoke to the queen. He told her that Columbus expected a reward only if he succeeded. This would be a small price to pay, the adviser said, to gain power for Spain.

The queen was convinced. She sent a messenger to bring Columbus back. At long last, he had won royal support for his great dream.

THE GREAT ADVENTURE

Months later, on August 3, 1492, three ships sailed from the port of Palos (PAHL-*ose*). The smallest was named *Nina*. It carried a crew of 24. The *Pinta*, middle sized, had 26 crew members. The largest ship was the *Santa Maria*. Its captain was Columbus. The *Santa Maria* had 39 crew members. Some of the sailors were boys only 12 years old.

There were windy days when the three ships traveled great distances. There were also calm days when they hardly traveled at all. The sailors looked for signs of land. They saw none. The days dragged on and on.

Then, on September 25, a sailor on the *Pinta* shouted, "Land ho!" The happy crew dove into the water. They swam and splashed like dolphins. But soon their joy turned to gloom. The "land" they saw was only a bank of clouds.

A Troubled Trip

Now the mood of the sailors changed. They grew angry, and for good reasons. The ships were leaking. They smelled terrible. Rats were everywhere. Drinking water was running low. The only place to sleep was on the ships' hard, wooden decks. No wonder the sailors wanted to turn back.

Still Columbus pushed ahead. Then, on October 10, he gave in. He said that he would turn around and go back to Spain if they did not see land within three days.

Soon after, the winds picked up. A branch with live blossoms floated by. Was land near after all? Hopes soared as the ships sailed to the west. The sailors' eyes searched the sea ahead. Finally, at two o'clock in the morning on

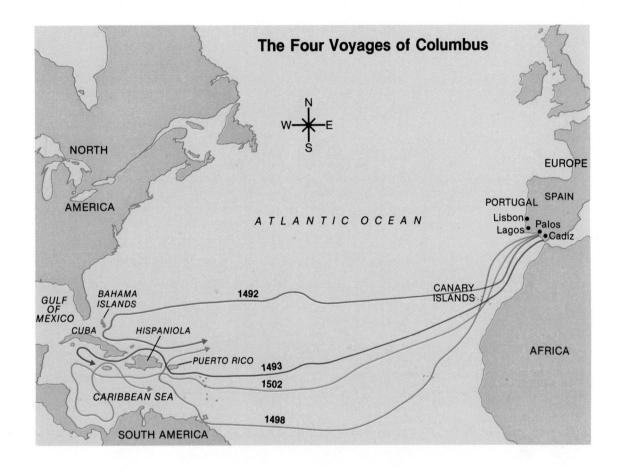

The Four Voyages of Columbus

October 12, a shout from the *Pinta* pierced the darkness.
"Tierra! Tierra!" (TYAIR-*ah*) Land! Land!

The New Land

At daybreak Columbus and some officers went ashore.
There they put up the green and white flag of Spain.

Columbus had landed in what would later be called
the New World. He had discovered the group of islands we
now call the Bahamas (*bah*-HAH-*muhz*). Between him and
Asia lay the two continents of North America and South
America. Columbus did not know this, however. He
thought he had reached the East Indies. So he called the
"very handsome people" who greeted him "Indians." The
Native Americans have been called this ever since.

Christopher Columbus and some of his crew come ashore on an island in the Bahamas. They carried the Spanish flag and claimed the land for Spain.

Columbus wrote a letter describing the people:

These people have no iron or steel weapons. They are very innocent, and they are very generous with everything they own. They never refuse anything they own, if asked for it. Just the opposite, they invite anyone to share it. They are also very intelligent and can navigate the seas around them.

Many months passed while Columbus and his fleet explored the nearby islands. They looked for gold. However, the only gold the Spanish saw was in the tiny rings worn in the ears and noses of the Indians.

On January 16, 1493, Columbus sailed for home. When Columbus sailed into the city of Palos, he was greeted as a hero.

A Broken Dream

Yet the dream of finding gold and the great lands of the East escaped Columbus forever. He made three more trips to the New World. Each one proved disappointing. Columbus believed that the islands he had first discovered lay just off the mainland of Asia. Yet he could not find the wonderful cities described in Marco Polo's book. He could not find the lands of spice and silk, gold and jewels.

King Ferdinand and Queen Isabella became unhappy too. They took away some of Columbus' titles. They would not let him rule the lands he had found. To them, Columbus was a failure.

At age 54, Columbus died a bitter man. He did not know that within 50 years, his discovery would make Spain the richest nation in Europe. He did not know that he had found the New World. He could not know that it would become the home of many great countries and many great peoples.

Columbus and other explorers used a new tool called the *astrolabe* (below) to help them find their way. You will read more about navigation in the next pages.

SKILL BUILDER

Finding North

Imagine you are a sailor on a small ship in the middle of the ocean. It is night. You want to sail east. How do you know which way to go?

During the day, you can find the direction by the sun. The sun is in the east in the morning and in the west in the afternoon. So, to go east, you go toward the sun in the morning and away from it in the afternoon.

Yet what if there is no sun to steer by? How do sailors find their way at night? In the time of Columbus, they used a **compass.** They still do today.

A compass needle is a magnet. It is balanced on a pin point. When the needle turns freely on the point, it always comes to rest pointing in the one direction—north. This is because Earth is a magnet. One of Earth's magnetic poles is the North Pole. The other is the South Pole. The magnetic force pulls the point of the compass needle north. The other end points south.

To use a compass, hold it flat and still until the needle stops moving. Then gently turn the compass until the **N** is at the point of the needle. You can then see all of the other directions.

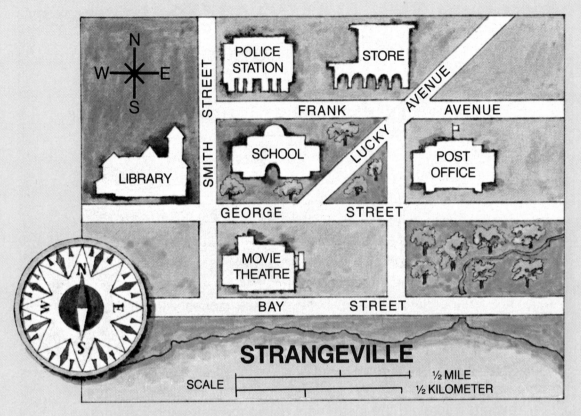

Suppose you are in a strange town. All you have is a map and a compass. How can you use them to find your way around?

First line up your compass needle with north on the compass. Then place your map next to the compass. Turn the map so that north on the compass rose points in the same direction as north shown by your compass.

Now you are ready to set out. You are at the corner of Smith and George streets. If you walk east, you will find the post office. Then in which directions must you go to reach the police station? Then in which way must you go to reach the movie theater?

Now suppose you are standing at the corner of Smith Street and Frank Avenue. In which direction would you walk to reach the store? In which direction would you walk to reach the library? In which direction does Lucky Avenue run?

How would you use the map to find directions if you did not have a compass?

THE NAVIGATOR

The voyage of Christopher Columbus changed the history of the world. But Columbus could never have made his voyage without the work of a man who, by 1492, had been dead for 32 years. The man was Prince Henry. He was the son of a king of Portugal. Prince Henry was called "the Navigator" (NAV-*i-gay-ter*) because he helped make tremendous advances in the art of **navigation** (*nav-uh-*GAY*-shun*), planning a ship's course.

In Prince Henry's time, Europeans had not sailed far out into the Atlantic Ocean. Many sailors were afraid of the ocean. They believed that monsters lived in it. These monsters, they believed, could swallow entire ships. Another belief was that the water near the equator was boiling hot.

Prince Henry did not believe these stories. He started a school for navigators. He brought together the best map makers, sailors, shipbuilders, and instrument makers. Together they shared their knowledge and made many advances.

Prince Henry's school helped sailors in many ways. Henry's experts improved the instrument called the astrolabe (AST-*ruh-labe*). It used the stars to tell sailors their location at sea.

Prince Henry's shipbuilders also built a new type of sailing ship. It was called the caravel (KA-*ruh-vell*). The caravel was built to sail much more easily on the open ocean. With it, Portuguese sailors were able to sail into the Atlantic Ocean and down the African coast.

Christopher Columbus made good use of Prince Henry's learning. He navigated with the astrolabe and sailed in caravels. Columbus couldn't have made his great discovery without the work of Prince Henry, the Navigator.

Prince Henry's school for navigators

Words to Know

Use each of the words listed below in a sentence.

colony   navigation

compass   saga

explore

Facts to Review

1. What skill helped the Norse discover so many new lands?
2. Why did Eric the Red choose the name *Greenland*?
3. Where do scientists today think Vinland was located?
4. Why did the European countries race to reach Asia?
5. What goods did the people of Europe want from Asia?
6. How did Columbus plan to reach Asia?
7. Why did Columbus call the people he found "Indians"?
8. What was wrong with Columbus' plan to reach Asia?
9. What conditions aboard ship almost convinced Columbus to turn back?
10. Why were Columbus, King Ferdinand, and Queen Isabella disappointed in the end?

Things to Think About

1. Pretend that you are a sailor aboard one of Columbus' ships. How do you think you might feel about the trip? What might you like about it? What might you not like about it? What might you fear? Write a short letter home to your friends and family in Spain. Tell them your thoughts and feelings about the voyage.
2. Put yourself in the place of the Indians as they watched the arrival of Columbus and his ships. Write a brief paragraph describing your reactions.

5 Race to the New World

VERACRVZ. N 2

Imagine how a bold sea captain of the late 1400's might feel if he heard this news:

"That fellow Columbus says he found gold by sailing *west* across the Atlantic. He says he found a shortcut to Asia."

Surely any captain who believed the story would want to point his ship west. Asia! The Indies! That was a place where a person could make a fortune.

This is what happened when Columbus returned to Spain. His reports caused great excitement in Europe. As Columbus set off on his later trips back to the New World, so did other brave sailors.

One of the first to make the trip was Amerigo Vespucci (*ah-muh-*REE*-go ves-*POO*-chee*). He was an Italian who sailed in the service of Portugal. It was Vespucci who finally realized that the lands Columbus had reached were not China and the Indies. Instead, according to Vespucci, they were "a new land." A few years later, a **geographer** (*jee-*OG*-ruh-fer*), someone who studies the world's geography, suggested that this new land be named for Amerigo Vespucci. The idea caught on, and this is how the Americas got their name.

Spain and Portugal led the way to the Americas. Soon other powerful countries followed. England, France, and the Netherlands joined the race for any riches in the New World.

All of these countries wanted to become richer and more powerful. In those days, the discoverer of a new place could "claim" it for his country. Then, if he could conquer the people of the new place, its resources would belong to his country. In this way, a country could get control over other lands and peoples.

On page 68: The man on the white horse is Hernan Cortes. He has just landed in Mexico. Aztec Indians with feathers on their heads offer Cortes gifts of gold and cloth.

The far-away lands that had been conquered became part of an **empire.** The country that had done the conquering could set up new colonies. Those colonies could grow food, mine gold, and add to the wealth of the empire.

So the race for empires was on. An exciting new age had begun. It was the Age of Discovery. It was the Age of Exploration. It was also the Age of Conquest.

SPAIN'S EMPIRE GROWS

Columbus had called the islands he had explored "land to be desired. Once seen, it is never to be left." It was not long before other Spaniards came to see for themselves.

Ponce de Leon (PON-*say day lay*-OAN) was a Spanish nobleman. In 1493 he sailed on Columbus' second voyage. In 1509 he conquered the peaceful and friendly Arawak (A-*ruh-wahk*) Indians on the island of Puerto Rico and set up a Spanish colony there. Ponce de Leon became its governor. He heard Indians tell about another island where there was a fountain of youth. The Indians said that anyone who drank from the fountain would remain young.

Ponce de Leon grew eager to find this fountain. So he set out in search of the waters that would keep him young.

On March 27, 1513, he sighted the coast of what is now the U.S. On April 2, he set foot on a beautiful land. It was filled with trees and flowering plants. Ponce de Leon called this place Florida, meaning "full of flowers." He explored its coast looking for the fountain. He never found it, and he finally returned to Puerto Rico.

In 1521 Ponce de Leon headed again for Florida. This time he wanted to set up a colony. Not long after he landed, he got into a fight with Indians and was killed by a poisoned arrow. Still, Ponce de Leon's explorations made Florida a part of the Spanish empire. It remained Spanish until the 1800's, for about 300 years.

Cortes Conquers Mexico

In 1519 the Spanish governor of the island of Cuba sent Hernan Cortes (*err*-NAHN *kor*-TEZZ) and soldiers to the coast of what is now Mexico. The governor had learned of a great Indian empire in Mexico. It was said to be rich in gold. The governor ordered Cortes to find the gold and claim the land for Spain.

When Cortes and his men landed on the Mexican coast, they learned that the rich empire was ruled by a group called the Aztecs (AZZ-*tecks*). The Aztecs were said to be very rich and powerful. They lived in a great city with many fine buildings and beautiful gardens. Cortes began marching toward the Aztec capital with his 600 men.

Along the way, the Spaniards met many Indians who hated the Aztecs. Cortes realized that if he could band together with the angry Indians he could capture the Aztec empire. He convinced thousands of Indians to join him.

Tenochtitlan, the Aztec capital, was a beautiful city of 100,000 people. It was built on an island in Lake Texoco. Raised roads connected the city with the mainland. There were many canals and lush gardens. Shown here is the central plaza. The tall flat-topped pyramids were used for Aztec religious ceremonies.

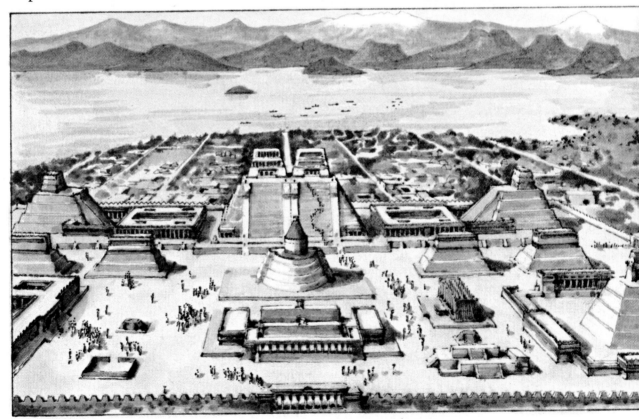

The Aztecs made beautiful objects out of gold (top) and colored stones (below).

The Aztec king, Montezuma (*mon-tay-*zoo*-muh*), had plenty of warning that Cortes was coming. Montezuma knew of these bearded white men. He had heard of the great "beasts"—the horses—they rode. He had heard of their "canoes with wings"—ships with sails. He had also heard of "sticks" that shot fire and could kill. (What were these?)

Montezuma wasn't sure what to do. He knew he should attack. He had many more soldiers than Cortes.

Montezuma couldn't forget an important Aztec legend, however. According to the legend, a great god was due to return to the land of the Aztecs. The god had white skin. The god had said that, when he returned, the Aztec empire would fall. Could Cortes be that great god returning? Should a king fight a war with a god?

Montezuma made his decision. He greeted Cortes in a friendly way and gave him beautiful gifts.

The Night of Sorrows

Cortes grew uneasy, however. He wondered: Was Montezuma plotting against him? So Cortes put the king in prison and took control of the capital. When the Aztecs discovered what had been done, they attacked the Spanish. A fierce battle was fought. Many Spanish fell wounded or dead. Cortes and only a few others escaped.

But Cortes was not finished with the Aztecs. He had his men make 13 small ships that could be carried in pieces overland and put together on the lake.

With the ships' parts, some Spaniards, and 100,000 Indian warriors from other groups, Cortes headed for the Aztecs' capital again. This time he cut off its supply of drinking water and burned its crops. Then, when his boats were put together, he attacked.

The Aztecs fought hard. This time, however, Cortes was the victor. On August 13, 1521, he marched into the Aztec capital. There Cortes became master of Mexico.

SPANISH POWER SPREADS

Now Spain controlled a great empire in the Americas. It controlled many islands in the Caribbean Sea, Florida, and much of what is now Mexico. More explorers would soon travel into what is now the U.S. Southwest and California. Others would conquer large areas of South America.

In 1528 a Spanish ship was wrecked near where the city of Galveston (GAL-*vuh-stun*), Texas, is today. Four men survived the wreck. One was Cabeza de Vaca (*kuh-*BAY-*sah duh* VAH-*kuh*). Another was a black man named Esteban (*ess-tay-*BAN).

These four men set out on one of the greatest adventures of all times. For six years, they wandered through Texas and Mexico. Along the way, the men heard tales from Indians about "seven cities of gold." The wanderers believed the stories of the golden cities.

Cortes (left) and Montezuma (right) travel to meet each other for the first time. The Indians had never seen horses before. Some of them thought man and horse were one animal.

Finally the explorers reached Mexico City. They had walked more than 1,000 miles *(about 1,600 kilometers)* through the wilderness. Of course, they told the Spanish in Mexico City that there were cities of gold to the north.

Coronado's Search

In 1540 the Spanish ruler of Mexico sent Francisco Coronado *(fran-*SISS*-koe kah-ruh-*NAH*-doe)* to hunt for the seven cities of gold. Coronado set out with 300 Spanish soldiers and about 1,000 Indians from northern Mexico.

For two years, Coronado searched in what is now Arizona, New Mexico, Texas, and Kansas. He saw "humpbacked cattle" (buffalo). He saw Indians who knew how to make poisoned arrows by making rattlesnakes bite the tips. But Coronado saw no glittering cities. He saw only Indian villages that *seemed* to shine like gold from afar.

Coronado returned to Mexico a poor man. His march, however, helped make Spain's claims to America's Southwest very strong. Later, Spanish colonists would follow Coronado's trail and start settlements there.

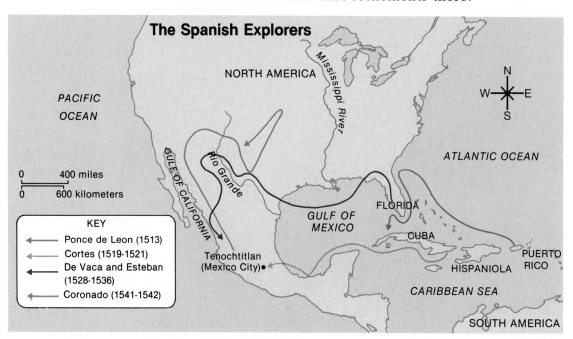

The Spanish Explorers

NORTH AMERICA

Mississippi River

PACIFIC OCEAN

ATLANTIC OCEAN

GULF OF CALIFORNIA

Rio Grande

0   400 miles
0   600 kilometers

GULF OF MEXICO

FLORIDA

CUBA

PUERTO RICO

Tenochtitlan (Mexico City)•

HISPANIOLA

CARIBBEAN SEA

SOUTH AMERICA

KEY
Ponce de Leon (1513)
Cortes (1519-1521)
De Vaca and Esteban (1528-1536)
Coronado (1541-1542)

The Pueblo of Acoma in New Mexico (top) looks much the same
as it did in the time of the Spanish explorers. Can you see
anything in this picture that explains why the Spanish thought
there were cities of gold in the desert? Francisco Coronado's army
(below) searched the Southwest for two years for those cities of gold.

OTHER EUROPEANS REACH THE NEW WORLD

Not all of the Spanish searches for riches were in vain. In Mexico and South America, the Spanish found a great deal of gold and silver. Each year, ships filled with gold and silver from the New World reached Spain. Other countries in Europe watched as Spain grew rich. So they too became eager to explore these rich, new lands.

The English Take an Interest

Only five years after Columbus' first voyage, John Cabot left England in a small boat called the *Matthew*. Like Columbus, Cabot was an Italian sailor from Genoa. Cabot, however, worked for the king of England. Cabot and his men were probably the first Europeans since the Norse to explore parts of North America. Cabot did not find gold, spices, or silks. Instead he discovered rich fishing grounds

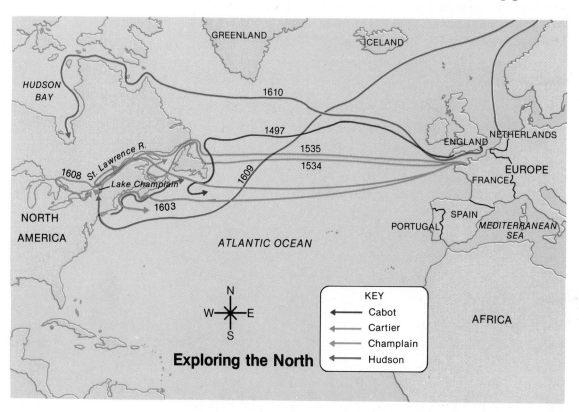

Exploring the North

KEY
- Cabot
- Cartier
- Champlain
- Hudson

off what was to become Canada. These waters, called the Grand Banks, were filled with cod and other fish.

Cabot's voyage opened up a rich fishing area. It also gave England a claim to land in the New World.

The French Move into Canada

In 1534 Jacques Cartier (*zhahk kahr*-TYAY) sailed from France. He hoped to find a way around North America that would lead to the Far East. Weeks later his two tiny ships entered the Gulf of St. Lawrence. When supplies ran low, Cartier returned home. His voyage gave France claims to parts of Canada.

On his second voyage, in 1535, Cartier traveled up the St. Lawrence River. He went as far as the present-day city of Montreal (mon-tree-AWL). Friendly Indians there gave him gifts of meat, fruit, and fish. After a long, hard winter in which many sailors died, Cartier and his men returned to France.

Champlain: Father of New France

By the 1600's, rich people in Europe prized the beautiful furs that came from North America. They especially liked hats made from beaver skins. The king of France decided to try to control the fur trade. In this way, France would become very rich. So in 1603 he sent Samuel de Champlain (*duh sham*-PLANE) to find a good place for a settlement in North America.

Champlain made two trips to the New World. In 1608 he started a fur-trading post on land overlooking the St. Lawrence River. It became Quebec (*kwe*-BECK). In 1609 he discovered the large body of water that now bears his name—Lake Champlain.

Champlain did so much to spread French rule in the New World that he was called "the Father of New France." Because of his discoveries, Canada and much of the land around the Great Lakes was claimed as French property.

Henry Hudson was a famous explorer. But he met with a sad end. He was abandoned with his son and others in a small boat on an icy bay in Canada. Today the bay is called Hudson Bay.

Claims of the Dutch

On a tiny ship called the *Half Moon,* Henry Hudson sailed from the Netherlands in 1609. Hudson was English, but he was sailing for the Dutch (people who live in the Netherlands). He crossed the Atlantic Ocean and then made his way along the coast of North America. He entered a large, beautiful bay and then sailed up a river. (Today this river is called the Hudson River.) Henry Hudson claimed all the land around the bay and river for the Dutch. Later the Dutch sent settlers there and started a colony called New Netherlands.

In 1610 Hudson was hired by England to explore farther in the New World. During this trip, he discovered the huge bay in Canada that now also bears his name. He thought it might be a body of open water that would lead to China. He sailed on and on aboard his ship *Discovery.*

The ship was trapped by ice for the whole winter. In the spring, Hudson wanted to push on, but his starving men rebelled. They put Hudson, his son, and seven others into a small boat. The nine men were never heard from again.

Europe's First Steps

By the beginning years of the 1600's, several countries had colonies in the New World. The Spanish claimed most of South and Central America. They also claimed Florida. The Dutch claimed the harbor at the Hudson River's mouth. France had a solid claim to parts of Canada. The English said Cabot's voyage gave them first claim to much of North America. The day of the great explorers was almost over. The time of the settler was beginning.

Explorers of the New World

Explorer	Date(s)	Country Sailed For	Major Achievement(s)
Ericson	1000	Norway	First European to reach North America.
Columbus	1492, 1493, 1498, 1502	Spain	Brought knowledge of America to Europe. Began exploration of the New World.
Cabot	1497, 1498	England	Discovered the Grand Banks.
Vespucci	1499, 1501	Spain, Portugal	Figured out that the land Columbus discovered was a new land.
DeLeon	1513	Spain	Discovered and explored Florida.
Balboa	1513	Spain	Discovered the Pacific Ocean.
Cortes	1519-1521	Spain	Conquered the Aztec Indians and claimed Mexico for Spain.
Magellan	1519-1522	Spain	Led first voyage around the world.
DeVaca & Esteban	1528-1536	Spain	Explored Texas and Mexico.
Cartier	1535-1536	France	Discovered St. Lawrence River.
DeSoto	1541	Spain	Discovered Mississippi River.
Coronado	1541-1542	Spain	Explored American Southwest. Claimed much for Spain.
Champlain	1608-1609	France	Founded Quebec. Discovered Lake Champlain.
Hudson	1609-1610	Netherlands	Found the Hudson Bay and the Hudson River.

SKILL BUILDER

Using Latitude and Longitude

You have already learned that there are imaginary lines that circle Earth. These lines were put on maps to make maps easier to use. Lines that circle Earth from east to west are known as parallels. One of these parallels is the equator. There are also imaginary lines that run north-south on the surface of Earth. These lines are called meridians. One of these meridians is the Prime Meridian.

Look at the drawing of the globe at the left below. As you can see, these lines form a grid. This grid helps us to find places on the globe. How is this possible? It is possible because map makers have assigned numbers to each parallel or meridian. Map makers call the numbered parallels **lines of latitude** (LAT-i-tood). They call the numbered meridians **lines of longitude** (LON-ji-tood).

The line of latitude around the middle of Earth—the equator—is zero degrees. Another way of writing this is 0°. Look at the middle globe below. What happens to the numbers of the latitude lines as they move north or south of the equator?

Now look at the globe at the right below. It shows lines of longitude. The Prime Meridian is the line of longitude numbered 0°. What happens to the lines of longitude as they move east or west of the Prime Meridian?

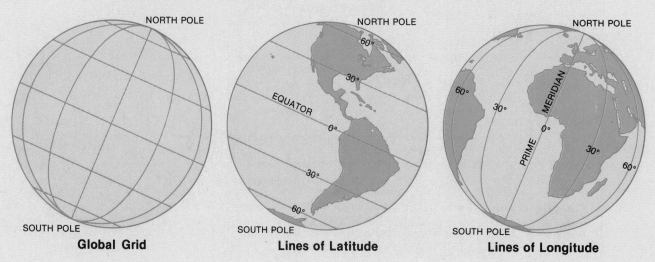

Global Grid

Lines of Latitude

Lines of Longitude

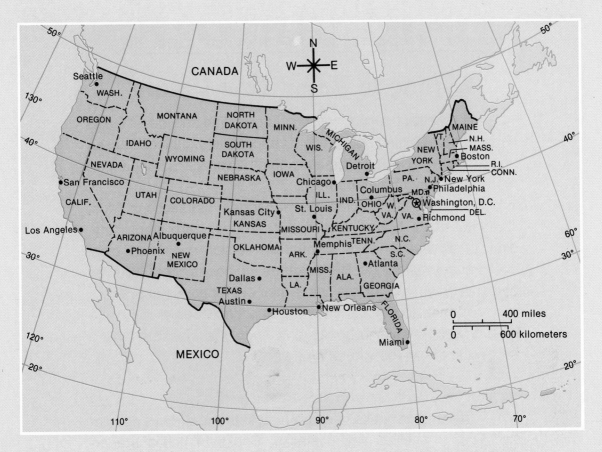

The map above shows how the latitude and longitude lines appear on a map of the United States.

If you live in Florida, you are between 25 and 32 degrees north latitude. This is written as 25°N and 32°N. At what latitude are you if you live in Maine?

If you live in California, you are at about 120 degrees west longitude (120°W). At what longitudes are you if you live in Texas?

You can use the grid to find places on the map. The city of Memphis, Tennessee, is at 35°N, 90°W. What city is at about 39° N, 95°W? What are the latitude and longitude for New Orleans, Louisiana?

Of course, not all places on Earth are located exactly where latitude and longitude lines meet. You can find Columbus, Ohio, at 40°N, between 80°W and 85°W. About what are the latitude and longitude for Albuquerque (AL-buh-kur-kee), New Mexico, and St. Louis, Missouri? What are the latitude and longitude of your community?

SKILL BUILDER

Getting to Know Your Library

A library is a treasure house of information and ideas. On its shelves, you will find books on just about every subject you can name. You may also find magazines, newspapers, maps, and many other kinds of information.

The books in the library are separated into sections. Most libraries have a **fiction** section. Fiction books are stories that didn't really happen. The **nonfiction** section contains factual books about real things. **Biographies** are books about the lives of real people. They too may have their own special place. There may also be a section for important **reference books** like encyclopedias, atlases, dictionaries, and almanacs. The librarian will be glad to show you where things are.

How Books Are Arranged

The books in a library are arranged on groups of shelves called stacks. Books of fiction are arranged in alphabetical order according to the author's last name. When there are several books by the same author, these will be arranged alphabetically by title. The first word of the title is used (not counting *a, an,* or *the*).

Books of nonfiction are arranged according to a system of numbers. Many libraries use the Dewey Decimal System. In this system of arranging books, all nonfiction books are divided into categories. There are special numbers for each category. For example, books on history, geography, and travel are numbered between 900 and 999. Books about American history are numbered 973. Those about the exploration of America are numbered 973.1

Finding a Book

Let's suppose you wanted to find a book in the library about explorers. How would you find out what number to look for?

You would go to the **catalog.** This is a set of books or cards that list every book in the library. There are subject listings, title listings, and author listings. All are filed alphabetically. All books in the library are listed by title and by author. Some are also listed by subject. Some will be found under more than one subject.

Look at the three cards below. Which is the subject card? Which is the author card? Which is the title card? If you wanted to find books on the explorers of America, you might go to the drawer labeled "A." You would flip through the cards until you came to subject cards like the top card below.

Suppose you already knew the title of this book. Under which of these drawers would you look for the title card? A-B? C-D? E-F? G-H?

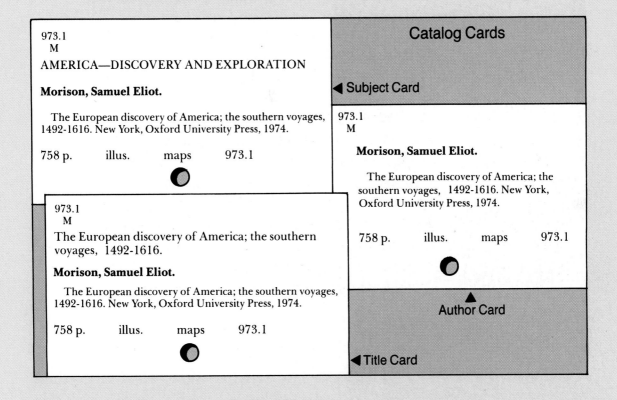

973.1
M
AMERICA—DISCOVERY AND EXPLORATION

Morison, Samuel Eliot.

   The European discovery of America; the southern voyages, 1492-1616. New York, Oxford University Press, 1974.

758 p.   illus.   maps   973.1

Catalog Cards

◄ Subject Card

973.1
M

Morison, Samuel Eliot.

   The European discovery of America; the southern voyages,   1492-1616. New York, Oxford University Press, 1974.

758 p.   illus.   maps   973.1

▲ Author Card

973.1
M
The European discovery of America; the southern voyages,   1492-1616.

Morison, Samuel Eliot.

   The European discovery of America; the southern voyages, 1492-1616. New York, Oxford University Press, 1974.

758 p.   illus.   maps   973.1

◄ Title Card

THE MAYA

You have read about the Aztec Indians who lived in Mexico. They were not the only great Indian civilization that had developed there. In another part of Mexico, there was another great civilization—the Maya (MY-*uh*).

A thousand years before Columbus landed in the New World, the Maya Indians invented their own way of writing and their own system of numbers. They built great cities in the middle of tropical rain forests. Inside these cities, they built pyramids 150 feet *(almost 46 meters)* high!

There were about 14 million Maya when the civilization was most powerful. These people lived and built their cities in a flat, thick jungle. The jungle was very beautiful. It was filled with giant trees, brightly colored birds, and bands of monkeys.

Most of the Maya worked as farmers. However, others were priests and rulers. Some of the Maya were great scientists. They studied the stars and created a calendar much like our own. Maya scientists were able to tell their people when to expect an eclipse of the sun, long before the eclipse took place.

Perhaps the Maya were the first basketball players! Almost every Maya city had a very long open-air grass court. Two teams played against each other on this court. Each player tried hard to put a rubber ball through a ring on a stone wall at the edge of the court. The game was so difficult that when one player made a point, his team was declared the winner.

About 800 A.D., the Maya began to leave their cities. By the time the Spanish came to Mexico, the Maya were no longer a great civilization. Their cities stood silent and empty in the jungle. What happened? No one knows.

Some Maya buildings still stand today.

Words to Know

Choose six words from the list below. Use each word in a sentence.

biography	fiction	lines of longitude
catalog	geographer	nonfiction
empire	lines of latitude	reference book

Facts to Review

1. How did Columbus start the Age of Discovery?
2. How did the Americas get their name?
3. Why didn't Montezuma attack Cortes?
4. How did Spain's experience in the New World encourage other European countries to explore here?
5. How did de Vaca's and Esteban's stories about the "seven cities of gold" influence the Spanish?
6. What gave the English claims in the New World?
7. Why did the king of France want to start a settlement in the New World?
8. How did the Dutch make claims in the New World?
9. What European countries had claims in the New World by the 1600's?
10. How can colonies contribute to a country?

Things to Think About

1. Pretend that you are an adventure-loving young person of the 1500's. You want to explore the New World. First, though, you need money and ships. Tell how you would go about convincing your king and queen to give you the money you need to make your voyage. Tell what reasons you would offer to win them over.
2. Did the explorers and soldiers from Europe have the right to take lands from the American Indians? Do you think people today think differently about this question than they did 400 years ago?

UNIT REVIEW

Using New Words

On a piece of paper, write the paragraph below. Fill in the blanks with the correct words from the list.

century   compass   explorers
colony   empires   navigation

The ___ who sailed the unknown Atlantic Ocean had to be good at ___ to find their way. These people had to be good at using a ___. Many of these people sailed in the service of nations that wanted to build up their ___. For example, John Cabot sailed for England in the 15th ___ in order to claim land for this nation in the New World. England could send people to this land to set up a ___. Explorers in the service of the king of Spain traveled through areas of what is now the United States Southwest.

Thinking About the Unit

1. Compare the different ways of life of the Indian groups you read about in Chapter 3. Why do you think their ways of life were so different?

2. Make a list of five explorers of the New World. What were the major reasons each had for exploring? How successful was each explorer in reaching his goals? Do you think these goals would have made you take the risks that these early explorers did?

3. Suppose you were offered a chance to explore a distant planet. Would you do it? Why? What would you hope to gain out of such a trip? Would you want to set up a settlement on the planet?

Sharpening Your Skills

1. Draw a political map of your state. On the map, show your community. Show the state capital and the largest city. Use an atlas or a relief map to find out the highest and lowest points of elevation in your state.

2. Use a compass to find the directions of your school and school grounds. In what direction does the front of your school face? In what direction are the school grounds?

3. Tear a piece of paper into six parts. On each part, write a date. Make half of them B.C. and half A.D. Have your partner make up a set of dates in the same way. Then exchange sets of six. Draw a time line like the one on page 50. Write the dates in the order they should appear on the line.

Expanding Your Knowledge

1. Write or present a report on one explorer. Find out as much as you can about the explorer's life before his explorations. What did the explorer look like? What happened to him after his explorations were over? In your opinion, what were the main contributions made by this explorer?

2. Choose one group of American Indians that interests you. Do a project about these Indians. You might want to build a model of their homes or draw pictures of their everyday lives. You might want to write a report or story about the group. Share your project with the rest of the class.

3. Keep a make-believe diary. Pretend that you are a young person on the ship of one of the explorers. Write about your excitements and your fears during the voyage.

Your Own History

This year you are going to be studying the history of your country. At the same time, you can learn more about your own state and community. There are many things you can do with what you learn. You might decide to make a scrapbook or a data book.

To start your investigation, find out what groups of American Indians lived in your state many, many years ago. Find out as much as you can about the ways of life of these Indians. Then find out which Indian groups live in your state today.

Next find out if any of the early explorers ever came into your state. Who came? What did they find? What did they do?

Unit Two
Europe Challenges the New Land

88

CHAPTER 6
England
Sets Down Roots

For almost four centuries now, an American mystery has remained unsolved. It is the mystery of the Lost Colony.

The mystery begins with an adventure-loving English nobleman named Sir Walter Raleigh (RAW-*lee*). He wanted England to spread its people and power in North America. He wanted to begin by founding a colony in what he called Virginia.

In 1585 he helped to set up such a colony on Roanoke (ROE-*uh-noke*) Island. This island is off the mainland of what is now North Carolina. This colony did not last very long, however. The colonists treated their Indian neighbors poorly. So the Indians attacked them a number of times. The colonists were not very strong, so they decided to return to England.

Still Raleigh did not give up. In 1587 he helped set up another colony. About 120 people, including 11 children, sailed to the New World. Their leader was a man named John White. They also built their settlement on Roanoke Island. There the first English child was born in the New World. She was named Virginia Dare.

Weeks later, John White returned to England for supplies. Because of a war, White was not able to get back to Roanoke until 1591. When he arrived, he was very surprised. Every single person had vanished.

The only clue was a word carved into a tree. It said: CROATOAN. This was the name of a nearby island.

What had happened? Had the settlers been killed? Had they been captured by Indians and carried off? Had they gone somewhere else? No one knows. The mystery of the Lost Colony lives on. The story reminds us of the difficulties of early colonists.

On page 90: The *Mayflower II* sails the Atlantic. This modern copy of the Pilgrims' ship sailed from Plymouth, England, to Plymouth, Massachusetts.

JAMESTOWN IS FOUNDED

Three small ships sailed from London one cold December day in 1606. Aboard were about 120 men. Their way was paid by an English company. In return, they were to start a colony in Virginia. There they were to look for gold and make a profit for the English company.

Sixteen men died on the long and stormy voyage. In May, the little fleet sailed into a river which they named the James River, after the new king of England. They chose a site for a fort and called it Jamestown.

Unfortunately, the settlers had picked a marshy and unhealthy spot. Mosquitoes that carried a sickness called malaria were everywhere. Many men became ill and died.

There were other problems too. Many of the settlers were rich men's sons. They were not used to working and refused to do things like chop down trees and plant crops. Also, the settlers got into arguments with neighboring Indians who then attacked. So many settlers were sick that it was hard to fight back.

"We had such famine and sickness that the living were hardly able to bury the dead," one man wrote. Often dinner was only worm-filled wheat and barley soaked in water.

John Smith Comes to Jamestown

Within six months, half the colonists were dead. More might have died if Captain John Smith hadn't taken charge. He was a tough soldier. He gave clear orders: Anyone who didn't work, didn't eat. Captain Smith didn't care who got blisters on his hands.

Smith also made friends with some of the Indians. He traded with them for more food. He made the settlers plant crops. He had them weave fish nets of reeds and grass, dig a well, and put up a church. The population grew to 500. One ship brought five Polish men and some Germans. It was no longer an all-English colony.

Then more bad luck hit Jamestown. Captain Smith was burned by an explosion and had to return to London. Once again, the settlers began to fight with the Indians. Winter set in. Food ran out. Of the 500 settlers, only 60 lived through the "starving time" that winter.

Finally, in the summer of 1610, new supplies and settlers arrived from England. Jamestown was saved.

Jamestown Grows

Now things went much better for Jamestown. Soon other small settlements were started nearby.

In 1619 the English company that ran Jamestown gave the settlers a chance to share in their government. Each of the 11 small communities nearby chose two men to represent them. The men were called **burgesses** (BUR-*jiss-iz*). Their assembly was called the House of Burgesses. It was a step toward democracy in America.

Jamestown was a growing settlement by 1614. The first houses outside of the walls had just been built.

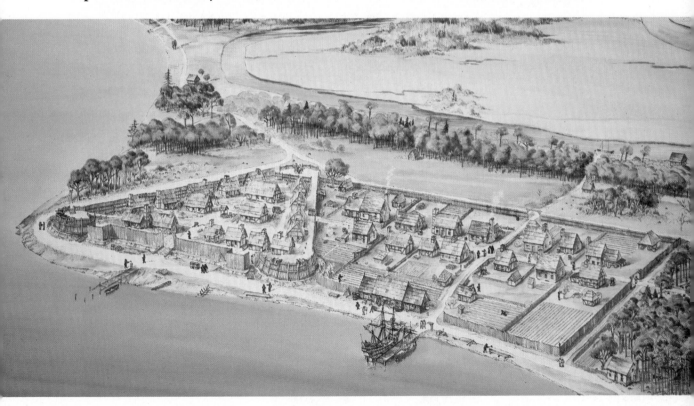

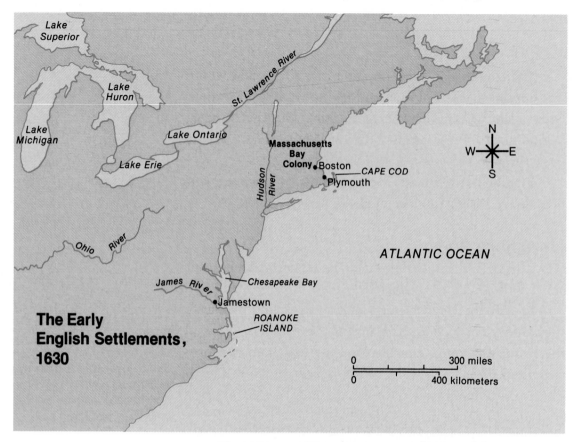

**The Early
English Settlements,
1630**

The House of Burgesses passed several laws. Among them were rules against getting drunk or loafing. The House of Burgesses also gave women the right to own property. This was unusual for the times. The burgesses said that on the large farms "it is not known whether man or woman is the most necessary."

In August of that same year, a Dutch ship arrived at Jamestown. Its supplies were running low. The captain traded 20 Africans for some food. These black men and women were not slaves in Jamestown. They worked as servants under contracts called **indentures** (*in-*DEN-*churz*). Many poor whites worked under the same kinds of contracts. Often **indentured servants** were people who wanted to come to the New World but didn't have the money. So they agreed to work for a certain amount of time—maybe three to seven years—to pay their way. When the time was up, the servants were free. Some of them bought land and had servants of their own.

Soon, however, the black Africans were being denied these rights. Gradually, ships began bringing black Africans to America as **slaves.** Slaves worked, without pay, for life for their owners. The children of slaves became the owner's property too.

In the next 40 years, slavery would spread throughout the Virginia colony and beyond.

A COLONY AT PLYMOUTH

The second English settlement in the New World was started because of religion. There had been great disagreements over religion in England for years. Many English people felt they did not have religious freedom.

In 1608 a group of these English people decided to move to the Netherlands. The Dutch didn't bother them about religion. Still, life was hard for the English in the Netherlands. They worried that their children were losing their English ways and forgetting their English language.

The group decided to build a colony of their own in America. First they went back to England. Then, in 1620, they sailed from the port of Plymouth (PLIM-*uth*) in a tiny ship called the *Mayflower*. They called themselves **Pilgrims**—people who make a trip for a religious reason.

The Mayflower Compact

More than two months later, they landed on Cape Cod on what is now the coast of Massachusetts. Before leaving the ship, they made an agreement, or **compact.** They called it the Mayflower Compact. It said everyone would have to work together in order to survive. It said the group would have to set rules and live under them.

The colony was to have "just and equal laws . . . for the general good of everyone." This agreement helped set an important pattern in America. People here would live under laws they helped make.

Plymouth Is Chosen

The Pilgrims spent a month looking for a place to settle. Finally, they found a hill where they could defend themselves. They found fresh water and cleared fields for farming. They named their colony Plymouth, after the English port they had sailed from.

Like the settlers of Jamestown, the Pilgrims suffered from cold weather, lack of food, and sickness. Half of the colonists died the first winter.

The Pilgrims' luck changed that spring, however. One day, an Indian named Samoset (SAM-*uh-set*) came to their settlement. He welcomed the Pilgrims in English. He had learned the language from the crews of English fishing boats. Samoset had even sailed for a while with an English captain.

Plymouth was an active settlement in 1627. Crops were raised in the fields just outside the fort.

Squanto, the Teacher

Days later Samoset brought another Indian to the colony. His name was Squanto (SKWON-*toe*). Squanto stayed and taught the Pilgrims many things. He showed them how to plant grains of corn with a dead fish to fertilize the land. He also taught them to watch the fields for a few nights to make sure that wolves and other wild animals did not dig up the fish. Often Pilgrim children got this scary job!

Squanto guided the settlers on hunting trips for turkey, deer, and other wild game. He showed them how to use herbs and roots for medicine and food. Most important, perhaps, Squanto helped the Pilgrims win the friendship of nearby Indians.

The Indians and the Pilgrims signed a peace treaty. That fall, the Pilgrims had a very good harvest. To celebrate and to give thanks, they planned a three-day feast.

The colonists spent many days getting ready. The Pilgrims hunted wild geese and ducks. They caught fish. The Indians brought deer and wild turkeys. Even the children helped by turning roasts on spits over the cooking fires. At last, it was time to eat. Everyone sat outdoors at long tables. It was America's first Thanksgiving.

In this painting, Pilgrims and Indians are shown sitting down to the first Thanksgiving dinner.

The Puritans were very strict with their children. They expected children to behave like "little adults."

MASSACHUSETTS BAY COLONY

As the little Plymouth colony struggled along, conditions back in England were getting worse. Charles the First became king in 1625. He made life hard for a group of English people known as **Puritans.** These were people who wanted to make the English church more "pure." They thought the church had become too fancy.

In 1630 nearly 1,000 Puritans sailed for Massachusetts. They brought with them a paper called a **charter.** It allowed them to run the Massachusetts Bay Colony. They brought the charter with them so the king couldn't easily take away their rights at some later time.

Among the Puritans were skilled carpenters, blacksmiths, and others. There were also educated, well-to-do people including ministers, merchants, and teachers. The Puritans had plenty of food, clothing, and tools. They were successful from the start. They started many villages. The most important of these was Boston.

Church and State

To keep the churches and the government under their control, the Puritan leaders made a strict rule. It said that only owners of property and church members could vote or hold public office.

A group of settlers who didn't own property were very much against this rule. They wanted to share in the government. So the rule was changed. Now Puritan men who didn't own property could vote if they were in good standing in their churches. Each town could send representatives to the general court. This was the **legislature,** the group that made the colony's laws. Thus, like Jamestown, the Massachusetts Bay Colony had the beginnings of democracy. As you will read on page 99, the people of this colony did not have as much freedom as we have today.

During the next 100 years, 11 more English colonies were started along the Atlantic Coast. (See page 125.)

FREEDOM OF RELIGION

The Puritans came to the New World so that they could worship as they pleased. In England, they had risked arrest for holding their own religious services.

In the New World, however, the Puritans were not fair-minded. They made laws that said everyone had to follow Puritan teachings and go to Puritan churches.

One young man, Roger Williams, began to wonder about these laws. He did not think they were right. So Puritan leaders put Williams on trial for holding "new and dangerous ideas." He was found guilty. Williams was told to leave the colony or he would go to jail.

In the winter of 1636, Roger Williams left the Massachusetts Bay Colony. It was cold. Snow covered the ground. Williams would have died if he had not been helped by Indians. They helped him build a new town, which he called Providence. It was the start of a new colony, called Rhode Island.

People with different religious beliefs were welcome in Rhode Island. The first Jewish synagogue in North America was built there in the city of Newport.

Because of Roger Williams, the idea spread that people of different beliefs could still be friendly. The idea that people should be free to worship as they please would become very important in America.

Roger Williams walked through the snowy wilderness to find a new place to live.

SKILL BUILDER

Interviewing

Do you know how your town or city was started? One way to find out is to **interview** someone who knows a great deal about its history. Interviewing is a valuable way to find things out. It is a skill that writers and reporters use almost every day.

To whom might you talk to find out about your community? Someone at a local historical society or museum might know. Perhaps there is a reporter on your local newspaper who covers town history. An older person whose family has lived in the town for a long time might be a good source. Such a person might have interesting family stories to pass along too.

Before setting out on an interview, you should remember these important things about a good interview:

- Most important—keep the reason for your interview clearly in mind. Know what it is you want to find out.
- Next, telephone the person or write a letter asking the person to set a time for the interview.
- Dress neatly for the interview and be on time.
- Plan your main questions before you go to the interview.
- Listen carefully to the answers and take brief notes to help you remember the answers.
- At the end of the interview, go over your notes to be sure all your questions have been answered.
- Then thank the person for talking with you.

To review: People in what two jobs must use interviewing almost every day? In what other jobs is it important to know how to interview? Name five important things to keep in mind during an interview.

Words to Know

Choose six words from the list below. Use each of the words in a sentence.

burgess indentured servant Puritan
charter interview slave
compact legislature
indenture Pilgrim

Facts to Review

1. What was the Lost Colony?
2. Why were some of the Jamestown colonists not suited for settling in the New World?
3. How did John Smith save the Jamestown colony?
4. What was the House of Burgesses?
5. Why did the Pilgrims decide to set up their own colony in North America?
6. What was the Mayflower Compact?
7. What problems did the Pilgrims face in their first winter in America?
8. What was the difference between a slave and an indentured servant?
9. In what ways was democracy starting in America?
10. What did the Puritans think about freedom of religion?

Things to Think About

1. What are some reasons why the American Indians might have wanted to be friendly with the Jamestown settlers? What are some reasons why they might not have wanted to be friendly? Pretend that you are an Indian living near the settlement. Would you be friendly? Why or why not?
2. The Mayflower Compact called for "just and equal laws." If you were a Pilgrim making a settlement in the New World, what sorts of things would you need to make laws about?

7 Europe in the New World

In the last chapter, you read how Jamestown, Plymouth, the Massachusetts Bay Colony, and Rhode Island struggled to survive. Yet these were just four of many settlements on a very large continent. England was not the only country that wanted colonies in the New World.

Spain also was settling the Americas. It was far ahead of England in building colonies in America. In fact, while Jamestown was still tiny and weak, Spain already had many prosperous settlements.

France too was settling the New World. Other European countries also were starting settlements. In this chapter, you are going to read about how settlers from four European countries settled here. These countries are Spain, France, the Netherlands, and Sweden.

As people from all of these nations came to the New World, they brought with them their own ideas and customs. The stories you are about to read show us how people from many different backgrounds helped build our country. They also show us how people of many different backgrounds were able to come together to create something new—the American people.

SPAIN IN THE NEW WORLD

Soon after the voyages of Christopher Columbus, Spanish people began settling in the New World. As you have read in Chapter 5, Spain took over Mexico. Spain also took over Central America and parts of South America. There was much gold and silver in these lands. Spain soon became the richest nation in Europe. Thousands of Indians were forced to work in the mines, digging the gold and silver out of the ground. Great ships then carried the treasure across the ocean to Spain.

On page 102: Indian cowboys round up wild horses at a mission in California in the early 1800's. Missions were important centers of religious and community life there.

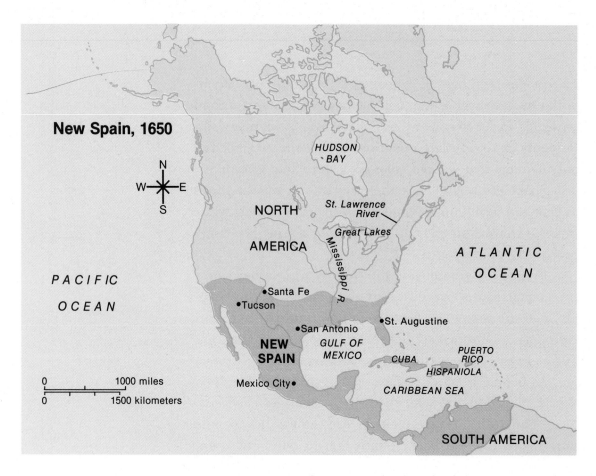

New Spain, 1650

HUDSON BAY

NORTH

AMERICA

St. Lawrence River

Great Lakes

Mississippi R.

ATLANTIC OCEAN

PACIFIC OCEAN

•Santa Fe
•Tucson

•St. Augustine

•San Antonio

NEW SPAIN

GULF OF MEXICO

CUBA

PUERTO RICO

HISPANIOLA

CARIBBEAN SEA

Mexico City•

SOUTH AMERICA

0   1000 miles
0   1500 kilometers

Many times, however, the king's ships were attacked by pirates. Sometimes the great treasure ships were captured. To help protect his ships against the pirates, the king decided to set up a fort on the mainland of North America.

The Founding of St. Augustine

In 1565 the Spanish sent a few hundred soldiers and sailors to Florida. They found the place along the Atlantic Coast in north Florida that Ponce de Leon had visited. Here they built a fort out of wood and mud. They called their fort St. Augustine.

St. Augustine was the first permanent settlement in what is now the United States. This means that from 1565 to today people have lived in St. Augustine. No other American city is this old. Today, if you go to St. Augustine, you can still see buildings that are hundreds of years old.

Santa Fe and the Southwest

St. Augustine was only a tiny part of the lands Spain controlled in the New World. Mexico was a much larger and more important part. Spanish settlers spread out over Mexico. They took over large pieces of land and set up farms and ranches.

The Spanish brought with them their language, their Roman Catholic religion, and their ideas about government. Slowly the Spanish spread to the north—toward the lands explored by Esteban and Cabeza de Vaca.

In 1609 the Spanish set up the settlement of Santa Fe (SAN-*tuh* FAY) in what is today the state of New Mexico. It became an important trading city. Soon the Spanish set up other settlements in the American Southwest.

A Spanish priest in the 1700's drew this picture of life at his mission in the New World.

In the next century, the Spanish built outposts in areas that are now New Mexico, Texas, and Arizona. Still later, the Spanish started settlements in California. The cities of San Antonio, Tucson (TOO-*son*), San Diego (*san dee*-AY-*go*), Los Angeles, and San Francisco were all started by the Spanish during this time.

Often the leaders of these settlements were **missionaries** (MISH-*uh-nerr-eez*). These were priests who wanted to convert the Indians to Christianity. The missionaries carried Spanish ways into the American Southwest. They learned Indian languages and taught many Indians to speak Spanish. They also taught many Indians new ways of farming and working with metals.

Sometimes the American Indians were eager to learn new ways. Sometimes they were not. Often Spanish soldiers fought with the Indians. If the Spanish won, the Indians would be brought into the missions. Many times, however, the Indians defeated the Spanish. Then all the Spanish soldiers, as well as the missionaries, would have to leave the Indian lands.

FRANCE IN THE NEW WORLD

Do you remember the name Samuel de Champlain? He was the French explorer who sailed into the St. Lawrence River and helped open up that part of North America to France. In 1608 Champlain climbed up a steep bank from the St. Lawrence. He raised the French flag high in the air and took control of this spot, called Quebec.

Champlain built a trading post at Quebec. The main business of Quebec was the fur trade. Indian and French fur trappers came to Quebec carrying the hides of beavers and other animals. Quebec traders bought the hides and then shipped the hides back to France. There they were sold to French hat makers at a very high price. In this way, the fur trade made money for the people of Quebec.

It was a hard life for people in the North. The winters were cold, and often there was not enough food. Champlain tells a story in his journal that shows how hard life there could be:

This picture shows Quebec as it looked in the 1700's. The fort high on the cliffs gave soldiers a good view of any attacking enemies.

On the fifth of February, there was a big snow storm. The wind was high for two days. On the 20th, some Indians came to the other side of the river. They called for us to help them. We could not, because large amounts of ice were drifting down the river.

These poor people were so hungry that they were desperate. So they decided—men, women, and children—to cross the river or die. They set out in their canoes. They thought they might make it through an opening in the ice made by the wind.

They made it to about the middle of the river. Then their canoes were caught by ice and broken into a thousand pieces. In the next instant, they were able to throw themselves on a large piece of floating ice.

As they rode the ice, we could hear them crying out. There seemed nothing before them but death. Then suddenly, another large piece of ice struck theirs. It hit so hard that it drove them ashore.

They looked like skeletons. They were very weak. I was amazed that they got across. I ordered that some bread and beans be given to them.

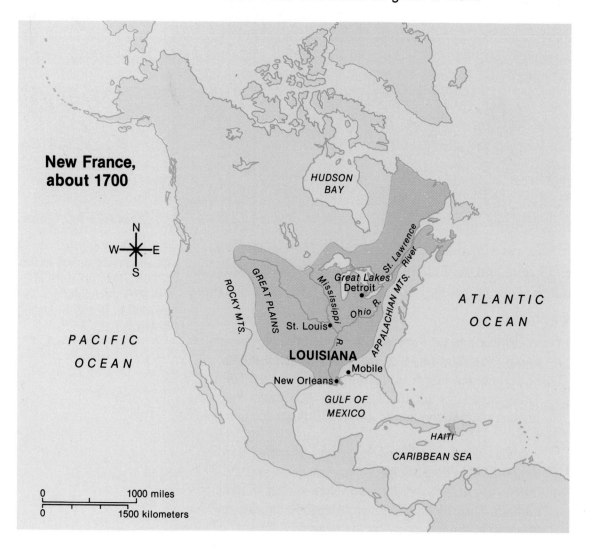

New France, about 1700

French Settlements

The French settlements in the New World were unlike the Spanish settlements in many ways. For one thing, the French did not build large farms and ranches. They were more interested in the fur trade. They were also not interested in converting the Indians to Christianity. Most of the French just wanted to trade with the Indians.

The French usually treated the Indians well. In return, the Indians usually were friendly to the French. French trappers traveled far and wide in search of furs. They went west to the Rocky Mountains. They went north to Hudson's Bay. They went south into the country of the Great Plains.

In this painting a French trader meets with the Indians to buy furs. The trader carries his goods in a sled pulled by dogs. He wears snowshoes that keep him from falling into the deep snow.

French Explorations

In 1673 Louis Joliet (JOE-*lee-et*) and Father Jacques Marquette (*zhahk mahr*-KET) set out on a long journey. They were searching for a great river the Indians said lay to the west. Marquette and Joliet wanted to see if this river might flow to the Pacific Ocean. They paddled in canoes through the Great Lakes and then down a number of small rivers and streams. Finally they reached the great river. It was the mighty Mississippi.

The river did not go west, however. It went south. Marquette and Joliet paddled down it for many miles. They realized that the river did not lead to the Pacific. After many hardships, they were forced to turn back. Nine years later, another French explorer, named Robert LaSalle, continued the journey. He led a group all the way down the river and found that it emptied into the Gulf of Mexico.

French explorers like these traveled by canoe across the Great Lakes and along the mighty rivers of the New World.

Because of these voyages, the French claimed much land in the middle of the North American continent. They named this land Louisiana after the French king, Louis. The French built many posts that later became great American cities. Some of these are Detroit, Mobile, New Orleans, and St. Louis.

Even though the French explorers and trappers were brave people, France was never able to back up its claims to land in the New World. There simply were never enough French settlers. Most of them were trappers who were scattered over a wide area. If more French people had come to this new land, perhaps today you would be reading this book in French instead of English.

THE DUTCH AND SWEDES IN THE NEW WORLD

In Chapter 5, you read about Henry Hudson, an Englishman sailing for the Netherlands. He explored the Hudson River in 1609. Soon the Dutch had begun trading with the Indians for furs. This trade was so valuable that the Dutch decided to set up a colony. They called it New Netherlands.

New Netherlands

The Dutch sent a governor to rule the colony. His name was Peter Minuit (MIN-*yoo-it*). He wanted to protect the colony from Indian raids. So he made a deal with the Indians. He bought an island named Manhattan from them.

The main Dutch settlement on Manhattan island grew and prospered. It was called New Amsterdam, after an important city in the Netherlands. New Amsterdam was a busy and bustling town. People from many different backgrounds walked its streets. There were Indians, Europeans, and blacks of African background.

In 1664 the Dutch went to war with England. An English fleet sailed to New Amsterdam and threatened to

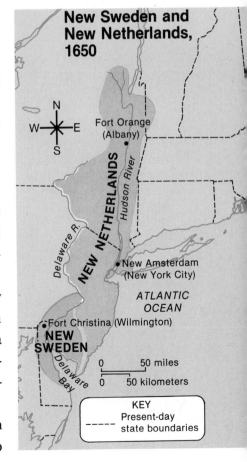

New Sweden and New Netherlands, 1650

Fort Orange (Albany)

NEW NETHERLANDS

Hudson River

Delaware R.

New Amsterdam (New York City)

ATLANTIC OCEAN

Fort Christina (Wilmington)

NEW SWEDEN

Delaware Bay

0   50 miles
0   50 kilometers

KEY
- - - - Present-day state boundaries

In 1661 the Dutch settlement of New Amsterdam was a small village. Today the skyscrapers of New York City stand on this site.

destroy the town. The Dutch surrendered. The king of England gave the whole colony to his brother, the duke of York. The colony of New Netherlands became New York and the city of New Amsterdam became New York City.

New Sweden

The Swedes also held land in North America. In 1638 Swedish settlers built a fort on the Delaware River. However, the Swedish settlement lasted for only a short time. It was soon attacked and taken over by the Dutch. Yet even in this short time, the Swedes made an important gift to American life. It was the Swedes who first built log cabins in the New World. Later other Americans copied their log cabins. Throughout our history, many famous Americans were born and raised in log cabins.

ST. AUGUSTINE

A year before St. Augustine was founded, a group of French soldiers settled in Florida. This made the king of Spain very angry. He said Florida belonged to Spain. The king sent a soldier named Pedro Menendez de Avilés (PAY-*droe muh*-NEN-*dace day ah-vee*-LACE) to teach the French a lesson. He also told Menendez to start a Spanish colony in Florida.

Menendez arrived in Florida in the summer of 1565. His soldiers built a wooden fort and some huts. Then they went off and destroyed the French settlement.

In the years that followed, St. Augustine grew slowly. Spanish colonies in Cuba, Puerto Rico, and Mexico were richer and bigger than St. Augustine.

The people of St. Augustine worked hard, though. They cut down the forest around the town. They planted grain and they raised cattle.

There was constant danger to St. Augustine. In 1586 the town was burned by Sir Francis Drake. Drake was a well-known English sea captain. He raided Spanish ships all over the world. The Spaniards called him *El Draco*—the Terrible One.

The people of St. Augustine built their town again. In the 1600's it continued to grow. Later, a new and stronger fort was built.

St. Augustine became a pretty town in these years. The city lay on a rise above a bay. Houses were built around a main square, or plaza. Many of the houses had grapevines clinging to the walls. Each house was built around a patio or courtyard. Inside the courtyards, settlers planted fruit trees and flowers.

This pleasant town remained the capital of Spanish Florida for almost 200 years. In 1819 Spain sold Florida to the U.S. Today you can visit St. Augustine and see how people lived hundreds of years ago.

SKILL BUILDER

Reading for Information

Suppose you wanted to learn more about the early days in Santa Fe. One place you might look is in an encyclopedia. You would read the encyclopedia for the same reason you do most of your reading in school—to gain information. The better your reading skills, the faster and more easily you will be able to get the information you want. What's more, reading will be much more fun.

It is true that some things have to be read very slowly and carefully. Other materials, however, may need only a light reading. Perhaps you need only to get an idea of what the subject is about. Perhaps you are reviewing something that you already know a lot about, or have already read. Such quick, light reading is called **skimming.**

A good skimmer can pick up a lot of information in a short time. The trick is knowing what "road signs" to look for.

To skim, move your eyes down a page slowly. Pause at headings and subheadings. These tell you what each section is about. Next, try to pick up the main idea from each paragraph or group of paragraphs. Often the main idea appears at the beginning of the paragraph in the form of a topic sentence. Other times it appears in the middle or at the end of a paragraph.

Also, you should notice key words—names, dates, places, for example. Pay attention to boldface words (like "skimming" in the second paragraph above). Finally, look at all photographs, maps, and pictures, and read the captions under them.

To review: What are some of the "road signs" to look for in skimming? Turn to pages 110-111. Look for the kinds of road signs mentioned here. Write a brief outline of what you have learned.

Words to Know

Use each of the words listed below in a sentence.

missionary   skimming

Facts to Review

1. What made Spain one of the richest nations in the world?
2. What was the earliest permanent settlement in what is now the United States, and why was it set up?
3. In what area of the present U.S. did the Spanish start many settlements? What was the purpose of many of these settlements?
4. In what ways were the French colonies different from the Spanish ones?
5. What did Marquette and Joliet find?
6. How did the Dutch lose control of New Netherlands?
7. What important contribution did the Swedes make to American life?
8. Describe what winters were like for people in Quebec.
9. What main problem did France have in controlling land in the New World?
10. What facts in this chapter point to rivalry among the European nations making settlements?

Things to Think About

1. Pretend that you are a missionary working among the Indians in a Spanish settlement. Write a letter home to Spain telling about your work. Tell how you communicate with the Indians. Tell how you teach them and what you in turn, have learned from them.
2. Draw a copy of the map on page 108. Now read what the text says about the explorations of Marquette, Joliet, and LaSalle. Picture in your mind the route that each followed. Then draw each route on your map. Label each one.

In this chapter, we are going to look at how people in the 13 English colonies lived in the middle of the 1700's. Ways of life differed from colony to colony in 1750. Black slaves in Maryland lived differently from white merchants in Massachusetts. German-speaking farmers in Pennsylvania lived very differently from large land owners living in Virginia.

Yet there were ways many people in the colonies were alike. For example, nine out of 10 colonists were farmers in 1750. Those colonists grew nearly all their own food. They also made nearly all the family clothing. If a family needed a new chair, the chances are that someone in the family made it. If a family needed a broom, a family member made it.

Land was easy to get. Almost anyone who worked hard could save enough money to buy some land. Almost everyone could expect to "get ahead." This didn't include slaves, though. It was possible for a slave to win his or her freedom, but it was very, very hard.

By 1750 the **population** (number of people) of the 13 colonies had grown to 1,207,000. Americans had large families, often with eight to 10 children. More immigrants arrived every year. By 1750 immigrants from many different countries were coming to the colonies to make their lives there.

Travel between the colonies was hard. To get from Charleston, South Carolina, to Baltimore, Maryland, it was easier to go by ship than to travel on horseback. Communication among the colonies was not very good either. As a result, different ways of life developed in the colonies.

On page 116: Settlers in the colonies cleared the wilderness. This painting shows a German settlement in Pennsylvania in the 1750's. Farming was important to each family in colonial times.

THE NEW ENGLAND COLONIES

Massachusetts, Connecticut, Rhode Island, and New Hampshire made up New England in 1750. Since much land in New England was rocky, farming was hard.

New Englanders lived close together in villages. Houses often were built in two rows that faced each other. Between the rows of houses, there was a field. There, cows and sheep could graze. This was called the village green. In time, the village green became the center of village life. On the green were the meeting house (which was often a church), a shop or two, and other public buildings.

A Living from the Sea

Fishing and shipbuilding became an important part of New England life. Many kinds of fish filled the waters near New England. Cod was the most valuable. Ships called schooners (SKOO-*nerz*) made cod-fishing trips three or four times each spring. They sailed between New England and the Grand Banks of Newfoundland. The fish were caught by

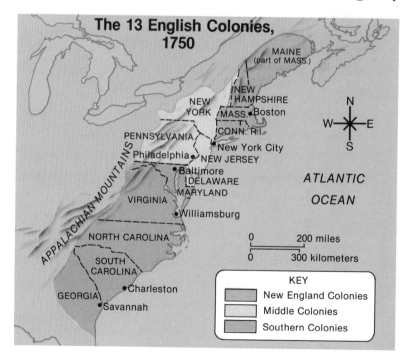

hand and by net. In order to preserve them, they were cleaned, smoked, or dried with salt. Then they were loaded aboard ships to be sent to Europe where there was a big demand for them.

When a fishing boat left port, a boy of about 10 or 12 was often aboard. He was called a "cut-tail." His job was to cut a wedge from the tail of every fish caught. These wedges were counted at the end of each trip to see how much each man was to be paid.

Sometimes the shout of "Thar she blows!" rang out. This meant the spray of a whale's spout had been sighted.

Whaling ships sailed from New England ports on long journeys. They often sailed as far as the South Atlantic Ocean. A journey sometimes lasted three to five years!

A large whale could provide tons of oil. Lamps that burned whale oil gave better light than did candles made of animal fat. So whale oil sold for a very good price.

Fishing and shipbuilding were important in the New England colonies. The harbors were busy places, with boats being built and repaired, with cargo being loaded and unloaded, and with fish being dried in the sun.

WANTED,

TO SETTLE IN

British North America,

700

FARMERS and LABOURERS,

WITH A FEW

TAILORS and SHOEMAKERS.

A Passage free, and One Hundred Acres of Land will
be given them on their arrival in the Colony.

*For further Particulars and a Passage, apply
to GEORGE MATTHEWSON, Atherton Street
Coffee House, Liverpool.*

Hours of Attendance from Nine o'Clock in the Morning until Noon,
and from Two until Eight in the Evening.

PRINTED BY SMITH AND GALWAY. POOL-LANE.

Posters like this one from
the 1700's urged people
to come to the colonies.

THE MIDDLE ATLANTIC COLONIES

Farmlands were richer in the Middle colonies of New York, Pennsylvania, New Jersey, and Delaware. Many new immigrants from England, Scotland, Germany, the Netherlands, and Ireland came to these lands.

The word *Pennsylvania* means "Penn's woodlands." The founder of this colony was William Penn. He was the son of a rich man. William Penn grew up in a castle with many servants. He wore fine silk clothes and was friendly with many of the best-known people in England. One of these friends was the king himself.

In 1665 a terrible sickness hit London. It was called the "Black Death." Many thousands of people became ill and died. Many people ran away from London to save themselves.

One group of people stayed in London. They were a religious group known as the Quakers. They stayed to take care of the sick and dying. William Penn liked these brave people. Before long, he became a Quaker.

In those days, it was dangerous to become a Quaker. England had a law saying that English people could belong to only one church—the Church of England. Quakers were not popular and were sometimes beaten.

William Penn became a leading Quaker. For this, he was thrown into jail a number of times. He was told to give up his Quaker beliefs, but he refused.

Penn began to feel that freedom of religion was impossible in England. He decided to start a colony in America. Here men and women would be free to worship as they pleased.

The king owed Penn's father a lot of money, but the father was now dead. So William Penn got the king to pay the debt with land in America instead of money. This land became Pennsylvania.

In 1681 Pennsylvania was set up. The colony was very democratic for its time. All male citizens had the right to

PENNS TREATY with the INDIANS made 1681 with out an Oath, and never broken. The foundation of Religious and Civil LIBERTY, in the U.S. of AMERICA.

In this painting, William Penn makes his treaty with the Delaware Indians. Penn paid the Indians for their land and protected their rights. Others did not treat the Indians as fairly.

vote. There was freedom of religion for all. Anyone accused of a crime was allowed to have a fair trial with a jury. These democratic ideas became very important in the colonies as time went on.

Settlers poured into Pennsylvania. It became a place where people of many different backgrounds could live together in peace. Quakers came from England. Scotch-Irish people came from the northern part of Ireland. There were many Germans and Swiss Catholics, as well as Jews from many parts of Europe.

The colony of New York grew more slowly. One reason was that much of the land was owned by just a few rich people. The lands they held were called **manors.** Workers who lived on them paid rent to the owner. The workers could not own these lands themselves. It was hard to find new settlers in the New York colony. That's because people would rather own their own land in some nearby colonies than pay rent on the manors.

A strong fur trade developed in the Middle colonies. Beaver hats were very popular in Europe. So tons of American furs were shipped to Europe from New York City.

THE SOUTHERN COLONIES

The Southern colonies of Maryland, Virginia, North and South Carolina, and Georgia were the most **rural** (country-like) of the colonies. In 1750 there was only one large town in the Southern colonies. This was Charleston, in South Carolina.

There were many large farms, though, called **plantations.** Their two main crops were tobacco and rice.

A Virginia plantation in the 1700's was a community. There was a main house, houses for workers, barns for the animals, and docks for unloading goods.

Profits from Indigo

Another big crop in the Southern colonies was indigo (IN-*dig-go*). This plant was used to make a bright blue dye. Indigo became an important crop in the South largely through the work of a teenage girl named Eliza Lucas. She was the daughter of a rich plantation owner. She was 16 when her father died. She then took over the running of three plantations in South Carolina.

In her spare time, Eliza Lucas liked to experiment with plants. She studied different plants to see if they could be improved, or if they could be made to grow in different places. She developed an indigo plant that would grow well in South Carolina.

Soon other planters in South Carolina heard about Eliza's indigo. They began to grow it and it brought them big profits. Eliza Lucas continued to experiment with plants as she grew older. She helped develop industries using hemp (which was used to make rope) and flax (which was used to make linen for clothes, sheets, tablecloths and other items).

Slavery Grows

Since many of the Southern plantations were very big, large numbers of farm workers were needed. However, it was hard to find white colonists to take these jobs. There was plenty of good farming land in the western parts of the colonies. Few settlers were willing to work on the plantations for someone else when they could get their own farmland in the west for almost nothing.

Thus, the owners of the big plantations turned to slaves to work the land. These slaves were black people who had been kidnapped from their homes in Africa. They were bought and sold like pieces of property. By 1750 there were about 250,000 slaves who lived and worked on Southern plantations.

This poster was for a cruel business—the buying and selling of human beings. Slavery brought misery to many people. Later it would divide the nation.

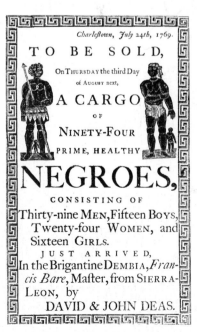

On the Frontier

Not all Southern farmers owned slaves. In fact, most Southern farmers did not own, or even want, slaves. Many of these farmers lived in the western parts of the colonies where the farms were smaller. Farmers there could work their farmlands themselves. This part of the country was known as the **frontier** (*frun*-TEER). The frontier was any land belonging to American Indian groups where colonists were beginning to settle. (The Western edges of the New England and Middle colonies were also frontiers.)

The people on the frontier had to clear forests to make the land ready for farming. They were too far from markets to buy many things. They bought things such as salt and gunpowder. They grew or made just about everything else themselves.

These frontier families were very independent. They had to stand on their own even more than other colonists. We call these people **pioneers.**

This pioneer woman stands outside her log cabin. The stumps from the trees used to build the cabin are all around. A pioneer family working very hard could build a cabin in two weeks.

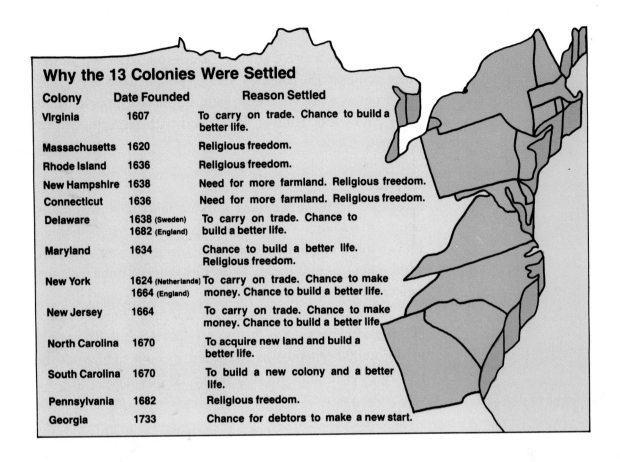

Why the 13 Colonies Were Settled

Colony	Date Founded	Reason Settled
Virginia	1607	To carry on trade. Chance to build a better life.
Massachusetts	1620	Religious freedom.
Rhode Island	1636	Religious freedom.
New Hampshire	1638	Need for more farmland. Religious freedom.
Connecticut	1636	Need for more farmland. Religious freedom.
Delaware	1638 (Sweden) 1682 (England)	To carry on trade. Chance to build a better life.
Maryland	1634	Chance to build a better life. Religious freedom.
New York	1624 (Netherlands) 1664 (England)	To carry on trade. Chance to make money. Chance to build a better life.
New Jersey	1664	To carry on trade. Chance to make money. Chance to build a better life.
North Carolina	1670	To acquire new land and build a better life.
South Carolina	1670	To build a new colony and a better life.
Pennsylvania	1682	Religious freedom.
Georgia	1733	Chance for debtors to make a new start.

CITIES IN THE COLONIES

The biggest cities in the colonies were on the coast. Merchants sent ships from them to England, the West Indies, France, and China. These ships carried products of American farms, fisheries, and forests.

The biggest city in 1750 was Philadelphia, in Pennsylvania. A British naval officer was surprised at how big a city it was. "I had no idea of finding such a place in America. It has nearly 2,000 beautiful brick houses," he wrote. He saw "streets paved and wide."

The most important city in New England was Boston. It was an important center of culture and learning. In the Middle colonies, New York City was slower to get started. It was smaller than Philadelphia.

To the south were Baltimore, in Maryland, and Charleston, in South Carolina. Charleston had some of the finest homes in the colonies. Its rich people lived very well. The women wore silks that were **imported** (bought from other countries). Houses were filled with imported furniture and dishes.

City Life

Most city people were hard-working folks busy earning a living. Philadelphia was known for its fine craftspeople. Philadelphia cabinetmakers made furniture you can still admire in museums today. Gunsmiths turned out a weapon called the Pennsylvania rifle.

In the cities, the great danger was fire. There were no fire departments such as the ones we have today. Everyone in the neighborhood was supposed to help fight fires. A leather bucket hung in every home. At the first cry of fire, everyone rushed out to help. Two lines would form

Here is a view of Philadelphia's busy waterfront. By 1775 more than 40,000 people lived in Philadelphia, the colonies' largest city.

between the burning building and a water supply. The buckets were filled and then were passed down the line to the fire. Empty buckets passed back up the "dry line" to be filled again.

FAMILY LIFE IN THE COLONIES

In 1750 almost every member of a colonial family worked. Often they worked from before dawn to long past dark. Only on Sunday did they stop. It took hard work to get the crops in, to preserve foods for winter, to keep the animals fed, to spin cloth, to make tools, to chop wood, to weave blankets, and to do a dozen other chores.

Some boys learned trades by becoming **apprentices** (*uh*-PREN-*tiss-es*). A family would sign their son up with a "master" of a craft at the age of about 12 or 14. The master

Fire was always a threat in colonial cities. With the buildings made of wood and built close together, a fire could wipe out many blocks before it could be put out by neighbors.

would teach the boy his craft. The boy lived and worked with the master until he was about 21. An apprentice might work as a carpenter, painter, clockmaker, blacksmith, or at other jobs.

Even in rich households, girls learned to sew. Almost every girl learned to spin. At the spinning wheel, flax grown by the family was spun into thread. Wool from the family sheep was also spun into thread. The colonists were proud that they could make their clothes entirely at home. In fact, they called them homespun.

Meals and Manners

A book of manners gave rules for children to follow at meals. It said:

- Never seat yourself until the blessing has been made.
- Then don't seat yourself until your parents have told you to be seated.
- Don't ask for anything.
- Don't speak unless you are spoken to.
- Don't throw bones under the table.
- Don't stare at anyone.

The noon meal was a large one. Breakfast and supper were smaller. Some families had exactly the same meal for breakfast and supper: bread and milk.

Enough food had to be saved to last the winter and early spring until the new crops came in. One thing that kept well was dried apples. Nearly every farmer planted apple trees.

A Swedish visitor to Delaware in 1758 wrote:

Apple pie is used through the whole year. It is the evening meal of children. In some places, the apple pie is made of apples that haven't been peeled or cored. The crust of the cake is so hard it won't break even if a wagon wheel goes over it.

This picture shows a young colonial woman all dressed up. How do you think today's fashions will look to people in the future?

Going to Church

Church-going was important in all the colonies. It was especially important in New England. Going to church there might fill up a whole Sunday. There was a morning session, a noon break, and an afternoon session. Sermons often ran for two or three hours. Anyone who dozed during a service was tickled or poked by a tithingman (TITHE-*ing-man*). He carried a long pole. At one end was a feather or squirrel's tail. At the other end was a knob.

Boys and girls each sat in special sections under the eye of the tithingman. His job was to keep them from giggling, squirming, sleeping, or doing anything else disrespectful.

THE NEW AMERICAN

By the middle of the 1700's, the colonists were almost a new kind of people. They were no longer just people who had come to the New World. They were people who had learned how to survive in a new land. They knew they had to work hard and use their time well. They also knew they had to solve problems and try out new ideas. Old ideas did not always work.

The colonies were under British rule, but many people began to grow apart from Britain. People in the settled areas wanted more say in their own government. People on the frontier had learned to take care of themselves. They too did not like to be ordered around by a government that was far away.

Then too, many people in the colonies had come from other European countries. They were not British and did not feel any special loyalty to the British king or any British laws.

The stage was set for big changes in the New World. You will read more about these in Unit Three, "Search for Freedom."

WOMEN IN THE COLONIES

In many ways, colonial America was a "man's world." The laws and customs favored men over women. Women could not vote. In some of the colonies, they could not own any property.

Still, women were very important in building colonial America. Here are the stories of a few of them.

Anne Hutchinson was born in England. She and her husband disagreed with the teachings of the Church of England. So, in 1634 they sailed to Boston with their 14 children.

Anne Hutchinson was a religious woman. She spent many hours reading and thinking about how to worship. Mrs. Hutchinson shared her ideas with friends. Before long, about 60 people were coming to her house for these discussions.

Other church leaders were alarmed by her popularity. They warned her to stop spreading dangerous ideas. Anne Hutchinson refused to keep quiet. So she was arrested and soon ordered to leave Massachusetts.

Years later the people of Boston put up a statue of Anne Hutchinson. They honored her for her courage and her belief in religious liberty.

Mary Rowlandson also lived in Massachusetts. In 1675 she was captured by Indians in a war. Her badly wounded nine-year-old daughter was captured too, and later died.

Mrs. Rowlandson lived with the Indians for the next 12 weeks. She marched through the woods, living on berries and nuts. She slept out-of-doors. She was one of the first white people to see how an Indian group really lived.

The Indians grew to like Mary Rowlandson. They admired her bravery. Finally they gave her back her freedom. She went home and wrote a book about her life in captivity. It became a best-seller.

Margaret Brent came to Maryland in 1638. She was a clever and hard-working woman. Before long she owned a large plantation. It was more successful than the plantations of her neighbors. They asked her for help. Margaret Brent soon was running several plantations. One of the plantations belonged to the governor of Maryland.

Men sometimes refused to repay her the money they owed her. They thought they could get away with it because she was a woman. Margaret Brent didn't let these men rest. She went into court and collected every debt. People in Maryland respected her as a smart businesswoman.

Phillis Wheatley came to Boston as a slave. A rich merchant, John Wheatley, brought her home. The Wheatley family taught her how to read and write. She was very intelligent and learned quickly. Soon she started to write poems. Phillis Wheatley became a famous poet. She visited Great Britain and published her first book of poems.

In 1776 Phillis Wheatley wrote a poem for George Washington and sent it to him. The general asked to meet this remarkable young woman. Phillis Wheatley wrote many more poems before she died in 1784 at the age of 31.

Reading a Pie Graph

We often speak of "the 13 British colonies." As you have read, however, not all the people were British. Look at the graph below. It gives some interesting information about the American population when it was first counted.

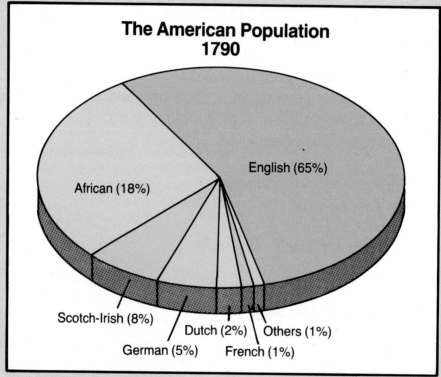

The American Population 1790

English (65%)

African (18%)

Scotch-Irish (8%)

German (5%)

Dutch (2%)

French (1%)

Others (1%)

This is a **pie graph.** A pie graph is a circle that is divided into wedges like the pieces of a pie. It can show the amounts of the different things that make up a whole group. The circle stands for the whole group. The wedges stand for each part of the group. The size of each wedge shows the size of each thing.

Look at the pie graph again. Into how many wedges is it divided? What do the wedges show? Look at the size of each wedge. Which group was the largest in the American population in 1790? Which was the second largest? Which group was the third largest? What were the smallest groups?

Words to Know

Choose six words from the list below. Use each word in a sentence.

apprentice   manor   plantation

frontier   pie graph   population

import   pioneer   rural

Facts to Review

1. Why did ways of life differ from colony to colony?
2. What were two important ways of making a living in New England?
3. Why was farming easier in the Middle colonies than in New England?
4. How did William Penn get the land for his colony?
5. Who was Eliza Lucas, and what did she do?
6. How were people on the frontier different from colonists in more settled areas?
7. Name four important colonial seaports.
8. Why do you think being an apprentice was a good way to learn a craft?
9. How did most colonists get their clothes?
10. Why do you think the colonists were developing into a new type of people?

Things to Think About

1. In which of the three groups of colonies would you have most liked to live? New England? The Middle colonies? The Southern colonies? Why?
2. Which type of common work in the colonies would you most liked to have done? Pretend that you are living in colonial times and must choose a career. Write a paragraph describing what job you want to do, how you will learn the job, and where you will do it.

UNIT REVIEW

Using New Words

On a piece of paper, write the paragraph below. Fill in the blanks with the correct words from the list.

apprentices   Pilgrims   Puritans
indentured servants   plantations

In colonial America, the ____ and the ____ were among the earliest settlers. In the Southern colonies, some people lived on large ____. Often cotton, tobacco, or rice was raised there. A good deal of the work of colonial America was done by slaves and by ____. Another important part of the work was done by ____, who were being trained for new careers.

Thinking About the Unit

1. Compare the ways the British colonies of Jamestown and Plymouth were started. In what ways were they similar? How were they different?
2. Tell how democracy began in the first colonies. Give examples to support your statements.
3. List five European countries that had settlements in the New World. In what part of the New World did each settle?
4. Suppose you were a boy or girl in one of the 13 colonies in 1750. Choose one colony and tell about your life there.

Sharpening Your Skills

1. Suppose that you are going to interview someone to find out why he or she picked a certain career. What kinds of questions would you ask? How would you set up the interview?
2. Turn to pages 122–124 in this text. Using the skimming techniques you have learned, find the following and write them on a piece of paper:
   a. headings and subheadings.   **c.** key words.
   b. topic sentences.   **d.** caption ideas.

   Now write a brief paragraph summarizing what you have learned from these pages.

3. Make a pie graph that shows how you spend a typical day. The entire circle should stand for 24 hours. Draw wedges in it that show how many hours you spend on each activity. Show time spent sleeping, going to school, eating, watching television, or any other activities in your typical day. Be sure that the size of the wedges shows the amount of time spent on each activity.

Expanding Your Knowledge

1. Make a dictionary of new words and terms you have learned in this unit. Arrange your words in alphabetical order. Write a sentence or two telling what each means. If you are not sure, reread the way the word is used in your text. Then check a dictionary too.

2. Find some cookbooks with colonial recipes. Choose one and plan to make it with your class. Consider each ingredient. For instance, if a recipe calls for flour, discuss with your class how the first settlers got flour. How will you get flour? Compare cooking in colonial times with the way it is done today.

Your Own History

In the first unit, you began gathering information about the first people who lived in your state or community.

In this unit you have read about how some cities were founded. Now it's time to find out how your town or city was started. Was it once an American Indian community? Was it a trading post for fur traders? Was it a fort built for protection? Was it a group of people who simply settled in the same place?

Find out too where the name of your city or town comes from. Does it have a special meaning? Is it an American Indian name? Did the first settlers name it? Is it a name from modern times?

Add the information you collect to your history scrapbook or files.

Unit Three
Search for Freedom

9 Road to Revolution

138

Once the troubles between Britain and the American colonies began, they grew quickly. By 1776 many colonists were ready for **revolution** (changing the government by force). They were ready to throw out the British and set up their own government. The war that they fought is known as the American Revolution.

Many years after the American Revolution, two famous Americans wrote letters to each other. Their names were John Adams and Thomas Jefferson. Both had taken leading roles in the Revolution. Both were later Presidents of the United States.

Adams wrote that he knew that the American Revolution had not started until the 1770's. He thought, though, that the years between 1760 and 1775 were just as important. During those years, he said, there was a revolution "in the minds and hearts of the people."

Oh, yes, he said, the American colonies belonged to Britain in those years. Big changes were taking place, though. People were coming to believe that the British king was unfair. Some were coming to believe that they would be better off if they were free of British rule.

In this chapter, we will look at the years before the American Revolution. We will see some of the changes that brought about a revolution "in the minds and hearts of the people." These changes led to the birth of our nation.

"THIS LAND IS OURS"

The French commander unfolded the letter. It was from the British governor of the colony of Virginia. It had been delivered by a 21-year-old Virginia officer named George Washington.

On page 138: Even before the American Revolution, colonists took action against Britain. Here, angry New York citizens pull down a statue of the British king.

In so many words the message said: We're amazed that you are building forts here. This land is ours. Leave!

The French leader replied: We're not budging an inch. In fact, we will put in prison any British person we find in these parts. After all, this land belongs to France!

The year was 1753. The place was the Ohio Territory (now Ohio and part of western Pennsylvania). France and Britain had fought in Europe several times recently. Now it looked as though they would fight in America. The winner could claim all land west of the Appalachian Mountains to the Mississippi River.

Britain controlled the colonies along the Atlantic coastline. France controlled Canada and had built forts along the Mississippi River. The French had also started a city, New Orleans, at the mouth of the Mississippi.

After receiving the French commander's reply, Washington and his small party raced back through the forests. They had to get to Virginia fast. Troops had to be sent to block the French. Forts had to be built.

British General Edward Braddock falls from his horse after being shot by a French soldier. The French and the Indians were more successful fighting from behind trees and rocks. Braddock's British army fought in the open, which was more dangerous.

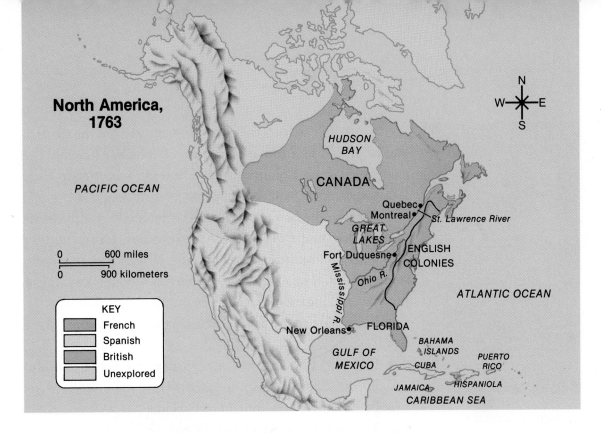

North America, 1763

HUDSON BAY

PACIFIC OCEAN

CANADA

Quebec
Montreal
St. Lawrence River

GREAT LAKES

Fort Duquesne

ENGLISH COLONIES

0   600 miles
0   900 kilometers

Mississippi R.

Ohio R.

ATLANTIC OCEAN

KEY
French
Spanish
British
Unexplored

New Orleans   FLORIDA

GULF OF MEXICO

BAHAMA ISLANDS

CUBA

PUERTO RICO

JAMAICA   HISPANIOLA

CARIBBEAN SEA

Washington advised the Virginia governor to build a fort at a key spot where two rivers join to form the Ohio River. But the French attacked and defeated the Virginians. The French now took over this land. They built their own fort there, which they called Fort Duquesne (*doo-*KANE). Today this is the city of Pittsburgh, Pennsylvania.

French and Indian War

France now controlled the Ohio Valley, but the fight had only started. It was to last for many years. It came to be called the French and Indian War.

British colonists outnumbered the French by at least 20 to one. The French, though, had many Indians on their side. Like the French, many of the Indians did not want to see British settlers move any farther west. So they joined with the French to stop the British.

The war started with a terrible loss by the British. An army of British soldiers and colonists from Virginia was advancing toward Fort Duquesne. About 10 miles from the fort, they were trapped in the woods by the Indians and the French. Hundreds were killed.

George Washington (above) and the English king George the Third (below) were on opposite sides in the American Revolution.

After this battle, the war went poorly for the British and colonists. The Indians and French attacked many of the colonists' farms. Colonists were often forced to leave their farms and move to larger villages for protection.

Finally, the British government decided to increase the fight. More troops were sent to the colonies. More supplies and more ammunition arrived. The British began to win some battles. They captured the city of Quebec in 1759. A year later, Montreal surrendered.

In 1763 France and Britain agreed to peace. As a result:

- Britain got all of North America east of the Mississippi River. (See the map on page 141.)
- Britain also won control of Canada.
- The frontier was open to British settlers again.

NEW PROBLEMS, NEW TROUBLES

For Britain, victory brought new questions:

- How can we pay the bills for this costly war?
- Who will pay for the soldiers, sailors, and supplies Britain still needs to protect its American colonies?
- Shouldn't the colonists help pay the bills?

The answers to these questions seemed simple in Britain. Britain thought the colonies should help pay. After all, the colonies had asked for British armies and navies to protect them against the French and the Indians. Giving this help had cost Britain a great deal of money. Now the colonies still needed British troops for protection. The colonists should be made to pay all these costs.

In 1764 the British lawmaking body, **Parliament** (PAHR-*luh-ment*), decided to tax the colonies. It said the colonists would have to pay a tax on certain goods. One tax was on sugar and molasses. **Customs officers** collected the tax. They were allowed to keep part of it themselves. Soon they were the least popular people in the colonies.

Polly and the Customs Officer

A ship named the *Polly* sailed into Newport, Rhode Island. The owner of the ship told the customs officer he carried 63 barrels of molasses. He paid taxes on this much and left.

Customs officer John Robinson got to thinking. The *Polly* looked like a big ship. He wondered if it didn't carry more than 63 barrels. He boarded another ship, raced after the *Polly*, and searched it. Sure enough, the *Polly* carried twice as many barrels as the owner had reported.

Robinson claimed the cargo for the government. Then his troubles started. The crew refused to sail the ship back to Newport. So he left the *Polly* and returned to Newport to get other sailors.

Then one night, 40 men rowed out to the *Polly*. They took all the cargo and wrecked the ship.

The owner of the ship went to a judge. "That customs officer, Robinson, must pay for my ship." the owner said. "It's his fault my ship is ruined." The judge agreed. He had John Robinson locked in jail until he could pay a big fine. It was three days before other British officials rescued John Robinson.

Scenes like this happened in many of the colonies. Both sides thought they were right. Neither side intended to give in.

The Stamp Act

The British Parliament passed more laws. Some were meant to help British trade. Colonists thought these laws helped British trade but hurt the colonies.

In 1765 Parliament passed a new law called the Stamp Act. Under this law, colonists had to buy a stamp for all kinds of paper products. Colonists had to buy stamps for such things as marriage licenses, playing cards, and even newspapers.

The colonists were used to paying some taxes. These taxes were voted by their own lawmaking groups, which

Colonists had to pay for tax stamps like this one on many items. Many people thought the Stamp Act was an unfair tax.

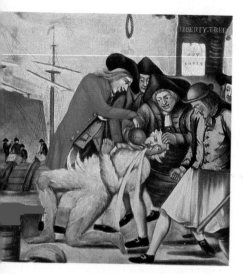

In the cartoon above, some colonists show their true feelings about British tax laws. They have covered a tax collector with tar and feathers and are forcing him to drink tea, on which there was a high tax. Colonial leader Samuel Adams (below) started the Sons of Liberty, also to protest British acts.

were the colonial legislatures. The stamp tax was voted by the British Parliament 3,000 miles (*4827 kilometers*) away. Colonists had no votes in Parliament. They could not elect any representatives to it.

James Otis, a young Massachusetts lawyer, called the act "taxation without representation." He said no parliament had the right to make people pay taxes unless those people had the right to vote for members of the parliament. The colonists did not have such voting rights.

Many colonists stopped buying British goods in protest. In some towns, people formed bands to protest. They called themselves the Sons of Liberty. They raided tax offices. They burned tax stamps in the streets.

Within a year, British lawmakers did away with the stamp tax. The colonists thought they had won.

But they were wrong!

MORE TROUBLE

In 1767 Parliament passed another law. This law placed taxes on many goods the colonists imported. Tea, glass, lead, and color for paints now were taxed. To make sure the taxes were paid, Britain sent more soldiers to the colonies. These soldiers had the right to search ships, businesses, and even homes.

Soldiers for defense were one thing. Soldiers who entered homes to search them were quite another.

Some colonists thought it was time to stop grumbling. It was time to organize. Samuel Adams of Boston suggested that leaders in the colonies begin to send each other letters and information. Adams helped form Committees of Correspondence to keep people in touch. They spread information about protests against the British.

It was an important first step in bringing the colonies together. Leaders in one colony now had a regular way to learn what leaders in other colonies were thinking.

Blood in the Streets of Boston

It was a March morning in 1770. A barber's helper noticed a British soldier passing by. The boy shouted: "There goes the fellow who hasn't paid for his haircut."

They argued. The soldier knocked the boy down.

Drawn by the shouts, groups of young men and boys ran to the scene. Stories of what happened spread through Boston. Someone started ringing the alarm bells.

The mob grew. They began throwing ice and snowballs at a British soldier standing guard. More soldiers rushed to help him.

From the docks came another group of men. Their leader was a tall man, about six feet two inches, part black, part Indian. Someone shouted, "Fire!" and the soldiers began shooting.

The first to die was the tall man, Crispus Attucks (KRISS-*pus* AT-*uks*). Four others were also killed. (For more on Crispus Attucks, see page 165.)

British troops fire at a crowd of colonists in Boston. This picture of the Boston Massacre was drawn by Paul Revere. Revere was a famous artist, silversmith, and colonial leader.

It was the first time blood had been spilled between the British and the Americans. The killings came to be called the Boston Massacre (MASS-*uh-kur*). Once again the colonists were greatly angered.

As a result, Parliament decided to end all taxes the colonists hated—except one. The king, George the Third, said there must be one tax so that his American subjects would remember that Britain still ruled them. This tax was on tea.

The Boston Tea Party

Because tea was still taxed, colonists stopped drinking it. They wouldn't buy it either. In Charleston, they stored it in damp cellars so it would rot. In Philadelphia and New York, they stopped tea ships before the ships could enter the harbors.

On the night of December 16, 1773, about 50 or 60 men boarded a British ship in Boston harbor. They had disguised themselves as Indians. For three hours, they

The Boston Tea Party was the most famous "tea party" in history. It also turned many people in Britain against the colonial cause.

threw chests full of tea overboard. More than 300 chests of tea were dumped in the water.

British war ships land soldiers in Boston harbor. Like the picture on page 145, this picture was also done by Paul Revere.

The "Boston Tea Party" sent the British into a rage. Valuable property had been destroyed. Someone must pay. As punishment, the British government passed harsh laws. The colonists called these laws the Intolerable Acts. This meant that the acts were unbearable, that they couldn't be accepted.

One law closed the port of Boston. No ships would be allowed to enter Boston harbor. The port would stay closed, the British said, until the colonists paid for the ruined tea.

Britain sent more soldiers to Massachusetts. "The New England governments are in a state of rebellion," said the angry King George. "Blows [fighting] must decide whether they are to be subject to this country or not." What do you think King George meant by this?

Talk in the Taverns

After these early troubles, colonists still argued among themselves. What should they do? Many colonists expected Britain to back down. A few people talked openly of breaking totally with Britain and forming a new government. Still the discussions went on.

Much of the talk went on in inns and taverns. There a visitor might hear such comments as these:

> If only we could send representatives to British Parliament. Then we'd have our rights as British citizens.

> The only way to save our liberty is to get free of Britain. We're different from them. They don't understand our ways.

> Sir, I've seen mobs run wild outside this very window. Are they to rule here in the colonies? If we break away from Britain, mobs will rule. No law will be obeyed.

> Britain is powerful. It has the best army and navy in the world. We are safe under Britain. I like that feeling.

> My family has lived here for 120 years. This is our home. What right has Britain to tax us? After all, we are Virginians. Next thing you know, they will want to tax our lands. They haven't the right!

THE FIRST CONTINENTAL CONGRESS

The British thought the new laws would silence the colonists. Instead, the Intolerable Acts only made the colonists angrier.

Some colonial leaders sent out a call for a meeting: Send two or three people from every colony. The date for the meeting: September 1774. The place: Philadelphia.

The people who met in Philadelphia had no power. But the meeting, called the First Continental Congress, brought together important leaders of the colonies. Such leaders as George Washington and John Adams were there.

These leaders wrote to King George. They demanded that the tax laws be changed. Then they agreed to meet again in the spring of 1775, if Parliament had not given up the Intolerable Acts.

Winter passed. The colonial leaders did not give up their demands. Parliament did not remove the hated tax laws. The colonies were on the road to revolution.

ABIGAIL AND JOHN ADAMS

"Alas! You are 300 miles from home. How many snow banks divide us. And my warmest wishes to see you will not melt one of them."

So wrote Abigail Adams to her husband John. John Adams was a member of the Continental Congress meeting in Philadelphia in 1774. Abigail Adams was with their children at their home in Braintree, Massachusetts.

John Adams was often away from home. He was a well-known lawyer and colonial leader. Abigail Adams was not a lawyer. She had not been to college. Yet her husband and friends knew that she was one of the smartest people in the colonies.

In colonial times, women were not supposed to have jobs or careers. They were expected to stay home with the children. Abigail Adams accepted this, though she didn't think it was fair.

John and Abigail wrote to each other often. He advised her to be ready to make sacrifices. To resist the Intolerable Acts, all colonists would have to make sacrifices.

Abigail Adams hoped that the Continental Congress would break away from Britain. Then they could make new laws.

And in the new laws which you will make, I wish you would remember the ladies. Be more favorable and generous to them than your ancestors. Do not put so much power in the hands of husbands.

Throughout the hard years ahead, John and Abigail Adams served as bright examples in the dark time.

Abigail and John Adams

SKILL BUILDER

Time Lines from Top to Bottom

A time line shows a length of time and some events that happened during that period. Some time lines show a time period as a horizontal line.

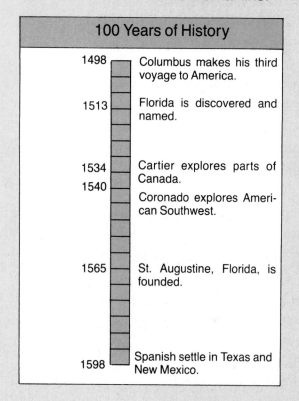

100 Years of History

1498	Columbus makes his third voyage to America.
1513	Florida is discovered and named.
1534	Cartier explores parts of Canada.
1540	Coronado explores American Southwest.
1565	St. Augustine, Florida, is founded.
1598	Spanish settle in Texas and New Mexico.

Horizontal time lines are read from left to right. Events that happened later in time are farther to the right than events that happened earlier.

Time lines that need a lot of words usually show time as a vertical line. Vertical time lines are read from top to bottom. Earlier events are placed above events that came later. Vertical time lines can show short lengths of time or long ones. The time line at the side of the page shows a century.

Time lines often show a group of events that are connected in some way. In this chapter, you read about a number of events that were connected. Taken together, they led up to the American Revolution.

Below is a list of those events in jumbled order. Go through the chapter and find when each event happened. Then make a vertical time line, showing them in order.

- Boston Massacre.
- France and Britain end French and Indian War.
- First Continental Congress.
- Boston Tea Party.
- Britain taxes colonies for French and Indian War.
- Britain passes Stamp Act.

How many years does your time line cover? How does this length compare with the vertical time line above?

Words to Know

Use each of the words listed below in a sentence.

Parliament   customs officer   revolution

Facts to Review

1. Why did many Indians choose to fight with the French against the British in the French and Indian War?
2. Which two Canadian cities did the British capture?
3. What were three results of the 1763 peace agreement between France and Britain?
4. Why did the British Parliament call for new taxes from the colonists?
5. Why did the taxes passed by Parliament make the colonists angry?
6. Who were the Sons of Liberty and why were they formed?
7. Did all the American colonists want freedom from Britain? Why or why not?
8. What did John Adams mean when he said that between 1760 and 1775 there was a revolution "in the minds and hearts of the people"?
9. If you had been an American colonist during this time, would you have wanted to stay under the control of Britain? Why or why not?
10. Why do you think the First Continental Congress was so important in American history?

Things to Think About

1. Pretend that you are an American colonist during the 1760's and 1770's. You have a close friend who still lives in Britain. Your friend has written you to ask why the colonists are so angry about British tax laws. Write a short letter in which you give reasons for their anger.
2. Think of some event that you read about in this chapter. How might a colonist have felt about it? Make up a poster that shows the colonist's feelings about the matter.

British troops took over Boston. No ships, except British ones, could sail in or out of the harbor. Still worse, the colonists were ordered to open their homes to the British soldiers. Families had to give the soldiers food and a place to sleep.

Such news made people angry in *all* the colonies. South Carolina sent rice and other food to help the people of Boston. In each colony, small bands of men met secretly, making plans in case of all-out war. They collected ammunition and stored it away.

Some British leaders thought King George was making a big mistake. One member of Parliament argued that British troops should be removed from Boston. He said:

> If I were an American, as I am an Englishman, when foreign troops were landed in my country, I never would lay down my arms! Never, never, never.

Many Americans felt the same way. Patrick Henry, a young lawyer, spoke his thoughts in Richmond, Virginia:

> Why do you stand here idle [not doing anything]? Is life so dear and peace so sweet that you would buy it at the price of chains and slavery? I know not what course others may take, but as for me, give me liberty or give me death.

In Boston, colonists were not standing idle. They formed an army of farmers, craftspeople, and merchants. They promised that they would fight Britain at a minute's notice. They proudly called themselves Minute Men.

On page 152: A young American soldier dies in the arms of a comrade at the Battle of Bunker Hill in Boston in 1775. The British won the battle, but the brave Americans proved they would not run under fire.

THE WAR BEGINS

British officers in Boston heard a rumor. The colonists were storing gunpowder in the village of Concord.

On the night of April 18, 1775, British troops left Boston on a secret mission. Their job was to find the gunpowder at Concord.

They tried to leave quietly, but they were being watched. The Americans had set up a signal to warn if any troops moved. The signal was to be sent from the tower of the North Church in Boston. One flash of the lantern would mean the troops were moving by land. Two flashes would mean they were moving by sea.

On the night of April 18, 1775, two lantern flashes came from the church tower.

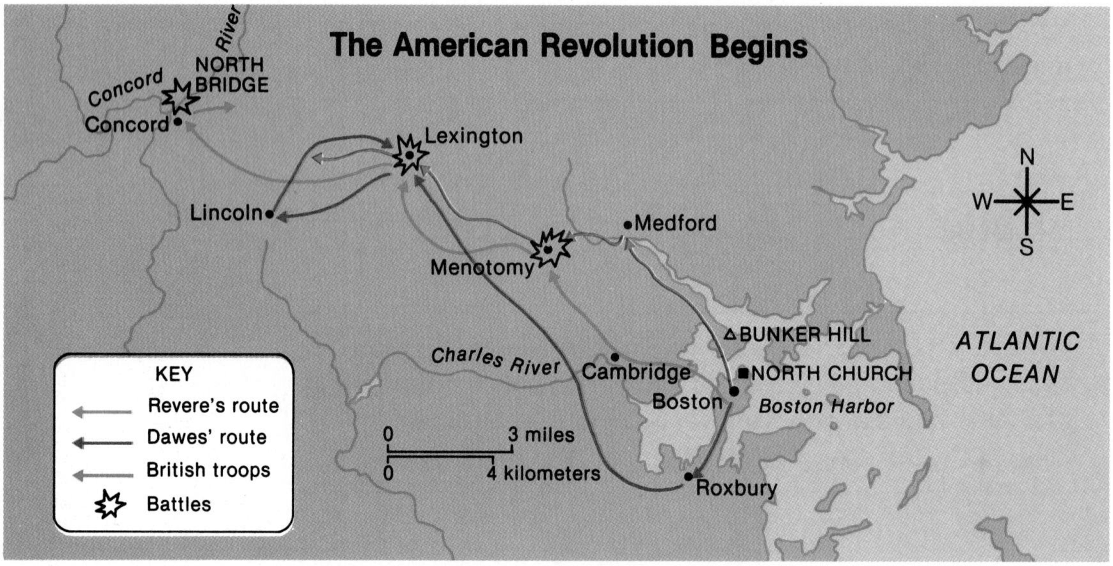
The American Revolution Begins
River
Concord
NORTH BRIDGE
Concord
Lexington
Lincoln
Medford
Menotomy
N
W
E
S
BUNKER HILL
ATLANTIC OCEAN
Charles River
Cambridge
NORTH CHURCH
Boston
Boston Harbor
0
3 miles
0
4 kilometers
Roxbury
KEY
Revere's route
Dawes' route
British troops
Battles

Lexington and Concord

Paul Revere and William Dawes rode out to spread the news. They rode from door to door, yelling, "The British are coming!" Minute Men rushed to their arms.

As the British troops marched toward Concord, they could hear church bells ahead, tolling the warning. Five miles from Concord, the British met the first Minute Men at the town of Lexington.

Shots were fired, and eight colonists were killed. The British pushed on toward the little village of Concord. They searched the town. During the night, the people there had hauled away most of the gunpowder and supplies. The British found little. Then, at the North Bridge, fighting broke out once again. Minute Men fired on the British troops and drove them away.

The British began the long march back toward Boston. By this time, Minute Men from other towns had spread out along the road. As the British soldiers passed by, shots came at them from behind trees, boulders, and stone walls. British soldiers fell dead or wounded all the way back to Boston.

That night colonists started arriving outside Boston, ready to fight. By morning hundreds of American soldiers ringed the city. The American Revolution had begun.

Bunker Hill

The American soldiers had the British nearly trapped in Boston. From a hill outside the city, the Americans could look down and watch the British.

On June 17, 1775, the British decided to attack the hill. Its real name was Breed's Hill, but the battle has gone down in history as the Battle of Bunker Hill.

The Americans were untrained as soldiers. The British were well-trained soldiers. Would the Americans have any chance against such a powerful force?

As the British troops climbed the hill, the American general, Israel Putnam, warned against firing too soon. "Don't fire until you see the whites of their eyes," he cried.

When the Americans finally fired, the British were forced to fall back. But they formed again and came back up the hill. Finally, the British managed to capture the hill. The Americans escaped.

These two American soldiers are shown fighting at the Battle of Bunker Hill. There were many free black soldiers in the American army.

These are some of the different uniforms that American soldiers wore in the war for independence.

The British had the hill now, but the cost had been very high. The Americans had proved that they could stand up and fight against the best soldiers in the world.

A General Is Chosen

The Second Continental Congress met in May 1775 at Philadelphia. The **delegates**—those who were chosen to attend the meeting—learned an unpleasant fact: King George had hired 12,000 German soldiers to fight in America. The German soldiers were known as Hessians (HESH-*unz*) because most of them came from the German state of Hesse. The delegates were outraged. This so-called king of theirs was hiring foreigners to shoot at them!

This Second Continental Congress had some important business. A Continental army had to be formed to fight the British. A commander had to be chosen for this new army. John Adams of Massachusetts stood up to suggest a name. He said that the best person for the job was George Washington of Virginia. Three days later, Congress approved. Washington became commander-in-chief of the Continental army.

Washington was a fine choice. He was an experienced soldier, having fought in the French and Indian War. Washington was well known for his loyalty to his soldiers, and his sense of honesty. He also strongly opposed the controls Britain had placed on the colonies.

Washington set out to build a strong army. This was not an easy job. He had little money to pay his troops or to buy supplies. Then too, many of his soldiers thought of themselves as Georgians or New Yorkers or Pennsylvanians —not as Americans. They didn't like taking orders from someone they hardly knew. Finally, many of the soldiers had agreed to join the army for only short terms—three or six months. After that, they were free to go home.

Would Washington be able to build a strong army in spite of all these problems?

THE DECLARATION OF INDEPENDENCE

While Washington tried to form an army, the leaders in Philadelphia were discussing a matter of great importance: Should the Americans break all ties with Britain?

Arguments sprang up again and again. Many of the delegates wanted a clean break away from Britain. Others wanted to keep some ties with the British government. Finally, the Congress asked Thomas Jefferson of Virginia and a few others to write a statement. In it they were to declare, or tell, what the American colonies intended to do. Then the whole Congress would discuss the statement.

Jefferson was one of the youngest delegates to the Congress. He had a brilliant mind and, as a member of the Virginia legislature, he had won respect as a wise writer of laws. He now wrote a statement that began with these words: "When in the course of human events. . . ."

These were the first words of our Declaration of Independence. This document told in clear language how the American colonists felt. It said that they were breaking away from Britain and told why. The Declaration listed the things the king had done wrong. It used words that have been quoted again and again around the world:

> We hold these truths to be self-evident: that all men are created equal, that they are endowed by their Creator with certain unalienable (*un-ALE-yuh-nuh-bul*) rights, that among these are life, liberty, and the pursuit of happiness.

The Declaration was saying that God gives people certain rights that cannot be taken away. It added that no government should try to take them away. If it does, the people have the right to make a new government.

The Declaration is one of the most famous documents in the world. When men and women in other countries and other times have talked about freedom, they have often used Jefferson's words.

Thomas Jefferson spent two weeks writing the Declaration of Independence. Working day and night, he produced one of the world's most famous documents.

The Declaration of Independence was approved on July 4, 1776. Copies of the Declaration were quickly printed. Riders were sent to every colony to read the statement in public squares and to have it printed in newspapers. (You can read more quotes from it on page 169.)

There was no turning back now. War with Britain was underway.

THE LONG STRUGGLE

Not all Americans supported the Revolution. Many, in fact, wanted to remain loyal to the king.

In the eight years of the war, Americans had to choose sides. Those who were for independence called themselves **Patriots.** Those who wanted to stay loyal to Britain called themselves **Loyalists.** Sometimes members of the same family were on different sides. Benjamin Franklin was one of the colonies' leading Patriots. Yet his son William chose the Loyalist side.

Retreat and Escape

In the summer of 1776, Britain showed its military power. A fleet of ships sailed into New York harbor. Aboard were 30,000 troops. The British commander-in-chief, General William Howe, thought it would be easy to defeat the Americans. He and his men did not think the Americans were very good soldiers.

For two years, Howe chased the Americans. Again and again he managed to defeat them. But each time, Washington was able to retreat (move back from the enemy).

In this way, Washington saved the American army. The British could never catch them.

Even so, Washington's army kept getting smaller. Men died of sickness. Some left to return home. The Continental Congress had a hard time finding money for pay or food. Winter came and some soldiers didn't even have shoes.

The Story of Trenton

By December 1776, Washington led only about 2,500 men. Many of them were sick and poorly clothed. Many were due to leave the army at the year's end. Something had to be done to raise spirits and to keep the men fighting.

Washington knew there were some Hessian troops in Trenton, in New Jersey. Washington also knew that the Germans would celebrate Christmas with parties and much drinking. He decided on a surprise attack.

On Christmas Eve 1776, a group of tough fishermen from Massachusetts waited at the bank of the Delaware River. Their job was to row Washington's entire army across the ice-choked river.

Washington crossed in one of the first boats. It was bitterly cold. Ice froze on the oarlocks.

Not until about three o'clock in the morning did the last man get across. Then the half-frozen men had to march nine miles in the bitter cold to the Hessian camp. Two soldiers dropped out of the line to rest. They froze to death in the cold.

Washington did not know that someone had found out about his plan. While he and his men were still on the frozen river, a messenger knocked on the door of the German commander's headquarters in Trenton.

George Washington leads the American army to victory at the Battle of Princeton in New Jersey. This battle was fought a month after the Battle of Trenton.

"The gentleman can't be disturbed," the commander's servant told the messenger. When the messenger insisted, his note was taken to the German commander. But the commander was too busy drinking and playing cards. He put the note in his pocket without reading it. It would have warned him of the American attack.

About eight o'clock the next morning, Washington's troops attacked the Hessian camp. Within an hour-and-a-half, the Americans had captured the whole camp. They took more than 900 Hessians prisoner.

The victory at Trenton was a big boost to American spirits. Some soldiers agreed to sign up for another term in the army. Bands of Patriots stepped up their raids on the British. However, the British army remained far stronger than the American army.

Winter at Valley Forge

The British army settled in for a comfortable winter in Philadelphia. Not far away, Washington's army camped on a frozen plain called Valley Forge. The soldiers were often hungry. They worked with frozen hands cutting trees to make huts. Their shoes, if they had any, were worn out.

American soldiers parade before General George Washington at Valley Forge. Some of the soldiers were dressed in rags. But their spirits were high. They liked the fact that General Washington stayed with them at Valley Forge.

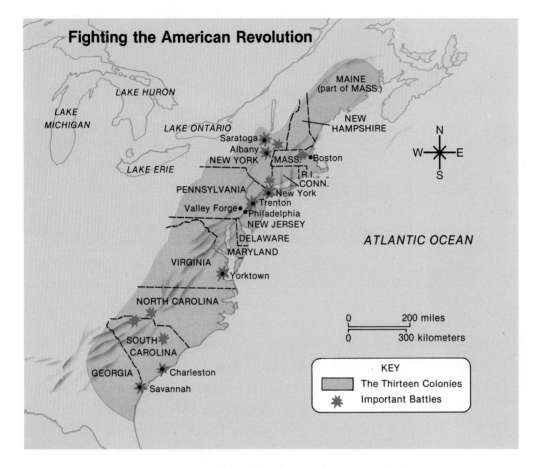

Fighting the American Revolution

KEY
The Thirteen Colonies
Important Battles

Washington wrote, "You could tell where the army had been by the blood of their feet on the snow."

He wrote many letters to Congress: Send food. Send clothes. Send powder. Do something!

Disease took hundreds of lives. Many Americans died that bitter winter at Valley Forge.

MOVING TOWARD VICTORY

While Washington struggled to keep his army together, Benjamin Franklin worked for America in Paris. He and other Americans urged France to enter the war. Britain and France were old enemies. The American victory at Saratoga in 1777 convinced France that the Americans were strong. In February 1778, France declared war on Britain.

One of France's richest noblemen had already joined the American cause. He was the 20-year-old Marquis de

At right: the Marquis de Lafayette meets George Washington.

Two other European soldiers who came to help America's fight for freedom: above, Baron Friedrich von Steuben; below, Thaddeus Kosciuszko.

Lafayette (*mahr*-KEE *duh lah-fay*-ET). He and some friends arrived in America in June 1777. He offered to serve in the American army as a private. Instead the Continental Congress named him a major general. Lafayette fought all through the war.

Spain and the Netherlands also gave their support to the Americans. They were eager for the defeat of Britain, their old enemy. So they lent money to the Americans.

Help came from other European nations too, in the form of good military leaders. Baron Friedrich von Steuben (FREE-*drik von* STOO-*bun*) came from Germany to offer his services. Count Casimir Pulaski (KAZZ-*i-mir puh*-LASS-*kee*) and Thaddeus Kosciuszko (THAD-*ee-us koss-ee*-USS-*koe*) came from Poland. These men all fought hard for the American cause.

Charleston Falls to the British

In the spring of 1780, the British captured the key seaport city of Charleston, in South Carolina. There they captured thousands of American troops. It was their biggest victory of the war.

The British controlled the sea, and they controlled important cities. They couldn't control the countryside and the frontier, however.

Small bands of Patriots raided British camps. They captured supply wagons. They made surprise attacks on scouting parties. The most famous of these fighters was

Francis Marion. His nickname was the "Swamp Fox." His band of fighters included men and boys, whites and blacks. Whenever the British chased them, the Americans disappeared.

The Last Battle: Yorktown

The British commander in the south was General Charles Cornwallis (*korn*-WAH-*liss*). He decided to move his army to Virginia. He thought he could end the war by taking control of Virginia.

It was a mistake. By now Washington's army had been joined by a French force. The French and American armies set out after the British.

Cornwallis had pulled his armies toward Yorktown, in Virginia. This city was on the coast of Virginia. There Cornwallis was trapped. The French navy blocked him from the sea. The French and American armies kept him from escaping on land.

Cornwallis knew he had lost. Through the mist and cannon smoke, a small figure stepped out from the British troops. Cannonballs roared past a young drummer boy. He began to beat out his message: *Stop. We want to talk*. Guns on both sides fell silent as surrender talks began.

At the Battle of Yorktown, American soldiers take down the British flag and put up the Stars and Stripes.

Two days later, Cornwallis surrendered. The date was October 19, 1781.

The American Revolution was over. The 13 colonies had won their independence. The British had decided that they couldn't fight the Americans and the French at the same time. So in 1783 Britain and the new United States signed a **treaty** of peace. (A treaty is an agreement or contract, usually between countries.) According to this agreement, almost all the land east of the Mississippi River and south of Canada became part of the United States. (Florida, though, remained part of Spain's empire.)

America had won its war. Now the Americans had the job of forming a government that would keep them free.

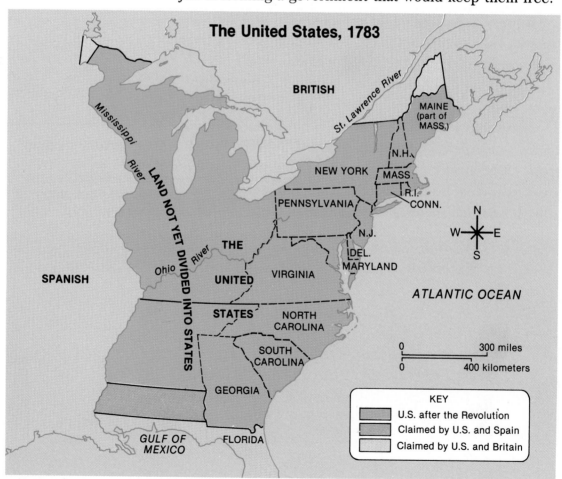

The United States, 1783

KEY
- U.S. after the Revolution
- Claimed by U.S. and Spain
- Claimed by U.S. and Britain

THEY HELPED TOO

The American Revolution was not won just by soldiers. Many other people helped make victory possible. George Washington, Benjamin Franklin, and Paul Revere are well-known heroes of the Revolution. Here are stories of some other heroes. They too helped in the American struggle for freedom.

Crispus Attucks was the first man to die in the fight against the British. He was born a slave in Massachusetts in 1723. His father was born in Africa. His mother was an American Indian.

Attucks was well treated by his master, but he wanted to be free. One day he ran away to sea. The tall, strong young man loved the freedom of life at sea.

Attucks was in Boston on the night of March 5, 1770. There was trouble between the people of the town and British soldiers. He was with a group of people when the trouble broke out. The British pointed their guns at the unarmed crowd. Crispus Attucks didn't move an inch.

Someone shouted, "Fire!" Crispus Attucks fell to the ground, dead. Others died that night too. But the former slave was the first to die for freedom.

Baron Friedrich von Steuben arrived in America in 1777. The German officer went to Valley Forge to offer his help. There George Washington asked von Steuben to teach American soldiers how to fight.

American soldiers had plenty of courage, but many of them were poor soldiers. They were used to fighting in the forests, shooting from behind trees and rocks. That was fine for some fighting. At other times, though, the Americans needed to fight the British out in the open.

Von Steuben taught the soldiers how to fight in the open. The baron did not speak English very well. At first the troops laughed at his accent. But they didn't laugh long. The baron was a stern teacher. From six in the morning to six at night, he made them march. Soon the Americans knew something about open-field fighting.

The following spring, the baron's teaching was put to use. Americans were fighting the British at Monmouth (MON-*muth*), in New Jersey. An American officer ordered a retreat. Then Washington and von Steuben rode up. Using the baron's lessons, the Americans stood and fought. They defeated the British in an important battle. Because of von Steuben, the Americans were beginning to fight like trained soldiers.

After the war, von Steuben became an American citizen. He lived the rest of his life in New York State.

The Battle of Monmouth was fought on a blazing hot day. **Mary Hays** spent all morning bringing pitchers of water to the soldiers. Because of this, some of the soldiers called her Molly Pitcher.

Her husband John was firing a cannon. Just as the order to retreat was given, he was hit by a bullet. Mary Hays ran to his side. She worked to stop the bleeding.

When she looked up, she saw soldiers running. She yelled at them to hold the line. Then she began to fire the big cannon. The soldiers were inspired by Mary Hays' courage. That, plus the appearance of General Washington, made them come back and continue the fight.

General Washington made her a sergeant in the American army. The soldiers cheered this heroine of the Revolution.

Haym Salomon (*hime* SAL-*uh-mun*) was a Jew from Poland. He had come to America to escape the harsh laws

Molly Pitcher at the Battle of Monmouth

against Jews there. Salomon was an early supporter of the fight for freedom. He served as a spy for the Americans. The British found out, arrested him, and sentenced him to die.

Haym Salomon managed to escape from jail. He went to Valley Forge. He was shocked at the sight of the soldiers in rags. Salomon's time in jail had left him too sick to serve as a soldier. He found another way to serve, though.

The American army was in desperate need of money to buy guns, bullets, and other supplies. The Continental Congress could not raise the money. It had no power to tax the people.

Haym Salomon was a successful business person. He had made a lot of money before the war. Salomon lent much of his own money to the American army. Then he worked night and day raising more money for the American cause. He was never repaid and he died penniless. Haym Salomon was another hero in the fight for American freedom.

SKILL BUILDER

Interpreting the Declaration of Independence

The Declaration of Independence is one of our country's most important documents. It deals with matters of life and death. The message of the Declaration was dangerous. It called for the American colonies to rebel against the British king.

The purpose of the Declaration was to convince and inspire the American colonists. It had to convince them that their cause was just. It had to inspire them. It had to make them willing to fight—even to die—for this cause. To do these things, the Declaration spoke in powerful, thrilling words. It appealed both to reason and to the strong feelings that stand behind the important things in life.

The four paragraphs on page 169 are not the whole Declaration. (Periods in a row, like this . . . mean that something has been left out.) They do show the main outline of this document. The first paragraph says that the Declaration will explain why the colonists separated from the British. The second paragraph tells what important rights all people should have.

The third paragraph tells some of the wrongs done against the Americans by the British king, their former ruler. The fourth says that the new country is here to stay. It says the signers are ready to give up their lives and property to defend it.

Many of the words in the Declaration are probably not familiar to you. The sentences perhaps are longer than those you usually read. Still, a dictionary and careful reading can make the meaning clear to you. In fact, you should be able to put the ideas of the Declaration into everyday words and short sentences. For example, the first paragraph can be written like this: "Sometimes it is necessary for one group to break off from another. When this happens, the group should explain its reasons."

Of course, these words don't really touch our feelings. They don't make us feel a part of something important. They do, however, help us to understand the meaning. Read each of the paragraphs carefully. Then rewrite each in your own words.

Our Sacred Honor

When in the course of human events, it becomes necessary for one people to dissolve the political bands which have connected them with another, . . . a decent respect to the opinions of mankind requires that they should declare the causes which impel them to the separation.

We hold these truths to be self-evident: that all men are created equal, that they are endowed by their Creator with certain unalienable rights, that among these are life, liberty, and the pursuit of happiness. . . .

The history of the present king of Great Britain is a history of repeated injuries. . . . [He] is unfit to be the ruler of a free people. . . .

We, therefore, the representatives of the United States of America, . . . appealing to the Supreme Judge of the world . . . do, in the name . . . of the good people of these colonies, solemnly publish and declare, that these united colonies are, and of right ought to be, free and independent states. . . . And, for the support of this declaration, with a firm reliance on the protection of Divine Providence, we mutually pledge to each other our lives, our fortunes and our sacred honor.

SKILL BUILDER

Reading Battle Maps

The Revolution's final battle at Yorktown grew out of a trap. A good way to see how the trap was set is to look at a map of the battle, like the one below.

As you can see, the map shows the different groups involved in the battle. Labels give the names of the person in command of each fighting force. Scales of miles or kilometers and a compass rose also help to show what was happening. Find each of these on the map.

Now trace what happened in the final battle. Where were Cornwallis' troops placed? From which direction did Lafayette come? From which direction did Washington come? How did Lafayette and Washington cut off any possible escape for Cornwallis by land? Where was the French fleet placed? How did the fleet cut off escape by sea?

Why would you say Cornwallis finally was forced to surrender to the Americans?

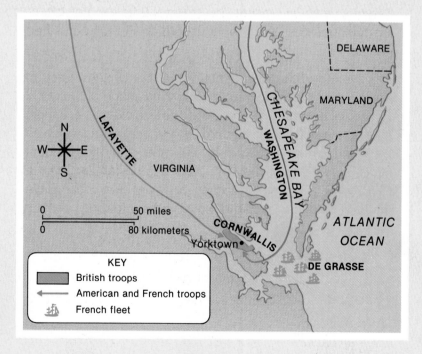

Words to Know

Use each of the words listed below in a sentence.

delegate   Patriot

Loyalist   treaty

Facts to Review

1. How did British actions in Boston in 1775 affect Americans in other colonies?
2. Where were the first two battles of the American Revolution fought?
3. What was the outcome of the Battle of Bunker Hill?
4. Why did people admire George Washington?
5. What job was Thomas Jefferson given by the delegates of the Second Continental Congress?
6. What beliefs did the Declaration of Independence present?
7. Why were the Americans able to surprise the Hessian troops at Trenton?
8. What problems did Washington face in fighting the war?
9. How did various European countries help the colonists?
10. How did Washington and Lafayette force the British to surrender at Yorktown?

Things to Think About

1. Go through the chapter and pick out the major events in the American Revolution from Lexington and Concord to the surrender at Yorktown. Be sure to note their dates. Then make a vertical time line of the American Revolution.
2. Pair up with a classmate. Pretend that one of you is a Patriot and the other is a newspaper reporter. Together write a newspaper article in which the reporter interviews the Patriot for his or her views on the Revolution. The reporter should supply the questions and the Patriot should supply the answers.

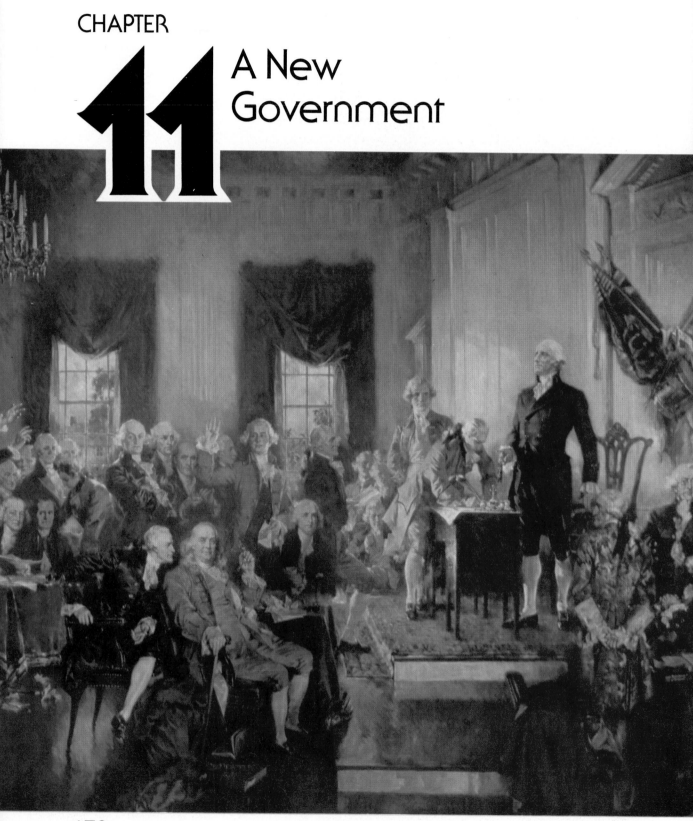

11 A New Government

It was Monday, September 17, 1787. Fifty-five delegates had been meeting six days a week for almost four months. Now their work was over. They could leave the heat and noise of Philadelphia. There would be no more hurried dinners at the inn. There would be no more late-night arguments. It was time to go home.

Just one final task remained. The delegates stepped forward to sign the document they had written. First was George Washington, who had run the meeting. Then the other delegates followed. They signed according to their home states, from New England to the South.

There was Jonathan Dayton of New Jersey. At 27, he was the youngest delegate. From Pennsylvania came Robert Morris, the richest man in America. He had not said one word during the whole time. Very different was a fellow Pennsylvanian, Gouverneur (*guv-er*-NEER) Morris (no relation). He had talked more than any other man there. James Madison came from Virginia. His notes are the best record of what happened at the Philadelphia meeting.

One delegate watched with special pride. Benjamin Franklin was 81, the oldest man there. He had often calmed angry feelings with a joke or a story. Now he looked at the back of Washington's chair. It was decorated with a sun at the horizon. Franklin said he had often looked at the chair and wondered if the sun were rising or setting. Today he wondered no longer. "I have the happiness to know that it is a rising and not a setting sun," he said.

A new day was indeed beginning for the United States. These delegates had written the United States **Constitution**—the basic law of our land. The Constitution set up a new kind of government. It has guided Americans for more than 200 years. It has helped the United States grow to become a strong and free nation.

On page 172: George Washington stands on the platform as the delegates line up to sign the United States Constitution.

Benjamin Franklin was the most famous American of his time. Franklin was a statesman, an inventor, a scientist, an author, and a businessman.

THE ARTICLES OF CONFEDERATION

In the last chapter, you read that the Continental Congress was a sort of national government during the American Revolution. Each colony sent representatives to the Congress. The Congress paid the soldiers—sometimes. It carried on dealings with other nations.

Late in the war, the colonies agreed to a group of rules, called the Articles of Confederation (*kun-fed-uh-*RAY-*shun*). The Articles set up a Congress that would handle the affairs of the whole nation. Each state had one vote.

The Articles did not set up a strong national government. People went on thinking of themselves not as Americans but as New Yorkers, or Virginians, or whatever.

Under the Articles, the Congress could ask for money from the states. The states didn't have to pay, however. The Congress could not control trade. There were no courts to settle arguments. The Congress was not very strong, but most Americans liked that. They had had enough strong government under the British.

One Nation—or 13?

The years after the American Revolution were hard. The United States was a small nation, with fewer than three million people. The country owed a lot of money. The British refused to give up forts they had in the west. Britain also kept American ships out of many ports that Britain controlled.

The government under the Articles of Confederation could do little. Other nations didn't take the United States seriously. In London, American statesman John Adams was teased. Did he represent one nation—or 13?

Several American leaders grew worried. George Washington was one of them. How could such a weak government defend the nation? How could the U.S. become great? These leaders felt that something had to be done. So they arranged to meet in Philadelphia in May of 1787.

A NEW PLAN OF GOVERNMENT

There were 55 delegates at the Philadelphia meeting. At first some thought they might just change the Articles of Confederation. Soon they knew that this was not enough. They would start over and work out a new government.

The delegates also agreed on another thing. The new government would not just be a loose grouping of states. It would be a government that mattered to each U.S. citizen. This is why the delegates began the Constitution, "We the people of the United States." They did not say, "We the people of New Hampshire, Massachusetts," and so on.

The Role of the President

Most of us take our system of government for granted. For instance, we know that there is a President at its head. The President serves for four-year terms. It seems natural to us because we are used to it.

The delegates at Philadelphia, however, thought about several ways for the government to be led. A few delegates didn't want a single head. Such a leader might become too powerful. They wanted a group of leaders instead.

"A single leader is best," said others. "But this leader should serve only one term. This way such a leader won't waste time running for reelection while still President."

"No, that won't work," said still others. "If a President knows it's not possible to run again, maybe that President won't try to do a good job. It should be possible for a President to be elected again."

Even this wasn't enough for some delegates. "The President needs to be strong. The President should serve for life."

The delegates talked it over. They took votes. Finally they made a decision about the President, and wrote it into the Constitution. The President would serve for four years. The President could also run for election again.

James Madison was a leader in the creation of the Constitution. Later he was the fourth President of the United States.

An Important Agreement

Have you ever tried to make up a set of rules for a group? If you have, you know it's not easy. People want different things. They feel strongly about them. You try to satisfy as many people as possible through **compromise.** This means each side gives in a little to reach an agreement. For example, Peter and Susan belong to the same club. Peter says that weekly dues have to be a dollar. Susan thinks 50 cents is plenty. They might agree on a compromise of 75 cents.

In the same way, back in 1787, making decisions about the new government required a lot of compromises. Delegates had to be willing to change. They had to give in to others from time to time.

The most important compromise of all involved setting up a legislature, a group that makes laws. The delegates wanted to have each state represented in this group. This was a problem, however.

Delegates from small states, such as Delaware, wanted a Congress like the one under the Articles. Each state had the same number of votes. All the states were equal.

This wasn't fair, said delegates from the big states like Virginia. The states with more people should have more representatives. Each state should have members in Congress according to the size of its population.

Finally a compromise was reached. The result was the kind of Congress we have today. It has two parts, each called a **house.** One house is called the Senate. Here each state has two votes. At the beginning, the Senate had 26 members—two for each of the 13 states. Today it has 100 members—two for each of the 50 states.

The other house of Congress is called the House of Representatives. Here each state is represented according to the number of people it has. The first House of Representatives had 65 members. Today's has 435. States with few people may have just one or two Representatives. States with large populations may have 40 or more.

Our Federal Government

Legislative Branch (Congress)	Executive Branch (President)	Judicial Branch (Courts)

Senate House of Representatives Makes the federal laws. Sets federal taxes. Approves appointments by President. May impeach the President.	Executive Departments Sees that federal laws are carried out. Approves or vetoes federal laws. Appoints ambassadors, judges, and other federal officials. Commands the armed forces.	The Supreme Court of the United States Lower Courts Decides what laws mean. Punishes lawbreakers. May rule that a law passed by Congress is unconstitutional (not in keeping with the Constitution).

A Federal System

The delegates knew that the national government had been weak under the Articles of Confederation. Now they worried that they might set up a government that had *too much* power. Americans had fought to be free. They wanted to stay this way. The question was, Who should have the power to govern?

One answer was the **federal system.** This means that power in our government is divided between the national, or federal, government and the states. The *national* government controls things such as defending the country, coining money, and dealing with foreign governments. The *state* governments control the *state* police, *state* school systems, *state* highways, and so on.

Another answer was the **separation of powers.** In our national government, power is divided among three branches. One branch is the **Legislative Branch,** or Congress. It makes our laws. Congress also has the power to tax citizens.

A second branch of the government is the **Executive Branch.** It is made up of the President and many assistants. They see that the laws are carried out. The President is also Commander-in-Chief of the armed forces.

Third is the **Judicial** (*joo-*DISH-*ul*) **Branch,** or the courts. The highest court in the land is the Supreme Court. The courts decide what different laws mean. They also punish lawbreakers.

None of the three branches can work all by itself. Each branch depends on the other, like parts in a machine. For instance, though Congress can pass a bill, the President has to sign it. Only then does it become a law. However, the President may **veto** (refuse to sign) it. Even if it becomes law, the Supreme Court may rule against it. The Court may declare a law **unconstitutional** (*un-kon-stuh-*TOO-*shun-ul*). This means that, if a law goes against what the Constitution says, it is no longer a law.

There are many other ways in which the three branches affect each other. They work in a system of **checks and balances.** Each branch can *check,* or limit, the other. In this way, power is *balanced* among the three branches.

The delegates signed the Constitution on September 17, 1787. It couldn't go right into effect, though. First an important step had to be taken. The states had to approve it. When nine states had done so, the new government would begin.

Would the Constitution be approved? It was hard to tell. The meetings of the convention had been secret. Most Americans did not know what the Constitution was like.

Sharp Words, Then Agreement

The Constitution was read all over the country. Many Americans were against it. The new national government, they said, would be too strong.

"What about the states?" asked some. "Most of their power is gone."

But the framers of the Constitution—the delegates who had written it—defended the document well. Yes, the new government would have more powers than the old one. Still, the people would have the final say. Besides, the United States needed a government that could act. Without one, the nation would not last.

The first state to approve the Constitution was Delaware. Four more states did so quickly. Then, after some struggles, Massachusetts, Virginia, and New York approved it. In June 1788, New Hampshire became the ninth state to approve. Now the Constitution was official. All 13 states finally approved the Constitution by 1790. Washington said it was a victory "for all mankind."

The Bill of Rights

Several states approved the Constitution only on one condition. They said it needed a **bill of rights.** By this, they meant a list of basic human freedoms—rights every person should have. They thought the bill of rights should be written in clear language to protect the rights of Americans.

The framers had provided a way to change the Constitution. Changes, called **amendments,** could be made. So in 1791, the 10 amendments, known as the Bill of Rights, became part of the Constitution. They spell out the freedoms of all Americans.

One of these is the right to worship as we please. Two others are the rights to speak and to write freely. Other amendments protect the rights of people accused of crimes. Many amendments have been added to the Constitution since 1791. None is more important than the Bill of Rights.

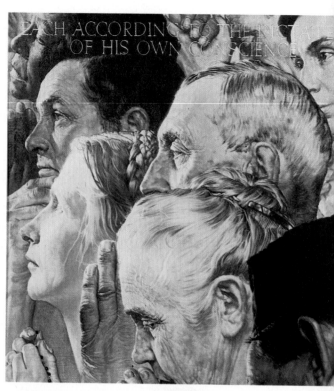

American artist Norman Rockwell painted these pictures to show freedom in America: freedom of speech (above left); freedom of worship (above right); freedom from fear (below left); and freedom from want (below right).

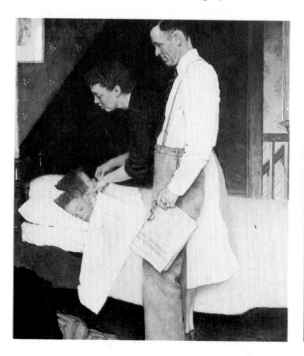

The Bill of Rights

What It Says

Amendment 1	**Basic freedoms.** Protects freedom of religion, freedom of speech, freedom of the press, freedom to hold meetings, and freedom to ask the government to correct problems. Keeps the government from creating an official religion.
Amendment 2	**Right to bear arms.** Gives the people the right to bear arms, subject to laws of the states.
Amendment 3	**Quartering of soldiers.** Protects people from having to give room and board to soldiers.
Amendment 4	**Freedom from unlawful searches and arrests.** Keeps the police from being able to search and arrest people unlawfully.
Amendment 5	**Rights of people accused of crimes.** Protects people accused of crimes from being taken to trial unfairly and being given unfair punishments.
Amendment 6	**Trial by jury.** Gives people accused of crimes the right to a speedy public trial by jury. Spells out how trial is to be conducted.
Amendment 7	**Civil trials.** Gives people involved in lawsuits the right to a jury trial.
Amendment 8	**Bails, fines, and punishments.** Protects people from unfair bails, fines, and punishments.
Amendment 9	**Rights to the people.** People have more than just those rights listed in the Constitution.
Amendment 10	**Rights reserved for the states and the people.** All powers not given to the federal government belong to the states or the people themselves.

OUR GOVERNMENT BEGINS

George Washington became our country's first President in 1789. John Adams was Vice President. Washington served two four-year terms. His job was not easy. He had to choose people to head departments in the new government. He had to find ways to pay for the huge debts run up during the Revolution. He had to work out agreements with foreign countries, especially those that still held land in North America.

At first the new President ran the country from New York City. Then, in the years between 1790 and 1800, Philadelphia was the nation's capital. Finally, in 1800, the capital was moved to a new location, a site on the Potomac (*puh*-TOE-*mik*) River. It was called Washington, D.C. (for District of Columbia).

By then, George Washington was dead. He had died in 1799. His work would have to be carried on by others. The young nation of 13 states would grow up to be strong and powerful. It would become a world leader. George Washington would be honored by Americans as the "father of his country."

George Washington comes ashore at New York City for the ceremony that will make him the first President of the United States. New York City was the nation's first capital.

FARMER WASHINGTON

George Washington never wanted to be famous. True, he is remembered as the "father of his country." He was happiest, though, on his farm, Mount Vernon, in Virginia.

Washington was born on a Virginia farm in 1732. He was a happy boy who loved games and horseback riding. Then his father and half brother died. The two deaths changed George Washington. The fun-loving child grew into a serious, hard-working man.

He worked on the frontier. There he served as an officer in the French and Indian War. After that war, Washington went back to Mount Vernon. He loved his plantation and his life with his wife Martha.

These were troubled times for the colonists in Virginia. Their ties to England were becoming very strained.

George Washington joined other colonists in opposing British taxes. Soon he became a leader in the Patriot cause. His fellow colonists trusted him. They knew he was not too proud to admit he had made a mistake. Soldiers knew he would not take unnecessary chances with their lives. Government leaders knew he could be counted on to see both sides of an argument and find a compromise.

After the Revolution, some Americans wanted to make George Washington king. He would not allow this. He would serve his country, though, as its first President.

George Washington served two terms (eight years) as President. In 1797 he left the government. He had started the U.S. on the road to growing strong. To Americans he was "first in war, first in peace, and first in the hearts of his countrymen." President Washington returned to Mount Vernon to be just Farmer Washington.

George Washington at Mount Vernon

SKILL BUILDER

Interpreting the U.S. Constitution

The Constitution is the supreme, or highest, law of our land. This means that everyone in this nation must obey it. It also means that all other laws must follow it. No law can say that something must be done when the Constitution says that it must not be done.

The framers of the Constitution knew they could not write laws that would cover every situation and problem. They also knew that the country would grow and change and that new situations would arise. The framers knew they could not write laws to cover these new situations.

As a result, the framers dealt only with certain basic ideas of how people should be governed. They hoped that Americans of the future would fit these ideas to new times and new needs.

The **Preamble** (PREE-*am-bul*), or introduction, to the Constitution states some very important goals.

> We, the people of the United States, in order to form a more perfect Union, establish justice, insure domestic tranquility, provide for the common defense, promote the general welfare, and secure the blessings of liberty to ourselves and our posterity, do ordain and establish this Constitution for the United States of America.

Like the words of the Declaration of Independence, many of these words are difficult. Below are some everyday phrases. They can be used in place of the underlined words or phrases in the Preamble. See if you can match them. Then rewrite the Preamble using ordinary phrases.

1. set up fair courts and laws
2. bring together in a better way the different parts of our country
3. the people who come after us
4. set up as law
5. keep peace at home
6. protect ourselves against our enemies
7. help people have better lives

Words to Know

Choose 10 of the words listed below. Use each word in a sentence.

amendment
bill of rights
checks and balances
compromise
Constitution

Executive Branch
federal system
house
Judicial Branch
Legislative Branch

Preamble
separation of powers
unconstitutional
veto

Facts to Review

1. Why did Ben Franklin say he had sometimes wondered if the sun on Washington's chair was rising or setting?
2. Name some weaknesses of the Articles of Confederation.
3. Why did people in London ask John Adams if he represented one nation or 13?
4. Why does the Constitution begin: "We the people of the United States"?
5. Why did some delegates object to the idea of a President at the head of government?
6. Why do we have two houses of Congress? What are they called?
7. What are the three branches of our federal government? What does each branch do?
8. What are changes to the Constitution called?
9. Why did several states demand a bill of rights?
10. Why was compromise used in writing the Constitution?

Things to Think About

1. Think about a problem you have faced recently in which there was a difference of opinion. Write the problem down, showing both sides. Then show a way that compromise might have been used to solve the problem.
2. Get together in small groups. Then choose a problem that is affecting your community right now. Choose one for which different people have different solutions. Think of ways to solve the problem through compromise. Present the problem and your compromise to the class.

Using New Words

On a piece of paper, write the paragraph below. Fill in the blanks with the correct words from the list.

bill of rights	Parliament
Constitution	Patriots
federal system	revolution
Loyalists	treaty

In the 1760's, _____ began passing new laws for the colonies to obey. The colonists were angered by some of these laws. Soon many of them were talking about _____. Those who favored independence from Britain were the _____. Those who wanted to keep their ties with Britain were the _____. By 1775 war had come. Eight years later, it ended when Britain and the new United States signed a _____ of peace. The new nation now had to work out a way to govern itself. In 1787 a new _____ was written. This document divided the power to govern between the nation and the individual states. We call this the _____. Several states refused to approve this plan of government until a list of human freedoms, a _____ , was added to it.

Thinking About the Unit

1. Why was George Washington a great leader? What qualities did he have that made people look to him as a leader?
2. Compare government under the Articles of Confederation with government under the Constitution. What differences between the two can you find?

Sharpening Your Skills

1. Think of some of the important events in your life. Write down the year and the event. Is the time between each event the same? Have two or more important events happened during one year, with no events at all happening in another? Make a vertical time line of these events.

2. What kinds of symbols might you find on a battle map but not on a street map? What kinds of information do these battle map symbols give?

Expanding Your Knowledge

1. Pretend you are a boy or girl living through the American Revolution. You are keeping a diary of your experiences. Write one day's entry in your diary. Describe some event that you have seen or tell how the war has changed your life in some way.

2. Design a bulletin board to show the Bill of Rights. Draw or cut out pictures showing each of these 10 amendments in action.

3. Choose one early American leader who interests you. Do some research to find out more about this person. Write a report that shows why the leader you chose made an important contribution to the U.S. Share your report with the rest of the class.

Your Own History

In this unit, you have read how the first 13 colonies became states. Since then, 37 more states have joined the Union. Find out when and how your state joined the Union. Who was President of the United States at that time? How old was the nation? Who was your state's first governor? Who were its first U.S. Senators? Make a data sheet telling about the history of your state. Add this to your scrapbook or your file.

Unit Four
From Sea to Shining Sea

12 The Pioneers

A man walks through the woods alone. He wears clothes made of buckskin. On his head is a raccoon skin cap with a tail. He carries nothing except his long rifle and a bag of bullets. His walk is silent. He stops to look at the ground and sniff the air. Then he moves on.

The man is Daniel Boone, and he is tracking a big brown bear in the Kentucky woods. It is 1769 and Kentucky is a wilderness. There are no settlers living here.

Soon though, all of this would change. Thousands of people would follow Daniel Boone to Kentucky. Hundreds of thousands more would continue going farther west. All of them wanted to settle on new land and start new lives.

But what about the people whose land they wanted— the American Indians? What about the Indians' rights to this land? It had been theirs for thousands of years. They had farmed it, hunted it, roamed it. Now they were being asked—and often forced—to leave it, piece by piece.

The Indians grew angry about what was happening. They were losing their land, and this was bad enough. They were also being forced to fight other Indians to gain rights to new lands for themselves. It is no wonder that their anger grew. So they decided to fight these settlers who were taking their land. A century of bitter battle between Indians and settlers was just beginning. So was a century of American movement ever farther westward.

THE STORY OF DANIEL BOONE

Daniel Boone was born in Pennsylvania in 1734. His family lived on the frontier. There were few neighbors, except for Indians. From young Indian friends, Daniel Boone learned the secrets of the woods. He learned how to walk silently.

One page 190: Daniel and Rebecca Boone crossed the mountains on their way to Kentucky. They knew how to find water and they knew which wild plants were good to eat.

He learned how to track animals and how to imitate (copy) their calls. He learned their habits. As the young man's knowledge of the wilderness grew, so did his fame as a clever **scout** (a person sent to find out what the enemy is doing or to find something).

When Daniel Boone was 19, his family moved to North Carolina. A few years later, he married a neighbor named Rebecca, and they had a family. Now he and Rebecca lived on a farm. Daniel Boone wasn't really happy, however. He missed the woods.

By the late 1760's, Boone thought North Carolina was getting "crowded." Of course, he had his own ideas about neighbors. He thought it was crowded because he had neighbors less than five miles away!

A Visit to Paradise

In 1769 Daniel Boone set off for a place called Kentucky. He went with another scout named John Finley. Finley had heard about Boone's skill as a hunter and scout.

It was a long trip. To get to Kentucky, they had to cross the mountains. In the mountains, they found an old Indian path. It led to a gap in the mountains. At the top of the gap, they stopped. Below them, as far as the eye could see, lay the Kentucky wilderness.

What did they see? On the hills and in the valleys, they saw huge herds of buffalo. Deer, bear, wild turkey, and other game roamed the land. The meadows were rich and soft. In all directions, there were huge forests. In them grew thousands of giant trees, tall and straight.

Daniel Boone knew he had found what he was looking for—his paradise. In the next few weeks, he and his friends explored the wilderness.

They were not alone in the wilderness, though. Indians hunted in Kentucky too. One day Boone and Finley were captured by a group of Indians. They were taken to the Indians' camp. At night, they were able to escape.

This was enough for Finley. He took off for home. Boone stayed alone in the wilderness for two years. He hunted and fished. Finally Daniel Boone went home to North Carolina. He knew, though, that he had to return to Kentucky.

The Wilderness Road

A businessman named Richard Henderson hoped to make his fortune in the new frontier. He asked Daniel Boone to help him. Boone was already famous for his years in the wilderness. Henderson wanted to build a road that would help people get to Kentucky. He chose Boone to lead the group who would build the Wilderness Road.

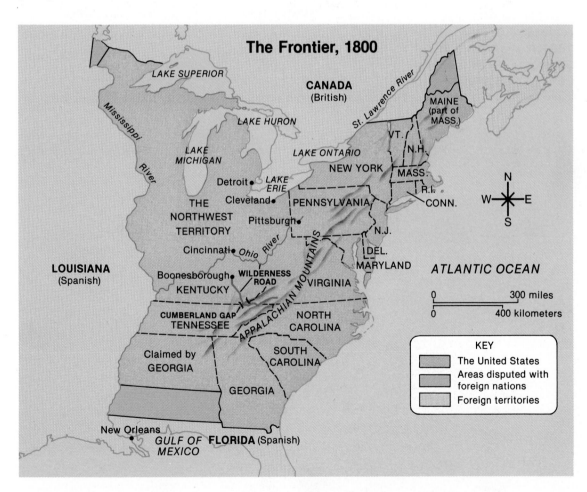

Boone and a group of 30 men set out for Kentucky. Boone went ahead and marked the trees to be cut down. Then the men put their axes into the trees. Boone also hunted buffalo and deer so the men would have food.

The Wilderness Road was not a road as we think of it. It was really just a path. At first, it wasn't even wide enough for wagons. But it was wide enough for people and horses.

When the road was done, the Boone family moved to Kentucky. They lived at Boonesboro (BOONZ-*buh-roe*), one of the first settlements in Kentucky. There, on the banks of the Kentucky River, Daniel Boone and the others built a fort. They needed it to protect themselves against attacks by the Indians whose land they were taking.

In one attack, Boone's son James was killed. His daughter Jemima was captured. Boone was able to rescue his daughter from the Indians. Later he himself was captured by a group of Shawnee (*shaw*-NEE) Indians. Luckily, the Shawnee chief, named Blackfish, liked Daniel Boone.

Travel to the West could be dangerous. But the pioneers still had fun. A crew man on a flatboat dances to the tune of a fiddle and a frying pan.

He adopted him as his son. Boone lived for a while as an Indian. But the Shawnee, though they liked Boone, were determined to drive the whites from Shawnee lands. Boone knew he had to escape.

Boone slipped out of the Indian camp one night. He followed a stream for miles, walking in the ice cold water. That way he would leave no trail. Boone reached Boonesboro in time to warn the settlers of the Shawnee attack.

Many Indian groups traded with the wagon trains of pioneers traveling west.

TRAVELING WEST

After the American Revolution, settlers began pouring into Kentucky and other western lands. They traveled along Daniel Boone's Wilderness Road. They also traveled by river. Thousands of settlers first went to Pittsburgh, Pennsylvania. There they boarded boats and floated down the Ohio River. In 1792 Kentucky became the 15th state in the U.S. (Vermont was the 14th in 1791.)

At first river travel seemed easy. There were no mountains to go over. The pioneers just floated downstream!

However, river travel was not always easy. The rivers had dangerous places where the water moved rapidly over falls. In other places, the rivers could flood in springtime.

Who Were the Pioneers?

In 1800 Kentucky was called the "West." It was west of the 13 original states. Fifty years later, the "West" would be California on the Pacific Coast. The U.S. would grow across an entire continent in those years.

Who were the people who came to this wilderness? Most of them were proud people looking for a new start. Some of them came from the older states in the East. Some came from Europe. The frontier offered land, adventure, and a chance to begin again. This pioneering spirit is what made the U.S. grow. It is a spirit passed on to us. It is part of our **heritage** (HERR-*uh-tij*) as Americans today.

Pioneer life was not easy. It required strength and patience. Pioneers could not be afraid of hard work.

A Home in the Wilderness

The first job of a pioneer family was to make a clearing so that they could plant corn. Most pioneers arrived at a settlement in the spring so they could plant a crop that season.

A father and his friend return home from a successful hunting trip. Now there would be food for the family.

First they cut down the trees. The whole family helped in cutting away the brush and pulling out the roots. Then they plowed the land and sowed their first seeds.

Next a family had to build a house. The log cabin was the home of most pioneers. Usually a few neighbors helped build it. The men had to cut down trees. With the logs, they built a one-room log cabin. Women and children worked too. They sealed the cracks between the logs with thick mud.

It took a few pioneers less than a week to build a log cabin. When it was done, the owners usually gave a house-warming party. Pioneers played as hard as they worked. There would be plenty of music, food, and dancing. Usually the party lasted from evening until sunrise.

Today log cabins sound cozy, but the log cabins of the pioneers were far from comfortable. They were dark because there were usually few windows. They were cold in the winter. Often the floor was made of dirt.

Pioneers made everyday jobs more pleasant by turning them into a party. At a quilting bee, people worked together on a quilt. They told stories and sang songs while they worked.

There was plenty of work to be done around the pioneer home. Food had to be found. In the early days, the woods were full of game. The pioneers had plenty of meat to eat. They shot wild turkeys, bears, and deer. They used traps to catch such smaller animals as beaver and raccoon. The animals were tasty in a stew. Their furs were valuable for clothes or as goods to trade.

In the early days, there were few stores. Most pioneers didn't even use money. Instead they traded things—furs for a bag of corn, cloth for a bag of gunpowder.

Frontier Housekeeping

Keeping the pioneer house was more than a full-time job. The whole family worked at it. Remember, these people had no modern appliances—no stove, no electricity, no running water. Even the simplest tools—brooms, bowls, spoons—had to be made at home.

Songs and stories were also part of a scutching bee. People worked together preparing the stalks of flax plants to be made into linen thread.

Pioneer families cooked over an open fire. They usually had just a few heavy pots. Favorite foods included lots of stews and soups. Pioneers had small vegetable gardens. They also planted fruit trees and pumpkins.

In almost every way, these people took care of themselves. Men and women worked together, sharing many jobs. They plowed, they built, they raised animals. They hunted, cooked, wove cloth. They made furniture, clothes, and tools. Their cabin was a workshop as well as a home.

The New American

The Declaration of Independence said, "All men are created equal." Still, money and family background gave some people an advantage in the new country. However, on the frontier, there was a new kind of spirit. The pioneers did not believe that anyone was better than anyone else. It didn't matter how much money a family had. There was no place to spend it. It didn't matter how important someone's parents were. Being important didn't cut down trees or put meat on the table. To the pioneers, all that mattered was how well you could shoot, chop, cook, spin, and weave.

As more people headed west, this idea spread in the U.S. A person was judged on what she or he did. All people started with the same things: a gun, an ax, a bag of corn, a few pots, perhaps a spinning wheel, and a dream.

THOMAS JEFFERSON

Thomas Jefferson was born in Virginia in 1743. He lived until 1826. In those 83 years, the United States changed from 13 struggling colonies to a young, growing country. Thomas Jefferson had a lot to do with this change.

Jefferson was shy as a boy. He loved reading books, walking through the woods, and riding his horse. He was a good student. As a college student, he spent 15 hours a day reading and studying.

As a young man, Jefferson was elected to the legislature in Virginia. He soon made a name for himself.

In 1776 the Continental Congress asked Jefferson to write the Declaration of Independence. Thomas Jefferson sat at his desk in the summer heat of Philadelphia. He thought and thought about liberty and human rights. Then he began writing. He poured all of his love for liberty into the Declaration.

If Thomas Jefferson had died in 1776, he would still be remembered as a great leader in the U.S. Instead he went on to serve his country in many ways. He was governor of Virginia during part of the American Revolution. Later he helped work out problems with foreign governments. He was Vice President of the U.S. under John Adams. In 1801 he became the third President of the U.S.

Jefferson was also an inventor, a scientist, a musician, and a designer of buildings. His own home, Monticello (*mont-uh-*SELL-*oe*), which he designed, is considered one of the most beautiful buildings in the U.S.

Thomas Jefferson became one of the best-known Americans in the world. Even in death, he was special. On July 4, 1826— exactly 50 years to the day after the signing of the Declaration of Independence—Thomas Jefferson died.

Thomas Jefferson

SKILL BUILDER

Making Decisions

The year is 1773. Will and Mary Reilly are poor farmers in Virginia. They have just heard about Daniel Boone's new Wilderness Road.

"Maybe we should go to Kentucky," says Will. "Our land is poor here. The land in Kentucky is fertile. The forests are full of giant trees. There's wild game everywhere. We could make a new start there."

"Oh, Will," Mary replies, "it's a hard life in that wilderness. Many of the Indians don't want us there. They'll fight to keep us out." She looks at their new baby sleeping in the crib. "I don't know if our baby could make it in such a place."

Will and Mary talk through the night. By morning they both have agreed to go West.

How did Will and Mary Reilly make this decision that would change their lives and the life of their child?

Will and Mary examined the problem carefully. They weighed the good and bad results of staying put or going to Kentucky. After thinking of all the benefits to be had in Kentucky, they outlined the costs. Then they thought of the benefits and costs of staying in Virginia. Finally they decided the chances were good for improving their lives in Kentucky. They decided to take the risks involved in the decision.

When we make decisions in life, we make choices. In making decisions, it is important to know what all our choices are and to weigh the good and bad in each one.

Imagine you were a poor farmer in Virginia about the time of Daniel Boone. List the benefits to be gained by moving to Kentucky. Then list the hardships to be overcome. Would you have made the same decision that Mary and Will Reilly did? Why or why not? Do all your classmates agree?

Now think about an important decision that you or your family has made. What were the choices involved? How did the decision affect your life?

Words to Know

Use each of the words listed below in a sentence.

heritage   scout

Facts to Review

1. How did Daniel Boone learn so much about the woods?
2. What did Daniel Boone see when he reached the gap in the mountains?
3. Why was the Wilderness Road an important step in opening Kentucky to settlers?
4. How did Daniel Boone use his knowledge of the woods to save Boonesboro?
5. What advantages did river travel have over land travel? What disadvantages did it have?
6. Why did people move to frontier places such as the woods of Kentucky?
7. What were some of the jobs men and women pioneers had to do just to survive on the frontier?
8. Why did Indians sometimes attack the pioneers?
9. How did pioneers get food on the frontier?
10. Why did people on the frontier develop a new kind of spirit?

Things to Think About

1. Pretend that you are a young Indian boy or girl. Your people have just been forced to leave their land because settlers are moving in. What are your feelings? Write a diary entry in which you describe your feelings and your reasons for having those feelings.
2. You are a young pioneer boy or girl. Six months ago, you and your family left a quiet, settled farming village in New England. Now you live in the Ohio wilderness. Write a short letter to a friend back in New England. Tell your friend what your new life is like. Say if it is better or worse than your old life and why.

13 Westward Ho!

When the U.S. won its independence in 1783, it stretched from the Atlantic Ocean to the Mississippi River. Beyond was the vast Louisiana Territory, owned by France. Beyond that was a large area controlled by Spain.

In 1801 Thomas Jefferson became President. One of Jefferson's goals was to win control of the port of New Orleans. This city was in the Louisiana Territory at the mouth of the Mississippi River. American farmers sent their crops down the Mississippi to New Orleans. The crops were then loaded on ships and sent to the large Eastern cities. Jefferson thought that the U.S. should control New Orleans.

The American government said to the French: "We'll buy New Orleans from you." The French answer shocked them: "We'll sell you more than New Orleans. We'll sell you the whole Louisiana Territory."

So, for 15 million dollars, the U.S. got one of the greatest land bargains in history. The Louisiana Purchase, as it was called, more than doubled the size of the U.S.

Almost nothing was known about this land in those days. Did it have good farmland? How did the Indians who lived there feel about settlers? Did the land contain valuable minerals? What was the safest way to get over the Rocky Mountains to the Pacific?

President Jefferson wanted to have answers to all these questions. He called in his private secretary, Meriwether (MERR-i-weh-ther) Lewis. He told Lewis to form a group to explore the Louisiana Territory. He told Lewis to find out everything he could about the land, the Indian people who lived there, the climate, the plants, and the animals.

Lewis asked his friend, William Clark, to join him on the trip. Clark was a scout who knew the wilderness.

On page 202: Miners look for gold in a California stream. Here, a miner pours water into a cradle filled with ore. The cradle was supposed to separate the gold from gravel. While some miners struck it rich, most ended up just with gravel.

A REMARKABLE JOURNEY

In 1804 Meriwether Lewis and William Clark set off from St. Louis, Missouri, with 40 men. On the way up the Missouri River, they saw huge buffalo herds grazing on the Great Plains. The explorers exchanged gifts with different Indian groups they met.

Help from Sacajawea

Near what is now Bismarck, North Dakota, Lewis and Clark spent the winter with the Mandan (MAN-*dan*) Indians. Living with the Mandans were a French trapper and his Indian wife, Sacajawea (*sack-uh-juh*-WEE-*uh*). She was a member of the Shoshone (*sho*-SHONE-*ee*) people. The Shoshone lived farther west. Sacajawea offered to guide Lewis and Clark on the difficult journey over the mountains. They eagerly accepted. In his diary, Lewis wrote of the many times Sacajawea helped the explorers: "Our journey would have ended in failure without her aid."

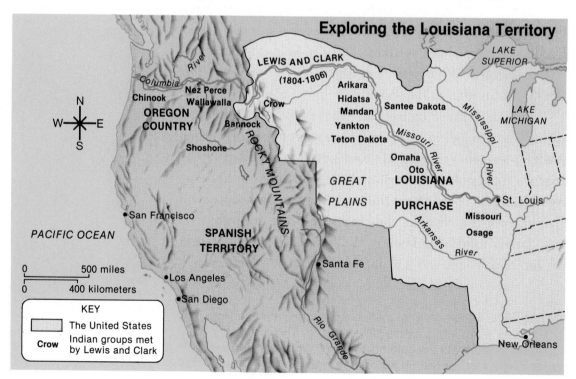

Exploring the Louisiana Territory

KEY

The United States

Crow — Indian groups met by Lewis and Clark

When they reached the mountains, Lewis and Clark planned to buy horses from the Indians there. They were in Shoshone country. The Shoshone were not happy to see the Americans, though. They were angry, for they knew what had happened to Indian groups in the East when the settlers had entered Indian lands. A meeting was arranged with the most important chiefs. The Indians showed up in war paint. Lewis and Clark stopped thinking about horses. Now they were worried for their safety.

Once again, Sacajawea rescued the explorers from danger. The head chief heard that Lewis and Clark had a Shoshone guide. He demanded to see her. When Sacajawea was brought in, the chief rushed to embrace her. It turned out that she was his sister. They had not seen each other for the five years years since Sacajawea had gone to live with the Mandans.

Reaching the Pacific

Now the Shoshone were eager to help Lewis and Clark. They sold horses to the explorers and helped guide them over the Rocky Mountains.

The Indians helped them build canoes from birch trees. Then they guided the explorers down the Columbia River to the "Great Pond"—the Indian name for the Pacific.

Sacajawea points out the way west for Lewis and Clark. She was the most famous of many Indian guides who helped explorers of the American West.

Lewis and Clark spent the winter of 1805 at the mouth of the Columbia River in what is now Oregon. They returned to St. Louis the next year. Almost the entire town turned out to greet them. People had feared the explorers would never return.

Lewis and Clark hurried to Washington, D.C., to report to President Jefferson. The President was impressed by the news of their remarkable journey. They had been gone two-and-a-half years and had traveled 8,000 miles (*12,872 kilometers*). They had explored much more than the Louisiana Territory. They had also explored and mapped the Rocky Mountains and the Oregon Territory.

Lewis and Clark were proud of their meetings with the Indians. They made friends with every Indian group they met. Lewis and Clark thought this would help settlers who later came to the West. The land seemed so big to Lewis and Clark. They thought there would always be room for both settlers and Indians in the U.S.

THE TRAIL OF TEARS

Things did not turn out the way Lewis and Clark had expected. In the years ahead, there was often trouble between settlers and Indians. Many treaties were signed

The forced journey of the Cherokee Indians was one of the dark moments of American history. Here are modern views of "the trail of tears." Which one do you think best shows what the journey was like? Which one best shows the sadness the Indians felt?

between the U.S. government and different Indian groups. In each of these treaties, the Americans promised to take a certain amount of land and no more. Time and again though, these treaties were broken and fighting began.

Sometimes it was started by settlers who wanted more land. Sometimes it was started by Indians who did not accept the treaties. They fought to save their lands. In the end, the Indians almost always lost.

One sad tale of Indian loss is called "the trail of tears." It began with a number of Indian groups living in the Southeast. Some of them had accepted many of the ways of the settlers. They farmed the land. One group, the Cherokee, grew cotton on their land. They had their own newspaper and had set up their own schools.

Then the American government told the Cherokee that they would have to leave their land. Settlers wanted it. The government ordered the Cherokee to move to an area on the other side of the Mississippi River.

During the winter of 1839, the Cherokee were forced to move. It was bitterly cold, and there was very little food. About one out of every four Cherokee people died during that march. It's little wonder that the Cherokee called the march "the trail of tears."

PUSH TO THE PACIFIC

The Louisiana Territory was only the first step west. Americans looked beyond it to lands to the south and west. Once they looked, they started to move.

Along the Santa Fe Trail

In 1820 there was a revolution in Mexico. Mexicans won their independence from Spain. Americans living on the frontier were pleased that Mexico was now an independent country. The Spanish rulers had not allowed Mexicans to trade with Americans. Now the new Mexican government changed this. It wanted Americans to trade with Mexico.

Soon Americans were traveling to the city of Santa Fe in what is now New Mexico. The route they traveled became known as the Santa Fe Trail. Some Americans got rich trading with the Mexicans. They traded cloth, tools, and hardware for Mexican silver and furs.

The American traders were impressed by what they found in Santa Fe. Santa Fe had beautiful mansions, churches, and public buildings. The Mexicans were dignified, cultured people. Americans were also impressed by men called **vaqueros** (*vah*-KAIR-*oze*)—Spanish cowboys. You will read about the vaqueros on page 215.

SETTLING IN TEXAS

Mexico was a large country, but not many people lived there in the 1820's. So the Mexican government invited Americans to settle in Texas, then a part of Mexico.

Soon there were more than 20,000 Americans in Texas. They outnumbered the Spanish-speaking Mexicans. Things went well at first, but soon the Americans in Texas decided that they wanted to govern themselves. This angered the President of Mexico, General Antonio Santa Anna (*ahn*-TOE-*nyo* SAHN-*tah* AHN-*ah*). He decided to teach the Texans a lesson.

The Road to Texas Independence

Santa Anna led an army into Texas in 1836. The army marched toward the town of San Antonio. A small force of Texans protected the town in a fort called the Alamo. Their commander was William Travis. Davy Crockett, a famous pioneer, was also at the Alamo. So was Jim Bowie (BOO-*ee*), who had invented the Bowie knife used in hunting.

Santa Anna's army surrounded the fort. Six thousand Mexican soldiers faced 184 Texas volunteers. For two weeks, the Texans held off the Mexicans.

On March 6, 1836, Santa Anna began an all-out charge. The Texans fought bravely, but by day's end all of them were dead.

Santa Anna thought he had crushed the Texas revolt. He was wrong. A month later, a small army led by an American, Sam Houston (HYOO-*stun*), was waiting for him at San Jacinto (*sahn hah-*SIN-*toe*). Houston caught Santa Anna in a trap. The Texans attacked yelling, "Remember the Alamo!" Santa Anna was captured. He signed a treaty giving Texas its freedom.

In 1836 Texas became an independent country with Sam Houston as its first president. The Texans wrote a constitution based on the U.S. Constitution. They designed their own flag showing a single star. Texans called their country the "Lone Star Republic." Nine years later, in 1845, Texas joined the United States. Now Texas was the Lone Star state.

A settler painted this scene of his Texas farm. The entire family worked to keep the farm running.

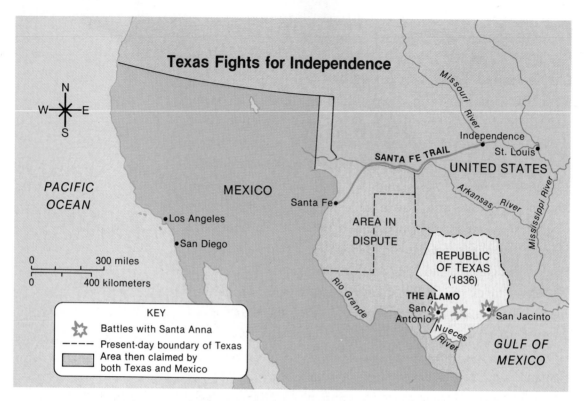

Texas Fights for Independence

KEY
⭐ Battles with Santa Anna
--- Present-day boundary of Texas
▢ Area then claimed by both Texas and Mexico

On the Oregon Trail

Independence, Missouri, was crowded in 1842. For more than 20 years, it had been the starting point of the Santa Fe Trail. Now though, the people coming to Independence were talking about another place—Oregon.

The Oregon Territory was larger than the present state of Oregon. It was the entire area of the Pacific Northwest—what are today the states of Oregon, Washington, and parts of Idaho, Montana, Wyoming, and Canada's British Columbia.

In the early 1840's, thousands of Americans traveled to Oregon on the Oregon Trail. Like the Santa Fe Trail, it began in Independence, Missouri. Wagon trains more than two miles long stretched across the Great Plains.

The wagon trains formed outside Independence. There the prairie was filled with wagons and tents. Pioneers waited until there were enough wagons to travel west safely. Usually an experienced scout came along to guide the pioneers. The pioneers elected their own leaders. When everyone was ready, the cry of "Westward Ho!

Wagons Ho!" rang out. The trip to Oregon took several months. Parts of the trail were over the rugged Rocky Mountains. It was a long and difficult trip, but hardy pioneers kept coming.

War Between the U.S. and Mexico

In 1846 the U.S. and Mexico went to war. Mexico was angry because Texas had become a U.S. state. Many Americans wanted to take valuable territory from Mexico.

The war lasted two years. Soldiers on both sides fought bravely, but in the end, the U.S. was too strong for Mexico. The U.S. Army invaded Mexico and captured Mexico City, the country's capital.

In 1848 a treaty was signed that ended the war. It gave the U.S. a huge block of territory. It included all of what are today the states of California, Nevada, and Utah. It also included parts of what are today Arizona, New Mexico, Colorado, and Wyoming. (See the map on page 214.) The U.S. now stretched "from sea to shining sea."

The trail west had many dangers. For this family, the collapse of their oxen meant they had to leave their wagon behind. Without food or water, they would not get far on their own.

SETTLING IN CALIFORNIA

Before the war between the U.S. and Mexico, California had been a Mexican territory. Most of the people living there were of Spanish or Indian background. There was little trouble between the groups who lived in California. This was partly because of the work of a very brave man. He was a Catholic priest named Father Junípero Serra (*hoo-NEE-pair-roe* SERR-*uh*).

Father Serra had come to California in the 1770's to convert the Indians to Christianity. He traveled up and down the California coast. Everywhere he went, he set up **missions** (communities where priests lived and worked). Father Serra and the other priests brought new crops to California—rice, wheat, oranges, and grapes. They also brought the first livestock—sheep and cattle. Father Serra learned from the Indians too. He learned Indian languages and customs. He learned about Indian arts. When Father Serra died in 1784, Indians and settlers alike missed this kindly priest.

After Father Serra's death, California continued to grow. Great ranches were laid out. Missions were set up along the California coast. Settlers from the United States also started settling there.

Spanish and Mexican customs were a part of life in the Southwest. Many of those customs have become a part of American life today.

By the time of the war with Mexico, there were about 15,000 Americans living in California. Soon after the war ended, something happened that brought thousands more to this land along the Pacific.

The California Gold Rush

One morning in January 1848, a man named James Marshall spotted some yellow pebbles in a California stream. He bent down and picked them out of the rushing water. Yes! He felt sure the pebbles were solid gold.

Marshall rushed back to his employer, John Sutter. The two men tested the pebbles. Sure enough, they were gold. The two men tried to keep their find a secret. However, someone at Sutter's Fort found out. He rushed into San Francisco yelling, "Gold! There's gold in the hills!"

Almost overnight, half of San Francisco disappeared. Shopkeepers left their stores. Sailors left their ships. In the valleys, farmers left their crops. Ranchers left their livestock. By the thousands, people streamed into the hills looking for gold. The Gold Rush had begun.

More than 50,000 people came to California in 1849. Still more came the next year. These travelers were called **forty-niners.** A few miners got rich. But most of them went "bust." This means they found nothing and spent all their money looking.

Some people got rich in other ways. They sold food, tools, and other needed goods to the miners. One of these people was Levi Strauss, a German-Jewish merchant. Strauss arrived in San Francisco with rolls of canvas cloth. He hoped to sell the canvas to miners who needed it for tents. He soon discovered that many other people were selling canvas for tents. Strauss saw the miners needed strong work pants. So he began making pants out of the canvas. They were perfect for hard work. Soon he was selling as many as he could make. These pants, which we call blue jeans, are still an American favorite.

Statehood for California

The Gold Rush changed California. Before the rush, San Francisco had been a little town of 800 people. By 1850 it was a bustling city of 35,000. Mining towns sprang up overnight. Some of them had colorful names like Hangtown or Rattlesnake Diggings. Life in the mining towns was rough. There was no police force to protect people. Miners usually slept with their guns in case someone tried to rob them of their gold.

Soon Californians realized they needed order in their land. A legislature was elected. California asked to join the Union as a state. In 1850 it became the 31st state of the United States.

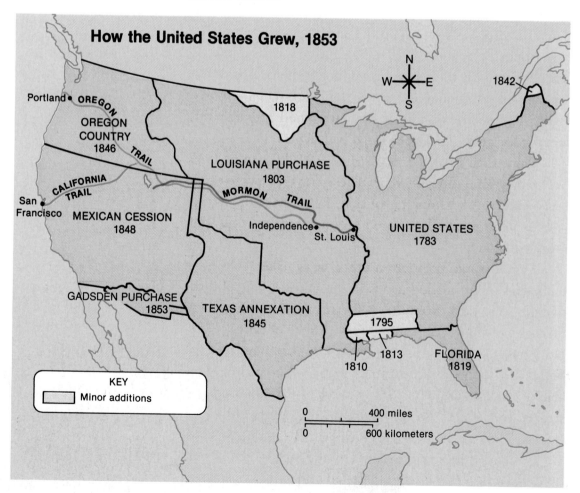

How the United States Grew, 1853

Portland •

OREGON

OREGON COUNTRY 1846

1818

1842

CALIFORNIA TRAIL

San Francisco •

MEXICAN CESSION 1848

LOUISIANA PURCHASE 1803

MORMON TRAIL

Independence •

St. Louis

UNITED STATES 1783

GADSDEN PURCHASE 1853

TEXAS ANNEXATION 1845

1795

1810

1813

FLORIDA 1819

KEY

Minor additions

0   400 miles

0   600 kilometers

THE VAQUEROS

People who saw them said vaqueros rode as though they had been born in the saddle. One of their favorite games of skill was to pick up a gold coin in the dusty street while riding in the saddle at full speed!

Vaqueros were the first cowboys. All year long, they worked on huge ranches in the Mexican territories of the Southwest. There they tended big herds of cattle.

Every spring, the vaqueros held a **rodeo** (ROE-*day-oe*). Today a rodeo means a show of Western riding and skills. In the old days, though, a rodeo was a roundup of the cattle. Many cowboy terms come from the Spanish that was spoken by the vaqueros.

Vaqueros carried no guns. Their main tool and weapon was the *lariat* (a long rope made out of rawhide). A skillful vaquero could bring down a charging bull with an expert toss of his lariat.

During a rodeo, a vaquero spent long hours in the saddle. Often it was hot and dusty. On his head, he wore a wide-brimmed hat to protect him from the sun and rain. Over his pants, he wore huge slabs of cowhide called *armas* (ahr-MAHSS). They protected his legs from the underbrush in rough country.

Today many Spanish-speaking Americans look back with pride on the days when the vaqueros rode the plains.

Vaqueros rope wild horses and bring them into the corral.

SKILL BUILDER

Comparing Distances

Going west was not easy. The trip was long and dangerous. You can see how long it was if you use the scale of miles or kilometers on the map below. Find out how far it is from New York to San Francisco, if you measure in a straight line.

People, though, did not travel over land in a straight line. They had to go where their wagons and animals could go. Some put their wagons on rafts and traveled on rivers when they could. On land they had to follow trails. Rivers and trails twist and turn. This makes a trip a lot longer than going in a straight line.

Try measuring the distance from St. Paul to New Orleans in a straight line. Then use a string to measure the distance following the curves of the Mississippi River. How much longer is the trip following the river? Say that you wanted to go from New York to New Orleans. What would be the distance if you flew in a straight line? Now say that you had to make the trip by boat. Is it more or less than flying in a straight line?

Turn back to the map on page 204 showing Lewis and Clark's route. How far did they travel? Why do you suppose they did not travel in a straight path?

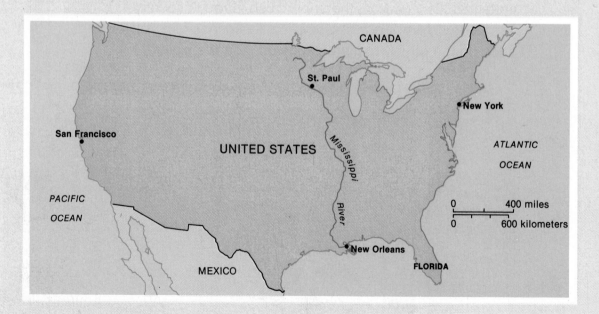

Words to Know

Use each of the words listed below in a sentence.

forty-niner   mission   rodeo   vaquero

Facts to Review

1. Why was the Louisiana Purchase a great bargain for the United States?
2. What were some of the things President Jefferson wanted Lewis and Clark to find out about the Louisiana Territory?
3. Why is the movement of the Indians out of the Southeast called "the trail of tears"?
4. How did Americans get to Santa Fe, and why did they come?
5. How did pioneers travel to the Oregon Territory? Why was the trip difficult?
6. Why do Texans "remember the Alamo"?
7. What did the U.S. gain as a result of war in 1846?
8. Who was Father Junípero Serra, and why was his work important?
9. How would you say the California Gold Rush changed the kind of work people did? How did it change the kinds of things they needed to live?
10. Why do you think California grew so lawless after the discovery of gold? How did people solve this problem?

Things to Think About

1. Say that you and your family are heading west in the 1840's. You must fit everything you need into a single covered wagon. You will be on the trail for at least four months. You will pass almost no stores or trading posts. What goods must you take with you? Make a list of them.
2. Pretend that you are keeping a diary to record your trip westward. Write an entry for your diary in which you describe what happened to you today on the trail.

CHAPTER

14

Democracy Spreads Across the Land

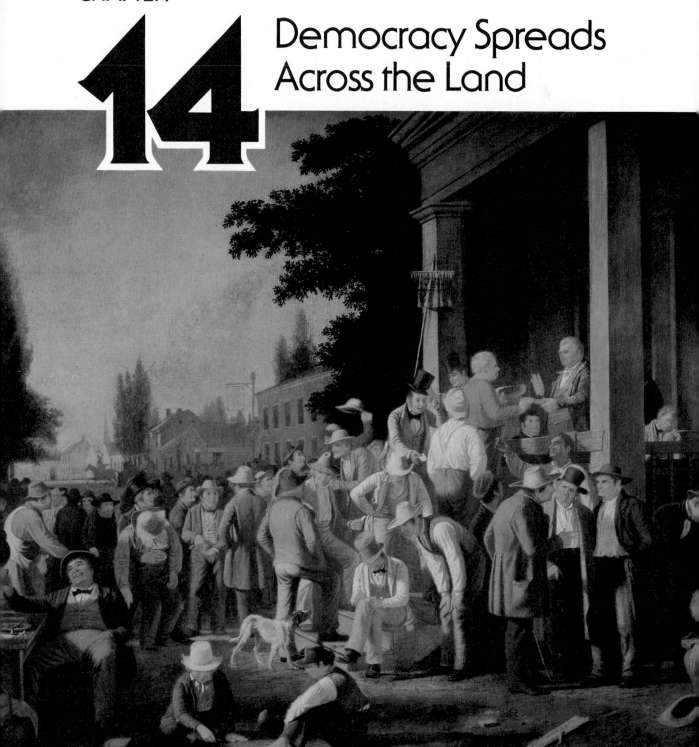

As you read in Chapter 11, Washington, D.C., did not become our nation's capital until a few years after our government had begun. In 1790 Congress created the District of Columbia from land given by Virginia and Maryland. A Frenchman, Major Pierre L'Enfant (*pyair* LAHN-*fahn*), then laid out plans for a new capital city.

L'Enfant's plan was a grand one. He thought that Washington, D.C., should grow in size and beauty as the nation did. He located the President's home, the White House, on high ground so that it would stand out. He did the same with the home for Congress, the Capitol. L'Enfant decided that the Capitol should be the center of the city. So he designed several main streets to start out from the Capitol, like the spokes on a wheel.

Thomas Jefferson was the first President to take office in the new capital city. In 1801 L'Enfant's plan was only beginning to be carried out. The city was made up of half-finished buildings on dusty dirt streets. The Capitol was only partly finished. Its famous dome had not yet been built. The White House too was not yet finished. Many of the streets still had stumps of trees in the middle of them.

Members of Congress lived in crowded boarding houses. They had to leave their familes at home. In the summer, dust from the unpaved streets blew in people's faces. Mosquitoes seemed to be everywhere.

Still our national government grew. Thomas Jefferson helped Americans feel that the city was theirs. Every morning the White House was open to visitors. Jefferson saw people in the order in which they came. **Diplomats** (representatives from other nations) and other important people often had to wait while Jefferson spoke to tourists.

On page 218: Election Day was like a carnival in American towns in the early 1800's. Notice the politician tipping his hat. He is asking the voter to remember to vote for him.

THE WAR OF 1812

President Jefferson served two terms. In 1808 James Madison, a fellow Virginian, was elected President. Madison faced a difficult problem. France and Britain were at war with each other. Neither side wanted the United States to trade with the other. So each told the U.S. to stop such trade. The United States would not stop because trade was an important part of the U.S. economy.

Soon the French were capturing American ships bound for Britain, and Britain was capturing American ships bound for France. Then too, British officers were coming aboard American ships and inspecting the crews. If a sailor on board a U.S. ship spoke with an British accent, the British took him back to their ship. The British claimed these sailors were **deserters** (escapees) from the British navy. Most of the time they were wrong. American citizens were being taken away against their wills.

The Call to Arms

Americans became so angry with Britain that there was a widespread cry for war. Finally, in 1812, Congress answered the cry by declaring war on Britain.

Captain Oliver Hazard Perry leaves a burning ship during the Battle of Lake Erie. Perry boarded another ship and led the American forces to a great victory over the British.

Luckily for the United States, the British had to put most of their military strength against France. Luckily too, the young American Navy was up to the British challenge. American ships, such as the U.S.S. *Constitution*, won several naval battles against the British. Isaac Hull, the captain of the *Constitution*, wrote a letter to the Secretary of the Navy to report one victory:

> We drew up alongside the (British) ship within less than pistol shot. We began firing at it with everything we had. We continued firing, damaging the ship badly and confusing its crew. Finally, we could see that the *Guerriere* (*gerr*-YAIR) was totally disabled.... I want to tell you how brave and gallant my officers and crew were during the action. Their fire was so well directed that it took only 30 minutes to disable the English ship. . . .

It was during this action that the *Constitution* won its nickname of "Old Ironsides." A cannonball from the *Guerriere* struck its strong oak side. The ball simply bounced off! Seeing this, a sailor shouted, "Hurray, her sides are made of iron!" The name "Old Ironsides" was born.

The Burning of Washington

Everything was not victory, though. In 1814 the British landed an army in Maryland. There they defeated a small American force and marched on Washington, D. C.

President Madison was out of the city. His wife Dolley worked all day packing important government papers. Friends kept telling her to leave. However, Dolley Madison did not scare easily. She told her friends to go ahead. She would leave when she finished her work.

Dolley Madison

Dolley Madison escaped just in time. The British marched into Washington without a fight. They walked into the White House. There they ate Dolley Madison's supper. Then they set fire to the White House.

"The Flag Was Still There"

Next the British marched to nearby Baltimore, Maryland. The British navy sailed into Baltimore harbor, which was guarded by Fort McHenry. They blasted the fort for hours. All day and into the night, the big cannons on the ships fired at the fort.

On board one of the ships was an American lawyer, Francis Scott Key. He thought the fort would have to surrender. At the first light of dawn, though, he could see the American flag still flying above Fort McHenry. This meant that the Americans still controlled the fort. Francis Scott Key wrote a poem about what he had seen. He called his poem "The Star-Spangled Banner." It became the **national anthem** (national song) of the United States. (For more on "The Star-Spangled Banner," see page 227.)

Francis Scott Key sees the flag still flying over Fort McHenry. Key had gone to the British ship to ask for the release of a friend the British were holding prisoner. After the battle, Key and his friend were let go.

On Christmas Eve 1814, Britain and the U.S. signed a treaty ending the war. Since the treaty was signed in Europe, news of it took several weeks to reach the U.S. So the war went on here.

On January 8, 1815, a large British army attacked the city of New Orleans. There, the British were met by a small force led by General Andrew Jackson. Jackson's band of rough fighting men easily defeated the large British army. The Battle of New Orleans made Andy Jackson an American hero.

ANDREW JACKSON—"OLD HICKORY"

Who was this man who was now such a hero? Andrew Jackson was born in 1767 on the Carolina frontier. His father died before he was born. So Andy Jackson was raised by his mother. The Jacksons were very poor. Young Andy did a grown-up's work on the small frontier farm.

During the American Revolution, Jackson was a messenger for the Americans. One day he was captured by the British. An officer gave the young scout an order: "Shine my boots." Jackson refused. The officer repeated the command. Jackson said, "I may be your prisoner, sir, but I am not your servant." The officer swung his sword at Jackson's head. Luckily, Jackson was quick and threw his arm up in front of his face. The sword made a deep cut in his arm. It also cut his face and left it scarred forever.

After the Revolution, Andrew Jackson became a lawyer and moved to the Tennessee frontier. He was one of the first lawyers in that new state, and he became rich. In 1796 he was elected to Congress. Jackson's frontier neighbors liked the idea that "one of them" could become successful in business and politics. Andrew Jackson became well known all over the West. People fondly gave him the name "Old Hickory." Hickory is the strongest and toughest of the trees that grow in the Tennessee forests.

Andrew Jackson was an American hero. This painting, done in the 1800's, shows him standing above the fury of the battle.

In 1828 Jackson was elected President of the U.S. His election worried some people in Washington. They were afraid that he would bring rough frontier people into government. These people thought only those who were educated and wealthy should hold important jobs in goverment. They were shocked by Jackson's frontier friends.

The Age of the Common Man

Over the past few years, however, ideas about government had been changing in the U.S. Most changes were coming from the new Western states. The original 13 states had not allowed everyone to vote. Only white males who owned some property had this right. This meant poor white men as well as women, blacks, and Indians could not vote.

People in the new Western states had different ideas about voting. They did not think less of a person who had no schooling. On the frontier, a person was as good as what he or she could do. In this way, these new states were more democratic than the old states.

The new states allowed all white men to vote. Soon the older states began to change their voting laws. By 1828 most states allowed all white men to vote. That's why this time is called the "age of the common man." (In this use, *common* means "ordinary.")

Today it is hard to see why this was so important. Women still couldn't vote. Blacks and Indians couldn't vote. Worse still, many blacks were slaves. What was so democratic about the U.S. in Andy Jackson's time, anyway?

American democracy did not happen all at once. It has grown in stages. In Andrew Jackson's time, allowing poor white men to vote was a big step for the U.S. It was saying that these people were worth something because they were people. As we now know, the age of the common man was just another step on the road to democracy in the United States. Yet it was a very important step.

GETTING AROUND THE U.S.

In its early years, the United States was a hard place in which to travel. The U.S. was a large country, even in those days. Its **transportation network** (the means of transportation that tied the country together) was very poor.

Today we take our transportation network for granted. Think for a moment, though, about a land where there are no planes, no superhighways, no railroads. There are no boats powered by engines. In fact, about all that exists are a few narrow, bumpy dirt roads and some rivers. The only means of power on land is muscle—the muscle of humans or the muscle of horses and mules. On sea, boats are moved by rowing, by water currents, or by wind power.

This is a picture of what the U.S. was like in the early 1800's. It was a picture that would soon change.

The National Road. At the beginning of the 1800's, Congress voted money to build a highway that would help link the American West with the East Coast. This National Road went from Cumberland, Maryland, to Wheeling, in what today is West

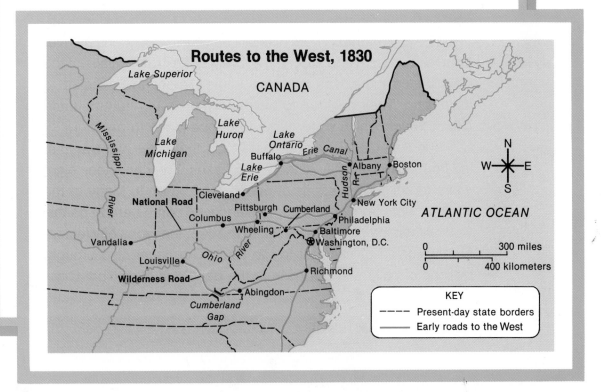

Virginia. Later the road was continued practically all the way to the Mississippi River.

Compared with the other roads of its day, the National Road was a wide highway. Thousands of pioneers in covered wagons used it on their way west. Farmers and ranchers drove livestock over it to markets in the East.

The Steamboat. One morning in August 1807, a strange looking boat left its dock on the Hudson River at New York City. People on shore laughed at the noisy boat as it puffed black smoke. They stopped laughing, though, when they saw how easily the boat could go upstream.

The boat was called the *Clermont* (KLERR-*mont*). It had been built by Robert Fulton. The power of steam drove its engines. Although the *Clermont* was not the first steamboat, it was the first one to go great distances.

In a short time, steamboats were carrying goods and people up and down rivers in many parts of the country. Because of the steamboat, many new towns grew up in the South and West. They were located along the rivers at spots where farmers could easily bring their crops.

The Erie Canal. There was still no way to get goods by river from the rich farmland around the Great Lakes to the cities of the East. Since there was no river, some Americans decided to *make* one. They decided to build a **canal** (a big human-made ditch through which water flows from one place to another).

The Erie Canal was the last link in the water highway that led from New York City to the Great Lakes. The canal took eight years to build. Thousands of people worked on it. Many of the workers were immigrants from Ireland who came here to do this work. When the canal was finished in 1825, the crops of Western farmers could quickly get to the East. The canal also brought millions of dollars in business to the people of New York City.

The American Flag

Are the following statements about the American flag true or false?

- It is not known who designed the flag.
- It is not known who made the first Stars and Stripes.
- It is not known if our flag ever flew during a battle of the American Revolution.

You may be surprised to know that all the statements are true. The beginnings of the red-white-and-blue flag we salute today are a mystery.

We do know that the Second Continental Congress adopted this resolution:

Resolved: that the flag of the United States be 13 stripes alternate red and white; that the union be 13 stars, white in a blue field. . . .

What is the importance of 13? How did that first flag differ from the flag we have today?

When Vermont and Kentucky joined the Union in 1795, two more stripes and two more stars were added to the nation's flag.

Congress soon realized, though, that the flag would grow too large if a stripe were added every time a new state joined the Union. So in 1818 Congress decided to go back to 13 stripes. Do you know what Congress decided to do about each new state?

The flag has inspired many poems and songs. The most famous is "The Star-Spangled Banner," by Francis Scott Key. It became our national anthem in 1931.

Here is the first stanza of "The Star-Spangled Banner":

Oh, say can you see by the dawn's early light
What so proudly we hailed at the twilight's last gleaming?
Whose broad stripes and bright stars thru' the perilous fight
O'er the ramparts we watched were so gallantly streaming?
And the rocket's red glare, the bombs bursting in air,
Gave proof through the night that our flag was still there.
Oh, say does that star-spangled banner yet wave
O'er the land of the free and the home of the brave?

How do you think Key felt when he saw the flag waving over Fort McHenry? What did the flag mean to him? According to this poem, how did Key feel about the United States? Use this poem to write a short story called "I Saw the Bombardment of Fort McHenry."

Until 1923 there were no rules for the flag's use. A list of them was writtten that year. But only in 1942 were these rules made into law by the U.S. Congress.

Did you know that:

- The flag should never be allowed to touch the ground.
- No other flag may be flown above the American flag on United States property.
- The flag should be hung upside down only as a signal of distress.

Study the way flags are hung in your school. Is the American flag always hung the same way? How? Why do you think there are laws about how to treat our flag?

Words to Know

Use each of the words listed below in a sentence.

canal   diplomat   transportation network

deserter   national anthem

Facts to Review

1. What did Washington, D.C., look like in 1801?
2. Why did the U.S. declare war on Britain in 1812?
3. What was the nickname of the U.S.S. *Constitution?* How did it get its name?
4. Who wrote "The Star-Spangled Banner" and under what conditions?
5. How did Andrew Jackson become an American hero?
6. What was the meaning of Andrew Jackson's nickname, "Old Hickory"?
7. What groups did not have voting rights in 1828?
8. Why was Jackson's time called the "age of the common man"?
9. What was the National Road? Where did it go? Who used it?
10. What made the *Clermont* different from other boats?

Things to Think About

1. Before "The Star-Spangled Banner" became our national anthem, "America the Beautiful" was our national song. Find the words to "America the Beautiful." What kinds of things does the song describe about the U.S.? Make a poster that illustrates two or three things it says about our nation. Either use pictures from magazines or draw the pictures yourself. Under each picture, write the quote from the song that you are illustrating.
2. You live in a country that has a democratic form of government. What signs can you see in American life that show this is true? Write a paragraph to tell what these signs are.

Using New Words

On a piece of paper write the paragraph below. Fill in the blanks with the correct words from the list.

deserters   heritage   national anthem   vaqueros
forty-niners   missions   scouts

The people and events of America's great growth period have left us a rich ____. Among the colorful people were the ____, who explored the wilderness. The earliest cowboys, the Spanish-speaking ____, were another colorful group. The priests who founded the ____ in the Southwest also left their mark on our history. So did the ____ who rushed to find gold in California. Among the important events of the period is the War of 1812. It began in part because the British navy was taking American sailors off American ships. The British said they were ____. This same war gave us the words to our ____, by Francis Scott Key.

Thinking About the Unit

1. Suppose you were Daniel Boone, alone in the wilderness of Kentucky for two years. What are some of the dangers you might watch out for? What skills would you need?
2. Tell which of the following would have been useful for a pioneer in Daniel Boone's time: cooking pot; hairdryer; gun; plow; television; automobile; seeds; camera; traps. Also tell *why* each would or would not be useful.
3. Make a list of the qualities you think a pioneer would have needed to make the long, hard trips on the Santa Fe or Oregon trails. Do you think you would have been a good pioneer? Why or why not?
4. Suppose you lived in one of the new Western states in Andrew Jackson's time. Also suppose you were in one of the groups—poor white men, women, blacks, Indians—who could not vote. What would you say to convince your state government that your group should have this right?

Sharpening Your Skills

1. Think of a decision you might have to make soon. List the things you should consider. Tell what choices you have. Tell the advantages and disadvantages of each one. Finally, make your decision and give your reasons for it.
2. Find a road map that shows where you live. Now choose a place on the map where you would like to go. Using the scale of miles or kilometers, measure the distance there in a straight line. Then pick out the route you would take to drive there. Measure its distance. Compare your answers.
3. As a research project, find out the correct way to fold the U.S. flag. Then demonstrate it to the class. Or draw a diagram that shows each step.

Expanding Your Knowledge

1. Make a poster advertising the wilderness of Kentucky to pioneers. Show a scene that would get people interested in moving there. Think of a catchy saying—for example, "Best Land in the West Land." Remember: To "sell" this wilderness to people, you have to present the good points.
2. Many tall tales and folk stories grew up around the miners of the Old West. Pegleg, Jeff Clarke, and Joaquin Murrieta (*hwah*-KEEN *moor*-YAY-*tah*) are just some of the characters in these tales. Find and read a mining story. Be ready to tell it to the class in your own words.

Your Own History

You read that Texas is known as the Lone Star state. Find out what nicknames your state has. How did it get these names? What is the story behind each name? Add this information to your scrapbook or file.

Each state has its own flag too. Find out what your state flag looks like. What is the story behind the design of your state flag? Draw a picture of your state flag and keep it as part of your history files.

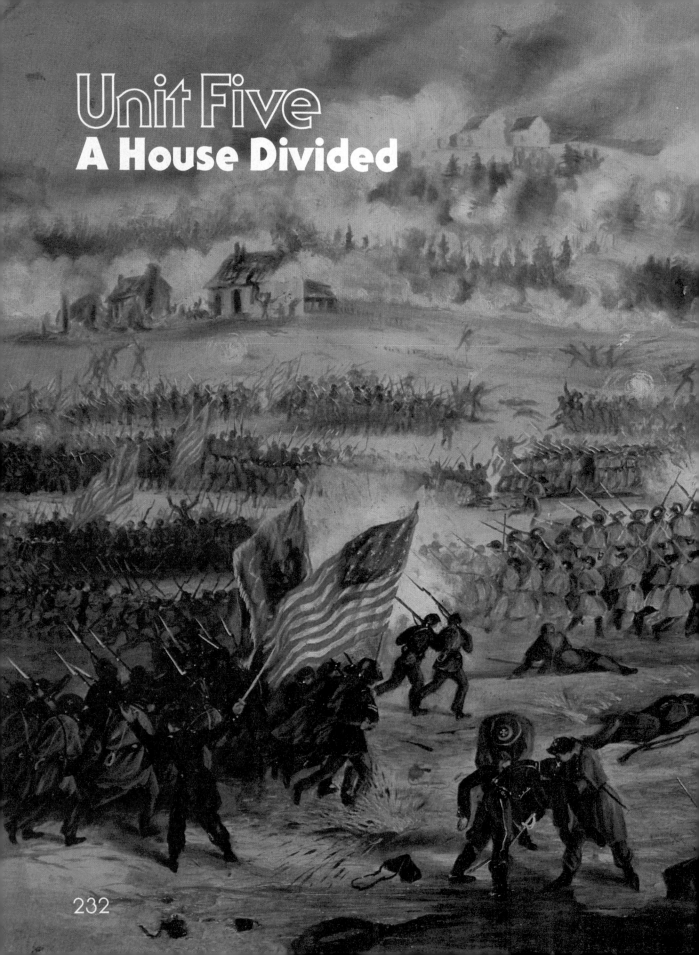

Unit Five
A House Divided

CHAPTER 15

The South Grows Strong

234

Eli Whitney, a young New England teacher, was visiting Georgia in 1793. Whitney loved to tinker with tools.

One day a Georgian showed Whitney some cotton. "You know, Mr. Whitney," said the man, "there is a fortune to be made here. We cannot sell this raw cotton until the seeds are removed from it. At present, this job must be done by hand. This takes too long and farmers can't make money on cotton. The person who invents a machine to clean cotton faster will certainly become rich."

Whitney set to work on the problem. A few weeks later, he had it—the first cotton gin. (The word *gin* was short for engine.) It could clean as much cotton each day as 50 people working by hand. Whitney's cotton gin changed the story of cotton—and the South—forever.

Before this time, Southern farmers had grown grain and vegetables for their own use. They had planted at least one other crop too. Instead of using this crop themselves, they sold it to make money. This was their **cash crop.** Important cash crops in the South were tobacco, sugar, corn, rice, and indigo.

With the invention of the cotton gin, cotton became the South's most important cash crop. There was a good market for cotton. Cloth factories in the North and in Britain both wanted all they could get. Now that farmers could produce cotton cheaply, it became "King" in the South. Soon huge plantations were growing it.

There were problems with cotton, though. For one thing, it called for more and more workers to grow it. Slaves had worked Southern farms for a long time. Now many more were used to keep the cotton crop coming in. Many Southerners came to believe that slavery was absolutely necessary to the life of the South.

On page 234: Many Southern plantations were the size of whole communities. This plantation in Kentucky had its own race track. Fans are shown arriving for a big horse race.

For another thing, cotton hurt the soil and made it less fertile. Farmers began to move westward and plant there. By 1817 Mississippi had been settled and was a state. Alabama followed in 1819. Texas and Louisana also became cotton-growing regions.

The two results of cotton's becoming king—more slavery and the spread of cotton farming to the west—would one day help split the nation. Till then, however, the South would grow stronger.

LIFE IN THE SOUTH

What was life in the South like about 1850? A lot depended on who you were. In the next sections, you will read about three ways of life in the South in those years.

Life on a Plantation

Plantations were important in the South because they affected the lives of many people. In a way, a big plantation was like a small town. It had just about everything needed right on it—blacksmith shop, barber shop, barns, stables, weavers, laundry, and, often, docks where ships could unload their goods. A big plantation had a large house or mansion where the owners lived. It had rows of cabins

The harvest was a busy time on this cotton plantation. Field workers picked the cotton. Then a team of mules dragged the bales to a steamboat at the river landing.

where the slaves lived. The following diary entry tells what life was like for the daughter of a plantation owner.

> June 1850, Barton's Acres
>
> Dear Diary,
>
> Today, after morning services, I rode with Father while he inspected the plantation. We checked the fences, some fields, and the blacksmith's shop. Riding out with Father is much more fun than visiting the kitchen pantry, linen closets, and other storerooms.
>
> Mother says I may go to the dance next week. I will wear a fine gown made from the silk that arrived last week from England. Next year, Diary, my brother Jonathan will go to England to finish his education. I shall miss him. Until tomorrow,
>
> Louise

Few women went to school in the old South. For the wealthy, however, there was often a private school for teaching manners and religion. Above, a graduation ceremony at a private school for women.

Slave Life

Few slaves could read or write. Teaching slaves such things was forbidden by law. It was thought that slaves who could read or write might get too many ideas, including ideas of freedom. Besides, the owners said, schooling would take the slaves away from their work for too much time.

Some slaves worked in the owner's home. They did the household chores, took care of the owner's children, and waited on the owner's family and guests. Other slaves worked in the buildings around the mansion. In the kitchen behind the house, they cooked the meals. In other buildings, they did the laundry, took care of the horses, and repaired the farm equipment. Some slaves learned skills, like blacksmithing and shoemaking. Then they could earn still more money for their owners.

Most slaves worked in the fields. They spent their days stooped over, picking cotton, sowing seeds, or plowing fields. These slaves usually worked in teams, called gangs. Their work was watched closely by the boss, or overseer.

The following letter tells how, many years later, one slave remembered his life.

August 1880

Dear Grandson,

You asked what life was like when I was a boy many years ago.

I lived then on a cotton plantation. My family and two others shared a cabin. It was very crowded and stuffy. It had no windows.

Each day before sunrise we were up and at work in the cotton fields. Often our work there went on until after sunset. Those who did not—or could not—work were punished.

Men, women, and children worked together. By the end of the day, our hands were sore, our bare feet were cut and bruised, and our backs were aching.

After our day in the fields, my father would then work on a small patch of garden near our cabin. Here he grew a few crops for our family. Our other food came from the plantation owner. Once or twice a year, we were given some clothes—a shirt, some overalls, and maybe a blanket. That's about all we had.

I ran away when I wasn't much older than you. It was hard for me to leave. You see, I left my parents and brothers and sisters behind. Except for one brother, I never saw any of them again. Maybe that's why I spend so much time at your house now—to be with my family.

Your grandfather, Nathan

Life on a Southern Farm

Most white Southerners owned small farms and did not live on plantations or own many slaves. Many did not own any slaves. Still these people looked up to the big plantation owners. The following letter is from a Southern farm boy to a cousin "up North."

July 1850

Dear Cousin Jeb,

    I enjoyed your letter. Your life in Connecticut sounds so different from mine! You asked what it's like here. Well, I'll tell you.

    Our house is really a cabin. It is built of wood and simply furnished. No fancy columns in front like our neighbors at Barton's Acres! We farm about 300 acres with 12 field hands. Dad and I work in the fields too. Dad was never able to get much learning, but several times a week I ride over to Louise Thorne's and sit in on lessons with her private teacher.

    For fun we go fishing or hunting. Sometimes we go to a camp meeting. There's a lot of singing and preaching and everyone has a good time.

    I hope you'll visit us someday.

                Your cousin, Thomas Hudnall

SLAVERY TROUBLES THE NATION

As slavery grew in the South, the South itself was also growing. So was the rest of the country. The North was growing strong with its industry. The West was becoming a center for farming and ranching. Each section tried to get the U.S. government to protect its interests. Southerners wanted laws that favored farming—and slavery. Northerners wanted laws that favored business and industry. Many Northerners objected to laws favoring slavery, which was not important in the North.

    Both North and South watched as the U.S. added land in the West. Both regions knew that someday new states would be created out of these new territories. New states would send Senators and Representatives to Congress. Their votes would help pass new laws. The North wanted these states to have no slavery—to be **free states.** The South wanted slavery allowed in these states—to make them **slave states.**

Slavery was the shame of the nation. When slaves were sold, families often were broken apart.

The Missouri Compromise

In 1820 there were 11 free states and 11 slave states in the Union. So, the North and the South had the same number of Senators in Congress. There was a balance of power.

Then Missouri asked to become a state. Northerners and Southerners fought angrily in Congress. Would Missouri be a free state or a slave state?

Finally, a settlement was reached. It was known as the Missouri Compromise. In this compromise, Missouri was allowed to join the United States as a slave state. At the same time, Maine joined the country as a free state. But a line was drawn westward from southern Missouri. No states north of the line could have slaves. States south of the line would choose whether to have slaves or not.

Many Americans believed that the Missouri Compromise had settled the problem of slavery in the new territories. They were wrong. The problem would soon return and it would cause a terrible war.

The Missouri Compromise, 1820

KEY
— Louisiana Purchase
— Missouri Compromise Line
Slave states and territories
Free states and territories
--- Present-day state borders

THE CALL FOR AN END TO SLAVERY

The year is 1842. A black man stands before a huge gathering of people. He speaks: "I appear before you this evening as a thief and a robber."

There is a gasp from the audience. The powerful voice continues: "I stole this head, these limbs, this body from my master, and ran off with them."

The man was Frederick Douglass. He was born a slave in 1817. In 1838 he escaped. From then on, he was a leader in the **abolitionist** (*ab-uh*-LISH-*uh-nist*) **movement.** This was a movement to do away with slavery. On this night, he was addressing the Anti-Slavery Society in Massachusetts. It was one of several groups formed to stop slavery.

Douglass also told about some of his experiences in the North. When he had escaped to New England, some white people there had refused to work with him.

In the years to come, Douglass often protested the way black people were treated. He walked out of a church that made blacks wait until white people had finished worshiping. He was dragged off a railroad car in which only white people were supposed to sit.

Fleeing at night, a slave family "follows the North Star" to freedom.

Frederick Douglass was the most famous slave who escaped to freedom. He devoted his life to helping his people. This early photograph was taken in 1856.

Harriet Tubman (above) led more than 300 slaves to freedom. Slave owners offered a $40,000 reward for her capture, dead or alive. A book written by Harriet Beecher Stowe (below) turned many people against slavery.

The Underground Railroad

Douglass also became a newspaper editor. In 1847 he started a paper called *The North Star*. In it, he suggested setting up an escape plan for slaves who wanted to go to the North. This system was called the "Underground Railroad." Escaping slaves, called "passengers," hid in the woods near their plantations. Then, when the coast was clear, they followed the North Star to the free states. On the way, they stopped at "stations." These were homes where they were safe. There, "conductors" hid them until they could go on. About 50,000 slaves escaped this way.

"Conductor" Harriet Tubman

One slave who escaped was Harriet Tubman. Once free, she promised to return to her home state, Maryland, and help the others to leave. Harriet Tubman made 20 trips and helped to guide about 300 slaves to freedom. When she reached a plantation, she would wait until dark. Then she would sing softly outside the slave cabins. Those escaping would know she was there. The song she sang was called "Steal Away." To the waiting slaves, it meant freedom.

Harriet Tubman's work was very dangerous. Congress had passed a law saying it was a crime to help runaway slaves. Rewards were posted for her capture. Slave catchers chased her, but she always managed to get away.

An Idea Spreads

In 1851 a white woman, Harriet Beecher Stowe, wrote a book called *Uncle Tom's Cabin*. The story told of the life and hardships of some slaves in Kentucky. It was based in part on true accounts.

Uncle Tom's Cabin was read by millions of people. It got them to think about the wrongs of slavery. It made them angry. More and more people came to think that slavery should be ended—not just in new territories, but all over the U.S. They began to work for this purpose.

QUEEN CITY OF THE MISSISSIPPI

The Mississippi River runs through the heart of the U.S. For hundreds of years, it has been a highway for people and goods. New Orleans stands near where the river meets the sea.

New Orleans has a very special past. It was settled in 1718 by French colonists. For many years after this, New Orleans was ruled by France, then by Spain, then by France again. Most of its settlers were from these two countries. The original French settlers were called Creoles (KREE-*olze*).

New Orleans became a stop for Americans going to the West. Many of them floated down the Mississippi to New Orleans on flatboats. Frontier people couldn't believe the sights. The "big city" buildings and the finely dressed ladies and gentlemen had a style all their own.

The years that followed were good ones for this "Queen City of the Mississippi." Steamboats carrying passengers and cargo made their way up and down the river. Inside, the boats looked like floating palaces. All kinds of colorful characters rode them.

New Orleans was also an interesting city because it had large numbers of free black people. Some slaves had been able to win their freedom. Many of them came to New Orleans. There were many black doctors, business people, and craftspeople living in the city. A newspaper run by blacks, the *New Orleans Tribune,* was read all over town.

New Orleans, 1852

SKILL BUILDER

Reading a Line Graph

You have already seen that the growth of "King Cotton" caused a great increase in the number of slaves in the U.S. One way to see this increase easily is with a **line graph.** A line graph is a good way to show a pattern of facts.

Look at the line graph below. Its title tells you what it shows—the growth of slavery from 1790 to 1860. Note the numbers running across the bottom of the graph. They show the dates the graph covers, in 10-year spans. Each year has a vertical line rising from it. Now note the numbers that run down the left side of the graph. They show the number of slaves in the U.S., in millions. Each number has a horizontal line running from it across the graph. (The horizontal lines without numbers show half millions.)

The dot on each vertical line shows how many slaves were in the U.S. in that year. To figure out how many slaves that dot stands for, look to the left and see which number it is closest to. For example, in 1810, the dot appears near the one million line. Near what line does the dot fall in 1830? In 1850?

The line drawn to connect the dots shows at a glance how sharp the rise in slavery was. How many more slaves were there in 1860 than in 1790?

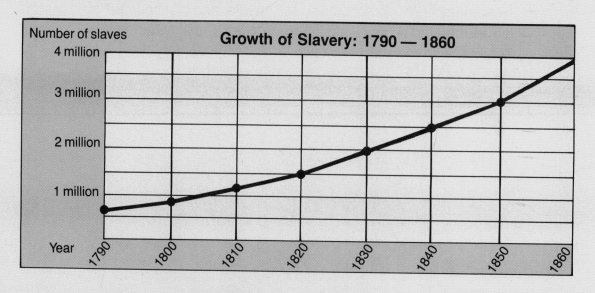

Number of slaves

Growth of Slavery: 1790 — 1860

4 million

3 million

2 million

1 million

Year   1790   1800   1810   1820   1830   1840   1850   1860

Words to Know

Use each of the words listed below in a sentence.

abolitionist movement   free state   slave state

cash crop   line graph

Facts to Review

1. Why was the cotton gin important to cotton growers?
2. Why did Southern planters feel they needed slaves on their plantations?
3. What special problems occurred when cotton became "king" in the South?
4. How was a plantation like a small town?
5. What kinds of work did slaves do on a plantation?
6. How was small-farm life in the South different from plantation life?
7. How were the interests of North and South different from each other?
8. How did the Missouri Compromise keep a balance of power between North and South?
9. What was the goal of the abolitionist movement? Was Frederick Douglass a good speaker for it? Why did Frederick Douglass say he was "a thief and a robber"?
10. Why do you suppose the Underground Railroad was dangerous for everyone involved in it?

Things to Think About

1. Do some research on Eli Whitney and the cotton gin. What was it made of? How did it work? Draw a sketch of Whitney's cotton gin. Then describe how it was run and how it cleaned the cotton.
2. Pretend that you are a young slave escaping by the Underground Railroad. Or pretend that you are a young person whose home is one of the stations. Write a paragraph that tells about your contact with the Underground Railroad. Tell about someone you met through it.

CHAPTER

16 The North Grows Strong

In 1789 a young worker from a cotton factory in England boarded a boat for the U.S. He had to disguise himself to get aboard. Why? Because cloth workers were not allowed to leave England. They knew too much about the new cloth-making machines that had been developed there. These machines could produce as much cloth in a day as workers could produce by hand in a month. England did not want any other nations to learn how these machines worked.

Young Samuel Slater wanted to come to the United States, though. He wanted to set up a new cloth factory here. So he memorized the plans for the new machines. With this valuable information in his head, he sailed for the United States.

Within only a few months of his arrival in the U.S., Slater had become a partner in a cloth-making business. His factory was located in Rhode Island next to a rushing river. He placed a big wheel in the river. The power of the rushing water turned the wheel. The turning wheel kept the factory machines moving.

Slater's factory was just the first of many. New England had plenty of fast-moving rivers. So there was water power for many machines. Soon New England had more factories than any other part of the country. In fact, Slater had begun a whole new **factory system** in the U.S. Over the years, machines would come to produce many more goods than people did. This change in the way goods were produced is called the **Industrial Revolution.**

Factories sprang up in other parts of the North too. They produced everything from shoes to guns to farm tools in great numbers. Factories changed the North in many ways. They helped it to grow wealthy and strong. They also helped to deepen differences between North and South.

On page 246: Many factories were built in the North in the 1800's.

A young girl works at her loom in a New England mill. This drawing was done by Winslow Homer, a famous American artist.

FROM FARM TO FACTORY

The new factories in the North needed workers. Many of the workers came to the factories from farms. Many of them were teenage farm girls. Working in the factories gave them a way of making a little money on their own. This was something they could not do on the family farm. They were used to long hours and hard work on the farm. So they were able to stand the 14-hour days they were expected to work in the factories.

Other farm workers were also taking factory jobs. Some simply could not support themselves on their small, rocky farms. Some were no longer needed on the farm. New farm machines were being invented. These machines cut down the need for people to work on farms.

Factory life was very different from farm life. Here, a child describes her life working in a cotton mill.

Boston, 1845

Dear Michael,

It's six months since we left the farm. Our life has certainly changed!

We live in a cellar. It is very crowded, but it is the only place Pa could find. Ma tries to keep it clean, but she is worn out after her day at the mill.

Katy Ann and I work at the mill too. We start at dawn and work till six or seven in the evening. The mill owner likes to hire children because we have small, quick hands to work the machines. He does not pay us much, though. Some of us are only eight years old. You should see the big machines we run! Sometimes there are accidents. Yesterday, Colin lost a finger in the machine.

Katy Ann and I go to school part of the year. Massachusetts has a law that says children under 15 can't work in a factory unless they went to school three months in the year before.

I wish we had more time for fun.

Your friend, Jennie

Factory life was often hard. Sometimes there were more willing workers than there were jobs. So those who would work for the lowest **wages** (pay) were hired. Many workers could not support their families on their wages. Often children had to go to work to help out.

THE GROWTH OF CITIES

As people left farms to take jobs in factories and mills, factory towns grew into cities. Small cities grew into larger cities. New buildings went up in these cities. Shops opened. Streets were paved.

People in cities depended on one another. A factory worker did not have time to grow food or make clothes. The worker needed to buy these goods. So stores and small businesses were started to serve these needs.

The cities had places of worship, eating places, hotels, theaters, and music halls. Books, magazines, and newspapers were sold. There was plenty of excitement and always something of interest to do or see.

Life in these fast-growing cities brought problems too. No one really planned *how* the cities would grow. As you saw in Jennie's letter, there was not enough housing. Often buildings were overcrowded and dirty.

The streets of New York City were busy even in the 1830's. Northern cities were centers of manufacturing and trade.

Railroads changed the map of America. The first trains were on the East Coast. In this painting of a railroad yard in Massachusetts, you can see oxen pulling freight wagons at the right.

Railroads to Link the Cities

In the years between 1830 and 1850, the U.S. also had a railroad-building boom. Many of these railroads were built by business people in the growing cities. They wanted an easy way to bring farm products into the city and take manufactured goods out.

Railroads helped greatly. In 1815, before the railroads, it took nearly two months to get from Cincinnati (*sin-si-NAT-ee*), Ohio, to New York City. By 1852 the trip by rail

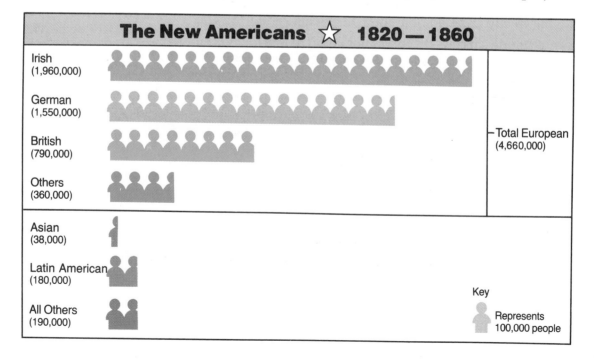

The New Americans ☆ 1820 — 1860

Irish (1,960,000)	
German (1,550,000)	Total European (4,660,000)
British (790,000)	
Others (360,000)	
Asian (38,000)	
Latin American (180,000)	
All Others (190,000)	

Key
Represents 100,000 people

took a week or less! The railroad soon became another strong link in our transportation network. It brought the farm produce of the West to markets in the East. It also brought the manufactured goods of the East—clothes, farm tools, saddles—to markets in the West.

A WAVE OF IMMIGRANTS

Between 1820 and 1860, eight million immigrants came to the U.S. Most of them came from countries in Northern Europe—countries such as Ireland, Germany, Scotland, England, Norway, and Sweden. Many of them could speak no English at all.

Often these newcomers were fleeing from problems in their homelands. (For example, in Ireland there was a terrible famine [FAM-*in*]—a time when there is not enough food for people.) People came to the United States to try and make better lives for themselves.

A young German boy tells what it was like to arrive in the U.S. in the 1840's:

> At five in the morning, the boat stopped. For 37 days, we had been crowded into this boat. Now we were in America.
>
> I got up and stepped over the other people and looked out. Water and fog were everywhere. I dressed and went on deck.
>
> Soon everyone had gathered there. Bags and bundles were piled in wild confusion. There were hundreds of us there, and all were on the deck. Finally a doctor and his staff examined us. Then more waiting. Two hours in the hot July morning sun.
>
> At last we were told to move again. Down the gangplank and onto the dock. No one knew what to do. "We'll get around to you," said the officials when asked. It took forever. Finally we were given our slips and could hurry out of the darkened dock and into the free sunshine. There, we took a good long look at the United States.

Most of the immigrants were poor, but hopeful. They came to find work, and most of them found it in the cities of the North. Some had read ads placed in European newspapers by American factory owners. These ads stated that there were many jobs to be had building railroads or working in factories.

MORE TROUBLES BETWEEN NORTH AND SOUTH

The North and the South were obviously growing in two very different ways. The North was building on a foundation of factories, cities, and railroads. The South was building on a foundation of plantations and farms.

It's true that the two sides needed each other. The North needed the South for its raw cotton and other crops. Northerners also needed to sell their manufactured goods to Southerners. The South needed the North as a market for its crops. Southerners also needed the manufactured goods that Northerners produced.

Yet each region fought fiercely in Congress to protect its own interests. The North wanted the national government to charge certain taxes that the South didn't want. The South felt that such taxes would hurt its agriculture while helping the North's industry.

The Compromise of 1850

In 1850 the old problem of slavery in the Western territories came up again. California wanted to enter the Union as a free state. At the time, there were 15 free states and 15 slave states in the Union. California would upset the balance of power in favor of the North.

Once again, arguments raged in Congress. Once again, a compromise was reached. California would enter as a free state. This angered many Southerners. To balance this, a runaway slave law was written. This law said that all runaway slaves must be returned to their owners. This angered many Northerners. Soon North and South were again arguing bitterly.

Abraham Lincoln Steps Forward

The year was 1858. A tall, awkward man named Abraham Lincoln was running for Senator from the state of Illinois. In one campaign speech, Lincoln made a statement that Americans would long remember:

> A house divided against itself cannot stand. I believe this government cannot endure [last] permanently half slave and half free.

Lincoln did not win the election, but people had come to know who he was. The Republicans knew what his ideas on slavery were. He did not believe it should be allowed in the Western lands.

The Presidential Campaign of 1860

In 1860 the Republican party asked Abraham Lincoln to run for President. Republicans were strong in the North. They said that their goal was to keep the country together as well as to keep slavery out of the Western territories. Lincoln promised, however, that if elected, he would not interfere with slavery in the South.

Many Southerners did not believe Lincoln. They thought he was a threat to their way of life. Some Southern states said that they would **secede** (*see*-SEED), or withdraw, from the Union if Lincoln was elected.

Here is what a Southern newspaper, the *Charleston Mercury* of South Carolina, said:

> The North has put forward an open enemy of slavery as a candidate for election. In every way, the whole Northern people have shown unfriendliness to us and to our most sacred rights. The South must not hesitate to rise up and say that we *will* be a free and independent people.

As a young man, Abraham Lincoln was famous for his ability to split logs. His neighbors called him the "rail splitter." This picture was probably shown at campaign rallies when Lincoln ran for office.

A Northern newspaper, the *Springfield Republican* of Massachusetts, replied this way:

> The South threatens to secede if Abraham Lincoln is elected. If a **majority** [more than half of those voting] cannot rule the country without the **minority** [less than half of those voting] seceding, it is time the country knew it. We will never have peace between the two sections of this country until the South has learned that the North is not its enemy, but its best friend.

When the campaign ended, Abraham Lincoln was elected President of the United States.

What would the South do now?

Help for the Farmer

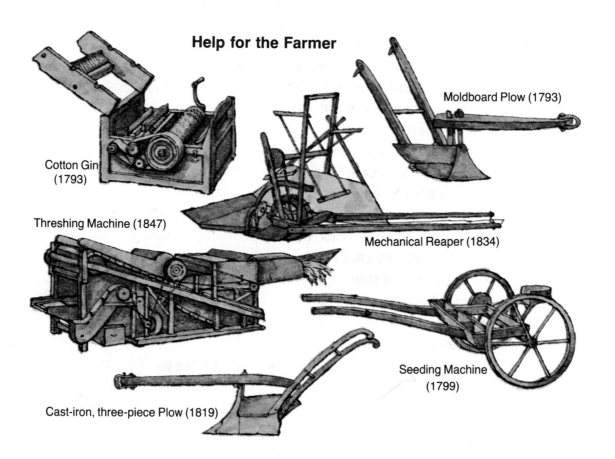

Cotton Gin (1793)

Moldboard Plow (1793)

Threshing Machine (1847)

Mechanical Reaper (1834)

Cast-iron, three-piece Plow (1819)

Seeding Machine (1799)

AMERICAN KNOW-HOW

"Why that's the strangest looking thing I ever saw," said one farmer.

"It will never work," said another.

"Try it," said a third. "We'll have a good laugh!"

The farmers were talking about a machine made by young Cyrus McCormick (SIE-*russ muh*-KOR-*mik*). McCormick had worked for years to build a machine that would cut down, or reap, crops at harvest time. At a local fair in Virginia in the 1830's, McCormick showed his new mechanical reaper (REE-*per*) for harvesting wheat. The reaper had a large knife which moved whenever the reaper moved. It made all kinds of clicking and clattering noises when it was pulled through the wheat by a horse.

McCormick pulled his machine out into the field. At first the horse was so nervous, it refused to move. McCormick spoke soothing words to it. Then the horse pulled. The farmers stopped laughing. The reaper worked! McCormick's reaper could do the work of six men.

The farmers were impressed. "That machine of yours could really help me," said one. "But how are poor farmers like us ever going to be able to afford one?"

The farmer had a good point. However, Cyrus McCormick was not only a clever inventor, but also a sharp business person. He knew the farmers could get high prices for their wheat. So he agreed to sell the reaper to farmers on the installment plan. This meant they first paid McCormick part of the money they owed for the reaper. Then every month they paid some more until the reaper was paid for.

At the same time, many other Americans were working long and hard on new ideas. Often people laughed at them, but these inventors pressed on. Some of them, changed the way Americans worked, lived, and traveled.

SKILL BUILDER

Dating Events and Sequencing

As you learn more about American history, you can become a history detective. You can figure out the dates when events took place even if your book doesn't tell you. The clues to do this aren't hard to find. For example, can you figure out the year in which the following conversation could have taken place?

Mr. Smith: Ellen, I'm home.

Mrs. Smith: Hello, dear. How was your first day at the cotton mill?

Mr. Smith: Well, it was strange seeing all those machines. But Slater says this is how cloth will be spun from now on.

The answer is about 1790. What were the clues?

On a separate piece of paper, try rearranging the events listed on the left in the order in which they happened. The list of inventions and their dates at the right will give you the clues you need.

- Farmers harvested more grain than ever before.
- New era in river transportation begins.
- Cotton becomes South's main crop.
- Railroads become important means of transportation.
- Shoe-making is moved to factories.
- Luxury comes to railway travel.

cotton gin, 1793

first U.S. locomotive, 1830

Pullman sleeping car for trains, 1858

shoe-sewing machine, 1858

mechanical reaper, 1834

steamboat, 1807

Words to Know

Use each of the words listed below in a sentence.

factory system	majority	secede
Industrial Revolution	minority	wage

Facts to Review

1. How did Samuel Slater help change American industry?
2. For what reasons did workers move from farms to factories in the early 1800's?
3. Why was factory life often hard?
4. In what ways did the growth of factories lead to the growth of cities?
5. Why did the railroad become so important between 1800 and 1850?
6. Why was there a great wave of immigration between 1820 and 1860?
7. Where did most of the immigrants come from during this period?
8. What compromise did Congress make in 1850 and why?
9. What problem was Lincoln talking about when he said, "A house divided against itself cannot stand"?
10. Why was the South so much against Lincoln's election as President?

Things to Think About

1. Pretend that you are a young person living on an American farm in the early 1800's. You are trying to decide whether to stay on the farm or move to the city for a factory job. Make a list of the advantages and disadvantages of doing either.
2. Choose one of the inventions listed in the box on page 254. Look it up in an encyclopedia. Then write a brief paragraph in which you tell who invented it and describe one way that it changed American life.

17 The Civil War

Abraham Lincoln took office on March 4, 1861. He was now President of the United States. However, the American states were no longer united. Several Southern states had carried out their threat and seceded from the Union.

South Carolina was the first to secede. Six more states—Alabama, Georgia, Mississippi, Louisiana, Texas, and Florida—soon followed.

The leaders of the seceding states explained their action this way: "Lincoln does not represent the whole nation. The North has elected him. He does not respect the rights of the Southern states. His government will wage a war against slavery. Our property will no longer be protected by the Constitution."

In February 1861, the seceding states met and formed their own country. They called it the Confederate (*kun-FED-uh-rit*) States of America. (Sometimes it is called the Confederacy.) Jefferson Davis was elected President.

Abraham Lincoln tried to convince the Confederate States to come back into the Union on their own. "We are not enemies, but friends," said Lincoln. "We must not be enemies." He then suggested that the Southern states stay in the Union and try to convince the other states that their cause was right.

Southerners did not listen to Lincoln. By the spring of 1861, four more states had seceded. They were Virginia, Arkansas, North Carolina, and Tennessee.

Still Lincoln tried to keep the Union together. He said, "No state can lawfully get out of the Union."

The stage was now set for the U.S. Civil War. In a **civil war,** people of one country take sides and fight against each other. Sometimes this means that friends or people in the same family end up on different sides.

On page 258: Dead Confederate soldiers lie in a field after the Northern victory at the Battle of Antietam in 1862. The Civil War was the first American war in which photography recorded the terrible results of war.

THE CIVIL WAR BEGINS

The U.S. flag waved in the April breeze. Below it, the soldiers in Fort Sumter waited. Food was running low. Soon the fort might have to surrender.

Fort Sumter was in the harbor of Charleston, South Carolina. South Carolina was part of the Confederacy. Yet soldiers of the U.S. government controlled the fort.

The leaders of South Carolina felt that the U.S. flag was the sign of a "foreign power" in Charleston. They wanted the U.S. soldiers to leave. They would not allow any supplies to reach the fort.

President Lincoln refused to give up Fort Sumter. He sent a message to South Carolina's leaders. "I am sending our soldiers bread," he said, "not bullets." It didn't matter. The Confederate cannons opened fire on the fort. For more than a day, the cannons boomed. Finally the soldiers in the fort surrendered.

The first shots of the Civil War had been fired. The war would not be over for four terrible years.

Abraham Lincoln acted quickly. He called for volunteers to join the Union army. The United States flag had been fired upon. People now realized that war between the North and the South could not be prevented.

No End in Sight

Both sides thought they would win the war easily. Many people thought it would take only one or two big battles and the war would be over. This is not what happened, though. There were many battles, with the South winning at first. Still, the North would not give up.

The North could afford to hold on for a long time. It had many more men who could fight. It had more supplies. The North had most of the country's ships, banks, and railroads. It had more factories to turn out more guns, cannons, uniforms, and other things used in war.

The South had some advantages too. It had many fine army officers. First among them was Robert E. Lee of Virginia. His bold attacks and clever planning won many

Union and Confederate Resources	UNION	CONFEDERACY
Population	23 million	8¾ million
Number of industrial workers	1⅓ million	110,000
Number of factories	110,000	18,000
Number of train engines	451,000	19,000
Miles of railroad track (Kilometers)	22,000 (45,000)	9,000 (14,000)
Value of property	$11 billion	$5½ billion
Value of farms and factories	$850 million	$95 million
Value of things produced	$1½ billion	$155 million

Young boys served in the Civil War. Above, a boy poses on a ship of the Union Navy. Below is a young Confederate soldier who was killed in battle.

battlefield victories for the South. Another important Confederate general was Thomas "Stonewall" Jackson. He got his nickname "Stonewall" at an early battle in the Civil War. Jackson and his men were greatly outnumbered. Yet, as another officer noted, Jackson stood his ground "like a stone wall."

As the Civil War went on, the South began to suffer from a lack of supplies. The North had placed its warships all along the South's coastline. In this way, it could **blockade** (seal off) Southern ports. The South could not bring in the clothing, tools, shoes, medicine, and war materials it needed. Nor could it ship out its cotton. Soon bales of cotton piled up unused on Southern docks.

On the Battlefield

On both sides, most soldiers in the Civil War were very young. Many were in their teens. They fought in army units from their hometowns. Relatives, neighbors, and friends fought side by side.

Most of the fighting took place in the South. The first big battle was in 1861 at Bull Run, a creek in Virginia, not far from Washington, D.C. The Union side was sure it would win. It was so sure, in fact, that people came out from Washington with picnic baskets to watch the "show." The Confederates won, and Union hopes of ending the war quickly were dashed.

Letter from Antietam

In the Civil War, the soldiers who fought on the Union side wore blue uniforms. They were often called Yanks or Yankees by the Southerners. The Confederate soldiers wore gray uniforms and were called Johnny Reb (for rebels) by the Northerners.

One of the bloodiest battles of the war was fought at Antietam (*an-*TEE*-tum*), near the border of Maryland and

Virginia. This letter from a Union soldier gives an idea of the hard life of a soldier in the Civil War.

Union soldiers hiding in ambush fire on the Confederates. Most Civil War battles were fought in the open by large armies. Sometimes small bands of soldiers fought each other.

> The Woods, Virginia
> September 19, 1862
>
> Dear Mom,
>
> Greetings from your soldier in blue. We finally pulled back from battle last night. I am unharmed by bullets, but weary from battle. We met Lee's army at Antietam Creek the day before yesterday. The losses on both sides were terrible. We lost two of the Reilly brothers from Springfield. Do you remember them, Ma?
>
> Tell Betsy that Ron's fever is down. He is still in the field hospital, but he is feeling much better. I wish all the fellows were so lucky. Getting sick in this war is just as bad as getting wounded.
>
> Our commanding general rode through camp on his horse tonight. The troops cheered and threw up their caps as if the war were over.
>
> Well, it's time for supper. Corn bread and cabbage tonight. Not like your home cooking, Ma. Boy, do I miss that!
>
> Be of good cheer.
>
> Your faithful son,
> Russell

Units of black soldiers like this one fought bravely in the Union army. Many of these soldiers were former slaves.

Bringing an End to Slavery

As you have seen, before the war Lincoln had promised not to interfere with slavery in the South. Now, though, as the war dragged on, he changed his mind. On September 22, 1862, he signed the Emancipation (*ee-man-suh-*PAY-*shun*) Proclamation. (To **emancipate** is to set free. A **proclamation** is a public announcement.) In this proclamation, Lincoln stated that all slaves living in the Confederate States were free after January 1863.

The Emancipation Proclamation did not really free all slaves right away. Slaves in the Confederate States had to wait until the Union army gained control of the South.

The Proclamation also announced Lincoln's decision to use black troops in the Union army. Soon about 186,000 black soldiers and 30,000 black sailors were fighting for the Union. They fought in hundreds of battles and many received medals for their bravery and daring. Lincoln called them "an important force" that the Union could not do without.

THE UNION BEGINS TO WIN

An observer watched the battle below from an air balloon. Soldiers in gray coats attacked soldiers in blue. Bayonets glistened in the sun. Flags flew as the soldiers charged. Soon dead and wounded men covered the battlefield. The smoke of gunfire rose everywhere. This was the battle of Gettysburg, Pennsylvania. The fighting went on for three long days.

The Union army won, but General Lee and many of his Confederate soldiers got away. As in other Civil War battles, the losses on both sides were very high. The South, though, was hurt more than the North. Never again would Lee have enough forces to mount a major attack.

Later that year, at the cemetery on the battlefield of Gettysburg, Lincoln made one of the most famous **addresses** (speeches) in U.S. history. It is the Gettysburg Address. (You will learn about it on pages 268-269.)

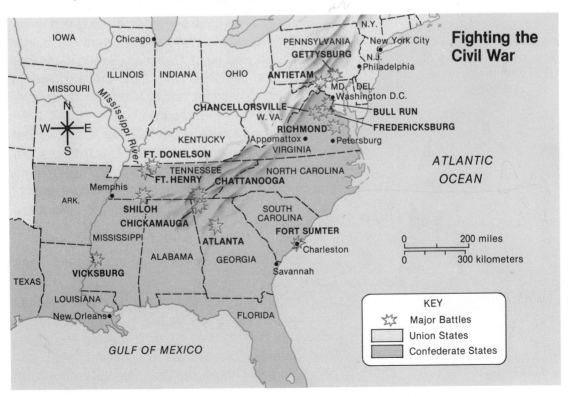

The Civil War took place more than a century ago. But photographs taken by Matthew Brady make it look like yesterday. In these photos of Ulysses S. Grant and Robert E. Lee, you can see the strain of war in both men's faces.

A New Union Commander

By 1864 the North was clearly winning the war. Part of the reason was that President Lincoln had found a great soldier. He was Ulysses (*yoo*-LISS-*eez*) S. Grant.

Grant had become known as a tough general who was as good as the Southern generals. He began defeating the Confederate army in the West. So, Lincoln put him in charge of all the Union armies.

Grant started an all-out attack against Lee's army near Richmond, Virginia, the capital of the Confederacy.

The diary of a young girl of Richmond, Virginia, tells what happened then:

November 23, 1864

Dear Diary,

Mother says not to worry, but the sound of fighting around Richmond goes on and on. General Grant does not give up. Nor does General Lee. So far Richmond has been spared from the Union army, but I know people are worried. I heard our dinner guests talking last night. One man described the way the soldiers live. He said they are huddled in trenches. Mud, insects, and sickness are as troublesome as the enemy weapons.

One thing I hate about this war, Diary, is that Cousin Bruce is fighting with the Union troops. He might be here with Grant now. It doesn't seem right that members of a family should have to fight against each other. I guess that's why Mother calls it the "Brothers' War."

April 2, 1865

Diary!

Tonight we flee Richmond. General Lee has said he can no longer save the city. Already his troops are burning their supplies to keep them from Union hands. The streets are jammed with carriages. In a few hours, the Union troops will be here!

On April 9, 1865, General Robert E. Lee surrendered to Grant at Appomattox (*ap-uh*-MAT-*uks*) Court House in Virginia. When Union troops cheered as the defeated Lee walked by, Grant ordered the noise to stop. "The war is over," he said. "The rebels are our countrymen again."

The Civil War brought hardship to civilians as well as soldiers. The residents of Richmond flee their burning city on April 2, 1865.

A WAR-WEARY LAND

The dream of the Confederate States was over. The Union had survived. The war had settled a very basic question: The nation would not be divided. States could not secede from the Union because they disagreed with the national government.

What was the price of the Civil War? More than 600,000 soldiers lay dead. Tens of thousands more were crippled or sick.

In 1864 Abraham Lincoln had been elected to a second term as U.S. President. Now he faced the great job of mending the nation.

SKILL BUILDER

Understanding the Gettysburg Address

At Gettysburg, Pennsylvania, on November 19, 1863, President Abraham Lincoln dedicated a new military cemetery. It was on land where part of the terrible Battle of Gettysburg had been fought. In this battle, 51,000 men were killed or wounded. The President's speech was short, lasting just two minutes. This is what Lincoln said in his Gettysburg Address:

Four score and seven years ago our fathers brought forth on this continent a new nation, conceived [*kun*-SEEVD] in liberty, and dedicated to the proposition [*prop-uh*-ZISH-*un*] that all men are created equal.

Now we are engaged in a great civil war, testing whether that nation, or any nation so conceived and so dedicated, can long endure. We are met on a great battlefield of that war. We have come to dedicate a portion of that field as a final resting place for those who here gave their lives that that nation might live. It is altogether fitting and proper that we should do this.

But, in a larger sense, we cannot dedicate—we cannot consecrate [*kon-suh*-KRATE]—we cannot hallow—this ground. The brave men, living and dead, who struggled here, have consecrated it far above our poor power to add or detract. The world will little note nor long remember what we say here, but it can never forget what they did here. It is for us, the living, rather, to be dedicated here to the unfinished work which they who fought here have thus far so nobly advanced. It is rather for us to be here dedicated to the great task remaining before us—that from these honored dead we take increased devotion to that cause for which they gave the last full measure of devotion; that we here highly resolve that these dead shall not have died in vain; that this nation, under God, shall have a new birth of freedom; and that government of the people, by the people, for the people, shall not perish from the Earth.

In his speech, President Lincoln, predicted that "the world will little note nor long remember what we say here." Lincoln was only partly right. Other speeches were given that day, and nobody remembers them. But Lincoln's speech will never be forgotten. Let us look at some of the reasons why this speech is one of the most important documents in American history.

First read the Gettysburg Address by yourself. You may need a dictionary to look up some of the words. Then think about the following questions:

1. A *score* of years is 20 years. How many years is "four score and seven"? What important year is Lincoln talking about in the first sentence? What important event is he talking about?

2. What does Lincoln think was the main point or purpose of the Civil War?

3. Who are the "brave men" of whom Lincoln speaks? Does Lincoln say for which army they fought?

Suppose you are a reporter that day in 1863. You are to write about President Lincoln's speech for your newspaper. Write a short news story about it—no more than 10 lines. Before starting, ask yourself the following questions.

- Whom are you writing about?
- What did he do?
- Where did he do it?
- When did he do it?
- Why did he do it?

Listen to your teacher or a classmate read the Gettysburg Address aloud. Write down words or phrases that touch your feelings in some way. How do they make you feel?

"HONEST ABE" LINCOLN

He stood six feet four inches tall in stocking feet. When he put on his shoes and hat, he added another foot. Abraham Lincoln was a giant in his day.

Lincoln was born in the Kentucky wilderness on February 12, 1809. His family followed the frontier westward as Kentucky became more settled. They moved to Indiana, and then later to Illinois.

Young Lincoln grew up to be a strong lad. He helped his father on the farm. He was good with an ax. He could cut down big trees and split them into "rails" for fences. His neighbors called him the "rail-splitter."

The young man did not have much time for school. Still, he loved learning. He read every chance he got. He often carried a book as he plowed the land. While chopping down trees, he would practice speeches. He pretended the squirrels and jackrabbits were his audience.

Once Abe took a trip down the Mississippi River to New Orleans. There he saw slave families being sold. He watched as mothers cried, saying good-bye to their small children. It was a sight that Abe Lincoln never forgot.

When he returned home to New Salem, Illinois, he worked in a store and studied law. Once a woman customer left the store without her change. Abe Lincoln walked seven miles after her to give her the money.

Now his neighbors called him "Honest Abe." When he became a lawyer, they sent him to Springfield to be in the state assembly. He was a good lawyer, and people trusted him. This trust would grow, just as his fame did, until it finally took him to the White House.

Abraham Lincoln's height (he was 6'4")
was a subject of humor in this cartoon.

CHAPTER 17 REVIEW

Words to Know

Use each of the words listed below in a sentence.

address   civil war   proclamation

blockade   emancipate

Facts to Review

1. Why did the Southern states secede from the United States?
2. What were the Confederate States of America?
3. What event started the Civil War? How?
4. In what ways was the North stronger than the South at the start of the Civil War?
5. What advantage did the South have?
6. How did Northern warships hurt the South?
7. What did the Emancipation Proclamation do?
8. What was the result of the Battle of Gettysburg?
9. Why is the Civil War sometimes called the "Brothers' War"?
10. What issue did the Civil War settle?

Things to Think About

1. Suppose that you are a newspaper reporter traveling in either the North or the South in the days before the beginning of the Civil War. Write a short report on what people in the region are saying about their cause.
2. Try to imagine that you are a young person in Richmond after the Union army has taken your city. Write a brief diary entry telling what you have seen and how you feel about it.

CHAPTER

18

The Nation Tries to Heal Its Wounds

It was Thursday evening, April 13, 1865. People in the city of Washington, D.C., were celebrating. Happy crowds marched in the streets, cheering wildly. A joyful feeling was in the air. The long war had finally ended.

In the White House, President Abraham Lincoln was already planning ways to bring the nation together again. Lincoln did not want to punish the South. Instead he wanted to work with Southern leaders to rebuild it.

At breakfast on the morning of April 14, Lincoln said how relieved he was that the killing was finally over. It was not over, though. That night one more gun was fired. It was a pistol aimed at President Lincoln. An actor, John Wilkes (*wilks*) Booth, shot Lincoln as the President watched a play at a theater. Booth was a Southern supporter who blamed Lincoln for the defeat of the South. By the following morning, Lincoln was dead.

Now the shouts of joy stopped. A stunned nation mourned the fallen President.

Vice President Andrew Johnson became President. Under the U.S. Constitution, if a President dies, the Vice President takes his place.

Johnson tried to carry out Lincoln's plans for a speedy peace. Soon, however, he and some important members of Congress clashed over these plans. These members of Congress believed that the South should be punished.

WHEN FREEDOM CAME

When the Civil War ended, there were about four million freed slaves in the South. What would happen to them?

They were free, but very few of them had money. Very few had land to settle on. All that most of them had were

On page 272: It took some time for the wounds of the Civil War to heal. However, by the 1880's, the New Orleans waterfront was a busy place once again.

the clothes on their backs. How were they going to stay alive? Frederick Douglass said of the former slaves: "They are free from the old plantation. But they have nothing but the dusty road under their feet."

Some blacks stayed with their former owners. Others wandered around the South looking for work. Most white farmers needed help, but few had any money to pay workers. So a system called **sharecropping** developed. In this system, a farmer would let workers live on his land and use some of it to grow crops. In return, the workers would give the farmer a share of their crops.

Here is how a sharecropper remembers the system:

> We sharecroppers never got ahead. We lived on other people's land and used other people's tools. Then, when our crops were grown, we had to give most of our harvest back to the farmer. Little was left for us to live on. So, we would go to the store and buy on credit. That's how we got seeds for next year's crops, a few clothes, and some food. In all my years as a sharecropper, I was always in debt. I rarely saw

money. We had little food, and the children were often sick.

Why didn't we leave? Well, even if we could pay back all our debts, where would we go? Few whites would hire blacks to do other jobs, and most of us didn't know how to do any work but farming anyway. It was just like being a slave all over again.

Some blacks did move to cities in both the South and the North. There they took whatever jobs they could get. Many cooked, waited on tables, took jobs as servants, or drove wagons. Some were able to practice a trade or get factory jobs. Others went on to become doctors, lawyers, teachers, and business owners. For most blacks, though, it was a very hard time.

HARD TIMES ALL OVER THE SOUTH

The Civil War had left the South very weak. Crops had been burned and farms destroyed. Railroads and bridges had been blown up. Many towns and cities had been burned to the ground.

Parts of the South were in ruins after the war. This photograph by Matthew Brady shows the ruins of the city of Richmond.

People all over the South felt very confused after the war. White or black, all knew that the Old South of slaves and King Cotton was gone. Somehow the South would have to be built up again. But how?

The Black Codes

Southern whites took charge of setting up new state governments. Then these governments began passing laws called Black Codes. Black people may have been freed from slavery. However, these codes tried to take away the rights blacks should have received with freedom. For example, a black without a job could be arrested and made to work for a white boss. Black people could not serve on juries or go to school with whites.

Many members of the U.S. Congress were very angry when they heard about these Black Codes. They said that the codes proved that the South had not learned any lessons from the war. They also said that the U.S. government would have to force the Southern states to change.

Life was hard for most blacks after the Civil War. This large family lived in a one-room cabin.

Freedom changed the life of black people. Now there were schools for black students to attend. The most famous was Tuskegee Institute in Alabama (above), founded by Booker T. Washington, a famous black leader. George Washington Carver, a famous scientist, taught at Tuskegee. In the first years after the Civil War, blacks were allowed to vote in elections (below right).

Congress Takes Charge

President Andrew Johnson did not agree with this view. The leaders of Congress proved more powerful than Johnson, however. Soon the U.S. government sent troops into the South to take charge.

Many Northerners moved to the South at this time. Some came to start new businesses. Some came to set up schools to teach blacks to read and write.

Now blacks began to vote in the South for the first time. Black leaders also were elected to Congress. Two blacks from the state of Mississippi, Hiram Revels and Blanche K. Bruce, served in the U.S. Senate.

At the same time that many blacks were being helped with elections, many whites were being banned from them. Congress said that whites who had been active in the Confederacy could not vote or run for office.

"THE FIRST VOTE."—Drawn by A. R. Waud.—(See next Page.)

Some white Southerners did not like carpetbaggers, shown in this cartoon. They said that the South should solve its problems without help from others.

Growing Bitterness

Many whites in the South hated these changes. They wanted to be left alone to work out their own problems in their own ways. They also hated the Northerners who had come to the South. They thought these Northerners were just trying to make money out of the South's problems. Southerners bitterly referred to these newcomers as "carpetbaggers." (Many Northerners had carried their belongings to the South in small suitcases made from pieces of carpet.)

There was a lot of bad feeling during this time. Many Southern whites were bitter about Northerners and former slaves running the government. Some whites even formed a secret group, the Ku Klux Klan, to threaten blacks and keep them from voting.

The bad feelings lasted many, many years and would trouble people in all of the United States. Even after the last U.S. troops were removed in 1877, there was much bitterness and dislike.

THE BEGINNING OF THE NEW SOUTH

In some ways, things were beginning to change for the better in the South. It was growing in many ways. By the 1870's, towns and cities were busy and new industries were being developed. After the Civil War, iron and coal were discovered in northern Alabama. Soon factories were being built to produce iron and steel. The city of Birmingham, Alabama, grew up around the factories. Birmingham became a large city and a leading center of industry. Atlanta, Georgia, became a business center.

Rivers and harbors were improved in the South. New post offices and other buildings went up. More railroads were built. Business and industry began to grow. It would be many years before the South recovered from the wounds of the Civil War. Still, it was making a strong start.

TRAVELER FOR TRUTH

At the end of the Civil War, black people looked to the future with hope. Slavery had ended. Blacks hoped the injustice of the past would soon be just a memory. Sadly, much injustice did return.

Sojourner Truth spoke out against injustice. She was named Isabella by her mother, a slave. After Isabella gained her freedom as an adult, she decided to travel—or sojourn (so-*jern*)—up and down the land spreading God's truth. She called herself Sojourner Truth.

She set off on her journey with 25 cents. "Do you know the best way to show your love?" she asked people. "By showing your concern for your fellow man," she would answer.

Sojourner also helped escaped slaves find homes and jobs in the North. She worked to improve living conditions for black people everywhere.

Sojourner Truth was the most famous black woman of her time. She traveled all over the country speaking out against slavery. She also spoke out for women's rights.

Once, at a big meeting, a well-known minister said that God did not intend women to be equal to men. Sojourner Truth drew herself up to her full six-foot height. In a loud voice, she said: "I have labored, I have planted and harvested crops. And aren't I a woman?"

During the Civil War, Sojourner Truth was invited to the White House by President Lincoln. When she died in 1883, hundreds of people paid last respects to this brave woman.

Sojourner Truth

SKILL BUILDER

Selecting Research Materials

Suppose you were asked to write a report on the Presidency of Andrew Johnson. Where would you look for information about the man and his years in office?

You might first consult a biographical dictionary such as *Webster's Biographical Dictionary*. Here you would find out the dates he lived, when he held office, and some important facts about him. Next you might consult a good encyclopedia. Remember, an encyclopedia is a collection of articles on many different subjects. Most encyclopedias consist of many volumes. The articles are arranged alphabetically. An encyclopedia can give you a quick introduction to almost any subject.

Once you get a general idea of who Andrew Johnson was and what he did, you will be ready to start gathering other information about him. Perhaps you would check the card catalog in your library to see if it had any biographies about him. A biography would tell you interesting facts about his life. In it you might learn what other people thought about him. You might also look for general books about the nation's Presidents and history books relating to the period in which he lived.

Which of these research sources might you use for each of the following topics?

- The Murder of Abraham Lincoln.

- John Wilkes Booth.

- The Ku Klux Klan.

- Life Among the Freed Slaves.

Pick one of these topics and write a report on it. For your research, use at least one book other than an encyclopedia.

Word to Know

In two or three sentences, explain what the word listed below referred to.

sharecropping

Facts to Review

1. What was Abraham Lincoln's goal after the Civil War?
2. What did Andrew Johnson try to do when he became President after Lincoln's death?
3. What problems did the freed slaves face after the war?
4. What was the South like after the war?
5. What did the Black Codes do?
6. Why did Congress take such a big role in running the South after the war?
7. Why did many white Southerners dislike the Northerners who came to the South after the war?
8. Who were the carpetbaggers? How did they get that name?
9. Why did bitterness and bad feelings between North and South continue after the end of the Civil War?
10. How did the South show it was recovering from the Civil War?

Things to Think About

1. Suppose that you work for a newspaper and are told to write an obituary (*oe*-BIT-*choo-err-ee*) about Abraham Lincoln after his death. (An obituary is a notice of a person's death and a brief account of his or her life.) What would you say about Lincoln's life in such a notice? Write a short obituary for Abraham Lincoln.
2. Make a list of things people of the North and people of the South should have done to make the time after the war a better one.

Using New Words

On a separate piece of paper, write the paragraph below. Fill in the blanks with the correct words from the list.

blockade   emancipate   slave states
cash crop   free states
civil war   secede

Abraham Lincoln ran for President in 1860. Many white Southerners thought Lincoln was a threat to slavery, which they needed to grow cotton, their ____. They also knew he wanted no ____ to be made out of the Western territories. He wanted only ____ to come out of these lands. When Lincoln was elected, the Southern states decided to ____ from the Union. After South Carolina attacked U.S. troops at Fort Sumter, the North and the South fought each other in a ____. The North prevented the South from receiving any goods from outside by using ships to ____ Southern ports. Lincoln decided to ____ the slaves in 1863. The war ended two years later.

Thinking About the Unit

1. Pretend you are a reporter. You are going to interview one of the people you have read about in this unit. Choose a person to interview. Make up a list of questions to ask this person about the problems of the times.
2. Suppose you were an immigrant boy or girl coming to the U.S. in the 1840's. What would you hope to find here? What would your dreams and plans for the future be?
3. In what ways is a civil war different from any other kind of war? Why is it more likely to divide people? Why does it sometimes take longer to heal the wounds of a civil war?

Sharpening Your Skills

1. Read the following part of a letter that might have been written in the time of the Civil War. What clues would help you date this letter? About when do you think it was written?

Dear Sister,
       Like our country, I feel at peace now. Do you remember our President's speech? His words about our government of, by, and for the people must guide our leaders forever. I wonder what the old "rail-splitter" will do now? We are fortunate to have such a President. Write soon.
                                                          Love, Laura

2. Write a short summary of the Gettysburg Address.

3. Suppose you want to write a report about the Gettysburg Address. You want to learn more about how Lincoln wrote the speech and about how he presented it. You also want to find out about the reactions of people at the time. What sources would you look in for information?

Expanding Your Knowledge

1. Do some research and use your text to find out more about a Southern plantation in the years before the Civil War. Make a diagram to show where the buildings and fields of a large plantation might be. Label your drawing.

2. Find out more about the life of Robert E. Lee. What did he do before the Civil War? What did he do after it? Why did his soldiers look up to him? Why was he well respected in the North?

3. Find out more about Ulysses S. Grant. What did he do before the Civil War? What did he do after it? Why did his soldiers respect him?

— Your Own History —

In 1789 Samuel Slater brought an industry to a town in Rhode Island. Find out what industries or businesses helped your town or city grow. When were they started? Who started them? Are they still there? Add your information to your history scrapbook or history files.

Unit Six
A Growing Nation

19 The Rise of Industry

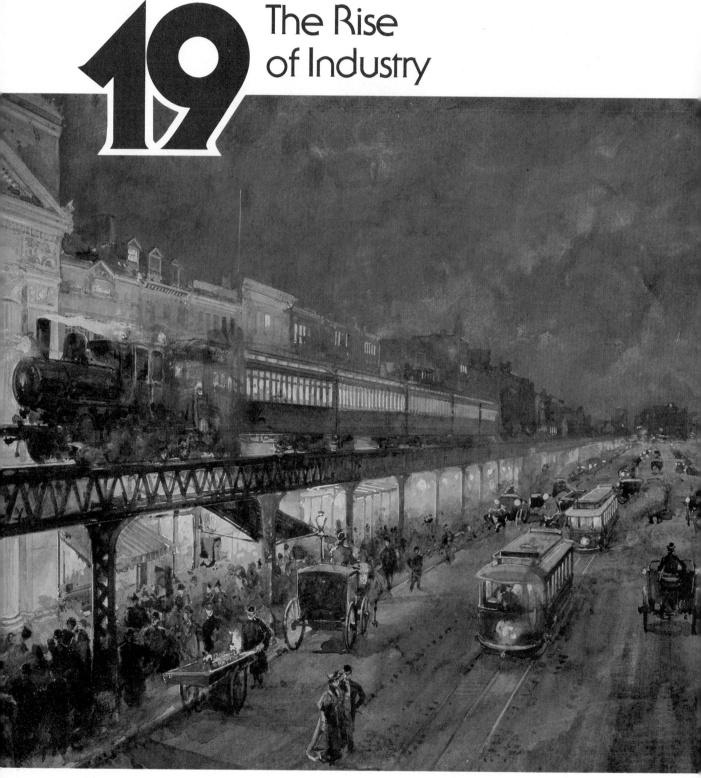

May 1869. A golden spike, or large nail, shines in the sun. A colorful crowd gathers around it. Work crews, cooks, dishwashers, soldiers, engineers, railroad officials, and government leaders all push forward to get a closer look. The governor of California raises his hammer and gives a few mighty swings. He hammers the golden spike into the ground. It is the last nail in the first railroad to link California with the eastern U.S.

This scene took place at Promontory Point, Utah. It marked the end of a great railroad-building race that had begun three years before. At that time, two railroad companies began laying track. The Central Pacific Railroad started in Sacramento, California, and worked eastward. The Union Pacific started in Omaha, Nebraska, and worked westward. Both companies built track as fast as they could. They wanted to see who could lay the most track before they could link up.

Both companies had a hard time. Workers for the Central Pacific had to dig tunnels through the Sierra (*see*-ERR-*uh*) Nevada Mountains, a high mountain range in California. Many of these workers were Chinese immigrants who came here to do this work. Most of the workers on the Union Pacific were Irish immigrants or American blacks.

Armed with axes, picks, and shovels, all these workers leveled the land, laid track, and built bridges. In summer, the men often fainted from the terrible heat. In winter, they had to build sheds over the tracks to keep going in the snow. In all kinds of weather the work continued.

A great era of railroad building was underway. Within 50 years, 254,000 miles (*about 409,000 kilometers*) of railroad track crisscrossed the nation.

On page 286: To you this 1890's New York City street scene probably looks very old-fashioned. But to the people of the 1890's, this picture showed off the latest inventions. How many "new" inventions of the time can you pick out in the picture?

The railroads changed America. They opened the West to settlement. They also helped industries and cities grow. Raw materials and finished goods, crops and livestock were all shipped by rail. Millions of immigrants came to the U.S. at this time. Some traveled by train to the West. Others took factory jobs in Eastern cities.

GROWING STRONG WITH STEEL AND OIL

Steel is the basic building material of modern times. Big things—bridges, buildings, airplanes, pipelines—all use steel. So do bicycles and thousands of other items.

Before the Civil War, this wasn't so. Many goods were made from iron then. Iron is not as strong as steel, however. Some steel was made, but it cost too much to be used in place of iron. Little by little, steelmaking was improved. Finally, ways were found to make steel cheaply.

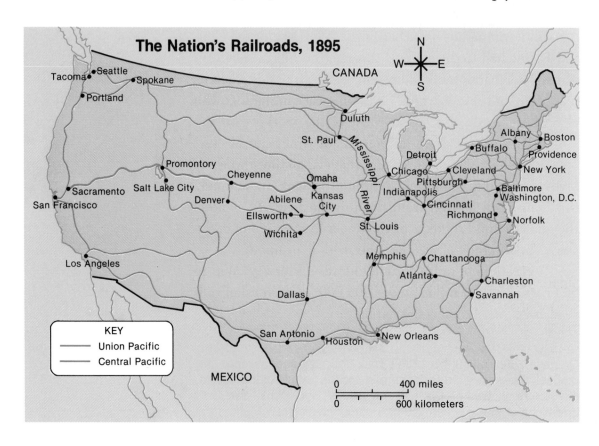

The Nation's Railroads, 1895

The old and the new cross paths in this picture. Trains made travel by covered wagon a thing of the past.

Other improvements followed. Soon steel was not only taking the place of iron, but also being used for many new things. Joseph Glidden, a farmer from DeKalb (*duh*-KALB), Illinois, invented barbed wire. By 1880 some 40,000 tons of it fenced in the prairies of the West. By 1884 a steel framework made it possible to build tall, many-storied buildings, called **skyscrapers.** That year the first skyscraper was built in Chicago. In the 1890's, steel tubing was made to be used in bicycles. By the early 1900's, steel became the backbone of another new industry—automobiles.

New uses for steel brought on new uses for oil. The skyscrapers that steel made possible had to be heated. Oil heat was often the answer here. The new steel automobiles had to have fuel. Again oil made into gasoline was the answer. Soon oil too was a booming business.

Andrew Carnegie and "King Steel"

One of the first people to see the possibilities of steel was Andrew Carnegie (KAHR-*nuh-gee*). Carnegie had come to the U.S. at the age of 13 as an immigrant from Scotland. For several years, he worked hard and saved his money. Then, in 1865, he went into the iron business and some years later began making steel.

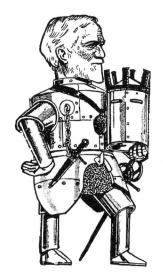

In the cartoon above, Andrew Carnegie wears a suit of steel. Steel was used to make the automobiles that Americans were buying. The oil that was used to run them was pumped out of oil fields like this one below.

First Carnegie built his own steel mill in Pennsylvania. Then he figured out ways to buy more and more mills. He didn't stop there, though. He went on expanding his business. He bought iron ore fields near Lake Superior in Minnesota. Then he bought ships to carry the ore across the Great Lakes. He bought coal mines and limestone pits, both needed in making steel. Finally, he bought railroads to carry the coal, limestone, and finished steel. Soon Andrew Carnegie owned the steel business from beginning to end. Ore dug up in his Minnesota mines on Monday could be made into steel rails in his Pittsburgh mills by Saturday night.

Black Glue Becomes Black Gold

The world has not always known the value of oil. Before the 1850's, most people had little use for it. A few settlers learned from American Indians that oil could be used as a medicine. To settlers in Pennsylvania who drilled for salt, though, oil was only annoying. It got in the way of their salt mining. Some called it "black glue."

Then, in 1852, a Canadian scientist, Abraham Gesner, discovered kerosene (KERR-*uh-seen*), which comes from oil. Kerosene could be used for lighting lamps and lanterns. The demand for oil began to grow.

In 1859 a well was dug in Titusville (TIE-*tus-vill*), Pennsylvania. It was the beginning of the oil industry. Other wells followed. Soon the pastures and cornfields of Titusville were dotted with oil wells. Towns sprang up overnight, and pipelines and railroads were laid to move the oil from the fields to a **refinery.** There it was made ready for sale.

In the years that followed, oil was found in Kentucky, Ohio, Indiana, Illinois, and Kansas. By 1910 it was also being drilled in Texas and Oklahoma. By that same year, gasoline-powered cars were on the road. Billions of gallons of oil were now needed. It had truly become "black gold."

The Man Who Could See Around Corners

John D. Rockefeller was responsible for much growth in the oil industry. Like Andrew Carnegie, he gained control of an entire industry and became one of the richest men in the world.

Rockefeller started as a bookkeeper in Cleveland, Ohio. He earned $3.50 a week. Soon after the Titusville boom, he went to Pennsylvania to look over the oil fields. By 1862 he was back in Ohio working hard in the business of oil refining.

Rockefeller had looked around the corner and had seen the possibilities for the future of oil. At the age of 30, he formed a company called Standard Oil. He also bought out the refineries of many other companies.

Like Carnegie, Rockefeller wanted to control his business from beginning to end. He built or bought his own oil fields, tanks, pipelines, and warehouses. He owned the oil cars of the Pennsylvania Railroad and got all the railroads to

John D. Rockefeller wears an oil barrel in this cartoon. Rockefeller changed the way big business was run in the United States.

give him special low rates to transport his oil. His barrels were made from Rockefeller-owned lumber and delivered to homes and businesses in Rockefeller-owned wagons.

Rockefeller's advice to young people starting out was, "Don't be afraid to work." Not everyone profited as much as Rockefeller, though. Many people in those days toiled long hours at hard jobs and remained poor. Their wages were low and their living conditions terrible. They wondered how their wages could be so low when companies' profits were so high.

The rise of big industries was making the U.S. a wealthy and powerful nation. It was also making the differences between the rich and the poor greater than ever.

MORE NEW INVENTIONS

It is 1876. The country is holding an industrial fair in Philadelphia to celebrate 100 years of American independence—and progress.

Inventions That Changed a Nation

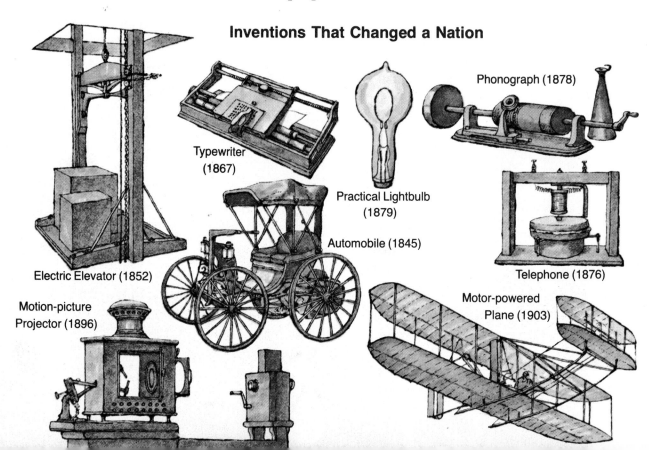

Typewriter (1867)

Phonograph (1878)

Practical Lightbulb (1879)

Automobile (1845)

Electric Elevator (1852)

Telephone (1876)

Motion-picture Projector (1896)

Motor-powered Plane (1903)

"Look, Mom! That machine prints newspapers."

"And see that one. It's called a typewriter. You press those keys, and letters appear on the paper."

"How much easier things are now."

With *ohs* and *ahs*, people wander about a great building called the Hall of Machinery. In it are hundreds of machines on display. The machines tell a story of progress and a changing way of life. There are now machines to do many tasks once done by hand.

"Look at the machine that spins cotton."

"Yes, and there is a home sewing machine."

Still other inventions do things that most people had never thought possible.

"Mr. Bell calls that a telephone. You can talk to someone on it."

To many, marvels of machinery were signs of the nation's greatness. Each invention brought more changes and made life a little easier. Said inventor George Westinghouse, "The more things we invent, the more things we need to invent."

Before and after: Life became easier for the homemaker in this 1880's advertisement when she switched from a coal-burning stove to an oil-burning one. Can you think of any recent inventions that have changed the way you live?

THE DEVELOPMENT OF AMERICAN CITIES

These new industries and inventions made it possible and necessary for people to live near each other in great numbers. During this period, many old American cities began to grow larger. Many new cities sprang up where only small towns had stood before.

Cities grew up where goods were made, where factories and mills stood, where railroads met, where opportunities were found. Corning, New York, grew because of the glassmaking industry. Grand Rapids, Michigan, developed because of furniture-making. Dayton, Ohio, became the home for the manufacture of a new invention, the cash register.

People moved to these places to work in their industries. These people needed to buy clothes and food. They needed homes to live in. They needed transportation between home and work, and between shopping and home. So, other people went to work selling them clothes and food, building homes, providing entertainment, and supplying public transportation.

Cities were growing fast—much faster than anyone expected. As they did, many problems arose.

Growing Pains

There were not enough places for people to live in the cities. Old buildings soon became overcrowded. New buildings called **tenements** (TEN-*uh-mentz*) were put up quickly and cheaply. They were often dark and narrow, and had poor lighting and plumbing. There were also few places to play and enjoy open spaces.

Factories were sometimes jammed next to these apartment buildings. As a result, noise, dirt, smoke, and bad-smelling fumes made life unpleasant—and unhealthful—for those living in the tenements.

Garbage and other wastes increased as the cities grew. Often these were dumped into drinking water sources. They caused disease to spread quickly. The writer Mark Twain said of one city, "It smells like a billion polecats."

The streets too were almost always dirty. They were muddy in the winter and dusty in the summer. Many were still unpaved.

People needed better ways to move around within the cities. Once they had been able to get everywhere by walking. As the cities spread out, though, distances became too great for people to walk everywhere.

The first steel bridge was built across the Mississippi River at St. Louis in 1874. Steel was used to build the bridges and skyscrapers of American cities.

Improving the Cities

In 1893 a big fair called the World's Columbian Exposition was held in Chicago. The fairgrounds were planned well and had all the services needed by a large city. People began to think more about city planning.

By 1901 New York City had passed the first **building codes.** These codes set standards for new buildings. They said how much space, lighting, heating, and plumbing a building had to provide.

Cities also began to pass **zoning laws.** These laws made sure that factories and homes were built in separate areas. Tunnels were dug under cities, and pipes were laid to bring in water, steam for heat, and gas for cooking. Sewers were built to take away wastes.

Cities also built railroads that were on raised platforms. In 1887, the trolley car was invented. It ran on tracks and was attached to wires overhead. The trolley helped the city grow by allowing people to travel greater distances to get to their jobs. Cities also began building parks and playgrounds. These gave city children safer and more pleasant places to play.

Thomas Alva Edison is shown in this painting with the phonograph that he invented. Despite a problem with his hearing, Edison used the wax cylinders to make sound recordings.

THE WIZARD OF MENLO PARK

The time: New Year's Eve, 1879.

The place: A research lab in Menlo Park, New Jersey.

The scene: Three thousand people wait in darkness. They have come by special trains to watch a demonstration. A scientist, Thomas Alva Edison, is going to show them his new lamp. Edison presses a button and suddenly a light goes on. The first successful electric light bulb glows steadily through the night. The visitors are amazed.

Word of Edison's invention spread quickly. He became known to the world as the "Wizard of Menlo Park."

Edison's work on the light bulb brought a kind of magic to the world. Other scientists had been working on the idea of electric light for years. Edison's goal, though, was to make small lights that could be used in homes and offices. He wanted bulbs that would burn for hours at a time. It took him two years to develop his light bulb. When Edison finally succeeded, he changed the lives of millions of people in the United States and all over the world.

Once his invention was perfected, Edison went on to organize the Edison Electric Light Company. He wanted to make his invention available to as many people as possible. Said Edison: "We'll make electric light so cheap that only the rich will be able to burn candles." He then developed the first power station to make and distribute electricity. This station, in New York City, began to operate in 1882.

In 1884 another man saw the possibilities of electric light. George Westinghouse organized a company to provide people with electrical current. By the early 1900's, many homes, farms, factories, stores, and offices had electric lights. Street lamps were lit by electricity. Children now studied at night by electric lights. The candles, fires, and gas and oil lamps of the past were soon forgotten as Americans lit up the dark by simply flicking a switch.

SKILL BUILDER

Predicting Change

In this chapter, you have read how the U.S. changed in some important ways after the Civil War. For example, you read how in 1869 the last tracks for the first coast-to-coast railroad were laid. The new railroad would help settle the West and unite the country. It would also help U.S. industry grow.

At about the same time, new ways to make steel were found and a way to turn oil into fuel was discovered. Later steel was used to make cars, and oil was used to make the gasoline that powered them.

Throughout history, inventions and discoveries of new fuels have created change. Some of the changes could have been predicted at the time. (To **predict** is to tell what will happen in the future.) Others could not have been. The builders of the first cross-country railroad knew that they were uniting the country and opening up the West. They probably could not have predicted how huge our cities would become and how fast the nation would become an industrial giant. It is even less likely that people at the turn of the century could have predicted that one day our supplies of oil would be scarce.

Today Americans are trying to learn to use **solar energy** (energy from the sun). Solar energy is cleaner than other energy sources. However, the devices that collect solar energy take up a lot of space. Suppose the day comes when all houses and buildings are heated by energy from the sun. Suppose too that someday cars, buses, trucks, and trains are powered by solar energy. What will our cities be like? How will our lives be changed? Try to imagine what life might be like without the use of any oil or coal. Draw a picture showing what your town might be like. Or write a story describing your life in the "new solar age." How will your life be different? How will it be the same?

Words to Know

Use each of the words listed below in a sentence.

building code	skyscraper	zoning law
predict	solar energy	
refinery	tenement	

Facts to Review

1. How did Andrew Carnegie become the leading steel producer in the U.S.?
2. Why did oil come to be called "black gold"?
3. How did John D. Rockefeller build his oil business?
4. What inventions were developed during this period?
5. What contributions did Thomas Edison make to improve American life?
6. What problems did rapid city growth cause?
7. What solutions were found for these problems?
8. How would you say the expansion of railroads changed American life?
9. How would you say the development of the steel and oil industries changed American life?
10. How were cities a result of the growth of industry? How did they lead to the further growth of industry?

Things to Think About

1. Think of some product that you would like to manufacture and sell. Draw up a plan of how you would do it. What materials would you have to buy? How would you get them to your factory? What kind of machinery would you need? How would you get your product to your buyers?
2. Review the problems that the growing cities of the U.S. faced in the late 1800's. List each problem. Think about your community or a community you have visited. Then, next to each problem, tell how this city or town deals with this problem in the present time.

CHAPTER
20
Closing the
Last Frontier

Sometimes a department store has a big sale. Customers line up outside, waiting for the doors to open. Then they rush in to grab up whatever bargains are offered. "You would think," say onlookers, "that they were giving something away free."

In 1889 people did get something free. The U.S. government offered free land to those people who got to it first. The land—in what is now Oklahoma—was the last free territory opened to settlers in the American West.

The government said everyone had to wait until noon on April 22. Settlers could then go claim their land.

So, people lined up on the border where Oklahoma meets Kansas to get in on the land boom. Thousands of settlers, nicknamed "Boomers," waited in carts, on horses, and on foot. U.S. troops rode up and down the border to keep people from crossing too soon. (Some settlers did slip over too soon, getting themselves the name "Sooners." Oklahoma later became known as the Sooner state.)

At noon bugles blew, guns went off, and the rush began. Settlers raced for the water holes and good land. By the time it was dark, 50,000 people had entered Oklahoma. Cities of tents and wagons sprang up overnight. Within months the last frontier had been closed. From then on, no really good land was left to be claimed for nothing.

FARMS FROM THE PLAINS

The settlement of other areas of the "Last West" had begun several years earlier. Many historians say that the West was won by **homesteaders.** A homesteader was a settler who made use of the Homestead Act of 1862. This law said that a citizen over 21 could have 160 acres *(64 hectares)* of public land. To keep the land, a homesteader had to live on it for five years and improve it.

On page 300: The gun has just sounded. Settlers rush into Oklahoma to claim the last open land in the American West.

Starting in 1862, these pioneer farmers made the long, hard trip to the Great Plains. Many of them came on the new railroads that now crossed the country. Some of them were from the Eastern U.S. Others were immigrants from Northern Europe, drawn by the promise of free land.

Life on the Plains

Most people found life on the prairie land hard and lonely. Wrote O.E. Rolvaag (ROLE-*vahg*), an immigrant from Norway: "This prairie had no heart that beat, no waves that sang, no soul that could be touched."

Instead there were miles and miles of hard land called **sod,** covered by tough grass—and few trees. Without trees for lumber, the early settlers had to build their homes from sod. There was little water, so farmers had to dig deep for wells. Sometimes they had to go down as far as 300 feet (*about 91 meters*). The weather was a problem too. It was very hot in the summer and terribly cold in the winter.

Besides the weather, farmers often watched their crops being destroyed by great clouds of grasshoppers. Wrote one farmer in the 1870's: "In a week, grain, fields, gardens, shrubs, vines had been eaten down to the ground or to the bark. Nothing could be done. You watched everything go."

Settlers sit for the camera in front of their sod house. This family had been slaves before the Civil War. Now they were landowners.

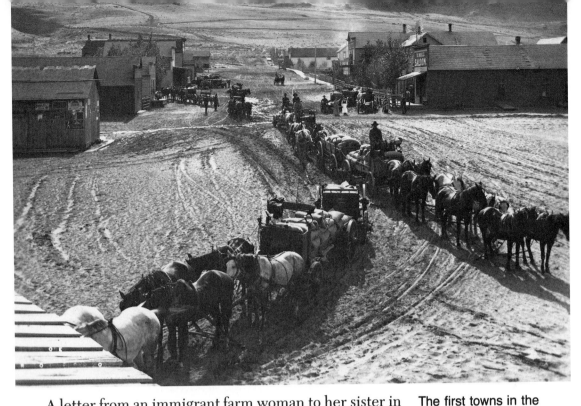

A letter from an immigrant farm woman to her sister in Norway tells what life was like:

The first towns in the West were no more than a few low buildings and muddy streets.

Dakota Territory, 1873

Dear Lisa,

Finally we are landholders. Just think—160 acres to farm!

It is a strange land, Lisa. There are no trees and not a bird, although a coyote (*kie*-OTE-*ee*) howls once in awhile.

Eric finds it hard to plow—the ground is so tough to break. Underneath, though, the soil is rich, and we are thankful for that. We are planting some wheat called Turkey Red. It was brought here by some Russian immigrants who came here to settle. It holds up well in this harsh climate.

Our house is built of sod. We call it "prairie marble" because it is the only building material that is easily available. A sod house, Lisa, is small, damp, and dark. The floor is made of dirt.

I miss the homeland, Lisa, and our friends and family. How far we have come to this vast land.

Yours in prayer,
Linde

A schoolteacher looks over her class in a pioneer one-room schoolhouse.

Farming Becomes Big Business

New farm machines worked miracles on the Great Plains. John Deere developed a strong plow that cut through the thick sod. As you recall, Cyrus McCormick had invented the mechanical reaper. Another machine, called a **thresher,** separated kernels of wheat from the stalks. Before its invention, farmers had to beat the stalks by hand or have animals walk over them.

A Colorado family sits down to an outdoor meal in this 1889 photograph. Farmers worked up huge appetites doing back-breaking work.

One result of this new machinery was that more land could be worked by one farmer. Farms of the Great Plains grew huge, stretching for many hundreds of acres. Farmers changed from pioneer growers to business people who planted one crop—usually wheat—and sold it for profit. The Great Plains became the "breadbasket of the U.S."

RANCHES FROM THE PLAINS

"How many more days till we hit Abilene (AB-*uh-leen*)?"

"I reckon maybe 10, maybe more."

The riders speak, then pass in the dark. Their job tonight is to watch over the cattle, to keep them calm, to let them graze until morning. These Longhorn cattle once roamed wild in southern Texas. Now they have been rounded up and are being herded north to the railroad.

In the distance, a campfire glows against the open sky. Near it, six more cowboys sleep, weary from the hard ride of the day. They call the trip the Long Drive. Indeed it is one. Driving 1,000 head of Texas Longhorns is no easy job. Ten miles a day for 100 days. That is 1,000 miles (*1,609 kilometers*) from the ranch to the railroad in Abilene, Kansas. All along the way, the cattle can graze free on the rich, open range. By the end of the drive, a skinny calf is a fattened steer. It is ready to be shipped by rail to the meatpacking plants of Chicago, Illinois.

Life Along the Trail

The days on the Long Drive are lonely and often dangerous. Rain or shine, day or night, the cowboy is outdoors. He is an expert horse rider and can throw a lasso, a skill learned from the *vaqueros*, the Mexican cowboys. He must be ever on the watch for signs of a stampede (*stam-*PEED). Any different sound or smell or the thunder and lightning of a rainstorm can start the cattle running. So can rustlers. A stampede is hard and dangerous to stop.

Women worked hard on the frontier. Often they tended the animals as well as cooking, taking care of the house, and raising children.

On each Long Drive, a cook comes along with his chuck wagon. Two hours before sunup, he wakes the riders for breakfast. At noon they stop again for dinner. Then the drive goes on until nightfall.

For the cowboy, it's a rugged open-air life with little pay. It does have a certain freedom, though. In fact, a favorite cowboy saying is, "Don't fence me in." Until about 1886, no one does.

The Coming of Cattle Kingdoms

By 1886 the free grazing lands of the Southwest were getting crowded. Wealthy ranchers were buying up great amounts of land and fencing it in with barbed wire. Huge cattle kingdoms began to dot the Southwest. No longer could herds move freely across the range as they had on the Long Drive.

At the same time, new railroads were being built. Now the cattle could be shipped all the way to market by rail. The Long Drive was no longer necessary.

Raising cattle became an important business. New breeds of cattle—Herefords (HERR-*uh-furdz*) and Black Angus—were introduced. Ranchers were able to fatten these cattle for market in a shorter time than the Longhorns took. The new rancher built barns and developed better feed. The American meat-packing industry grew to be the largest in the world.

A cowboy rides herd on a long line of longhorns. Big cattle drives lasted for weeks. At night cowboys would sing to the cows to help keep them quiet. Some popular cowboy songs were first sung on these Long Drives.

MINING THE PLAINS AND MOUNTAINS

It was not long before great mineral resources were discovered in the West. The race was on to "strike it rich."

The first miners were **prospectors**—people who hoped to get rich quickly by finding valuable metals. They rushed from place to place, hoping to discover metals such as silver or gold. They used simple tools—picks, shovels, and wash basins. They hardly ever got rich, but they did get to live in mining towns with colorful names. Tombstone in Arizona, Deadwood in the Dakotas, and Last Chance Gulch in Montana were among them. Some mining towns turned to dust when the ore gave out and the miners left. Miners, like cowboys, had little interest in settling down.

Company Mines, Company Towns

By the 1870's, mining was no longer a one-person kind of work. To get gold and silver from deep underground, miners had to dig shafts and make tunnels. Special chemicals were needed to get the ore from the rocks. All this cost money—more than any prospector ever had. So companies were formed to run these mines. Miners went to work for these companies.

The work was hard, and the pay was low. Often these workers lived in ugly towns that grew up by the mines. The streets were piled with leftover rocks. The homes were shacks that had been put up quickly. The air was filled with smelly smoke. A railroad chugged through town to take the ore away, and the nearby streams grew dirty from the wastes of the refineries.

The large companies soon saw that other minerals were useful for industry. Copper, bauxite (BAWK-*site*), salt, and lead were mined to make copper wiring, aluminum, electric storage batteries, and many other products of the modern world. The mines of the West seemed to give the U.S. an endless source of raw materials.

Naturalist John Muir (right) and his friend, John Burrows, rest during a hike. They worked hard to save wilderness areas in the United States.

A Call for Conservation

John Muir (*myoor*) looked out over the land of the West and said, "This nation will one day run out of valuable resources." Muir was an immigrant from Scotland who had a great love of nature. He was an explorer and writer who spent many years hiking through the U.S. and other lands. Muir wrote that people needed to protect the environment. He made a 1,000-mile (*1,609-kilometer*) hike from Wisconsin to the border of Mexico. He wrote about what he saw. In his writings, he said that the U.S. government should protect some of the beautiful parts of the country. It should make national parks and wildlife areas.

Yosemite (*yoe-SEM-it-ee*) National Park in California is one result of Muir's work. The park was created in 1890.

Many people in those days did not want to listen to John Muir. They did not agree with his thinking. The nation was young and still growing. It needed resources— minerals, lumber, land—to build its industry. In the late 1800's, few people wanted to look into the future. They did not try to see how what they were doing would change the environment in the next 100 years. They never imagined the problems of air, water, and land pollution that their actions would one day create.

PEOPLE OF THE BUFFALO

For years the Indians of the Plains lived by following the buffalo. Their life depended on hunting these animals. The buffalo provided meat for food, hides for clothing and shelter, bones for tools, gut for bow strings, and chips for fuel. To the Plains Indians, the buffalo was life itself. Luckily the buffalo was the most plentiful animal on the Plains.

The Desire for Indian Land

In 1859 there was a gold strike at Pike's Peak near Denver, Colorado. This was in Indian territory. The Indians were forced to give up their land. In 1875 gold was found in the Black Hills of the Dakotas, sacred land to the Sioux (soo) Indians. Again prospectors rushed in. This time the Sioux formed a great war party with braves from many groups. The party was led by chiefs Sitting Bull, Rain-in-the-Face,

Chief Sitting Bull was a Sioux Indian who fought to save his people's land.

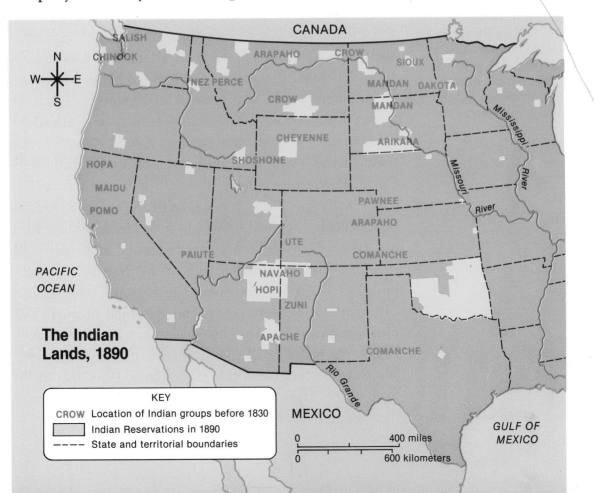

The Indian Lands, 1890

KEY
CROW Location of Indian groups before 1830
Indian Reservations in 1890
State and territorial boundaries

0 400 miles
0 600 kilometers

and Crazy Horse. A U.S. colonel, George A. Custer, went looking for them. In June 1876, he and his cavalry met 3,000 Indians near the Little Bighorn River. Custer and all his men were killed.

The railroads wanted Indian land too. Workers put down miles of track over Indian hunting grounds. Often the Indians attacked, but in the end the tracks were built.

Hunters came also. From 1872 to 1882, hunters killed a million buffalo a year. Said one hunter, "A man could have walked 20 miles *(32 kilometers)* on their dead bodies." By 1893 the buffalo were nearly gone.

Settlers wanted Indian lands too. The Oklahoma Territory was Indian land. Then the government opened much of it to the Boomers in 1889. The Indians were ordered to other areas set aside for them, called **reservations.**

This Navajo woman named Juanita (above) was part of a group of Indians who traveled to Washington, D.C., in 1874. They tried to make peace between Indians and the U.S. government. Chief Joseph (below) was a famous Indian warrior and leader.

Old Indian Life Ends

The Indians did not give up their land easily. Each time another group wanted it, the Indians fought. Between 1869 and 1874 alone, there were hundreds of battles. Said one U.S. general: "We took away their country, and their means of support. We broke up their way of living, their habit of life, and introduced disease and decay among them. It was for this and against this that they made war. Could anyone expect less?"

Finally the Plains Indians had to give up. With the buffalo gone, they had no way to live. Much of their land was taken. Many of their leaders were old and weary.

One Indian—Chief Joseph of the Nez Perce *(nezz-purss)* in Oregon—used these words to tell how he felt: "The white men were many, and we could not hold our own with them. We were like deer. They were like grizzly bears. We had a small country. Their country was large. We were content to let things remain as the Great Spirit made them. They were not, and would change the rivers if they did not suit them."

CHIEF JOSEPH OF THE NEZ PERCE

The story of Chief Joseph and his people is one of the saddest stories to come out of the closing frontier. The Nez Perce lived in the beautiful Wallowa (*wahl*-ow-*uh*) Valley in Oregon. They were a gentle people. They farmed the land, hunted, and raised horses.

The Nez Perce made an agreement with the U.S. government. U.S. leaders agreed that the Wallowa Valley belonged to the Nez Perce. Then settlers decided they wanted the land. The government gave in to the settlers, and told the Nez Perce to move to a reservation many miles away.

Young Nez Perce braves wanted to fight. Chief Joseph refused to go to war, though. He hoped to find a peaceful solution. Then one day, settlers attacked the Nez Perce. They killed women and children, and stole many horses. The young Nez Perce braves lashed out in anger. They killed several settlers. Now war could not be prevented.

Still Joseph tried to avoid any more killing. He decided to lead his people to safety in Canada. The Nez Perce began their desperate journey.

Thousands of American soldiers chased the Nez Perce across 1,000 miles *(1,609 kilometers)* of rugged land. Close to the Canadian border, Joseph and his now tired and starving band stopped to rest. In a bitter snowstorm, the U.S. Army attacked. Joseph saw that his cause was lost. Rather than see his people killed, Chief Joseph surrendered. His speech to the Army generals shows the great spirit of this leader:

> My people ask me for food, and I have none to give. It is cold and we have no blankets. My people are starving to death. Where is my little daughter? I do not know. Perhaps, even now, she is freezing to death. Hear me, my chiefs. I have fought; but from where the sun now stands, Joseph will fight no more, forever.

SKILL BUILDER

Writing a Summary

You cannot remember everything you read in a chapter. You should try to remember the main ideas, though. One way to help you to remember is to write a **summary** of the chapter. A summary gives you a short version of the longer chapter. In a summary, you include only the major facts in the chapter, the most important things in the chapter. For example, read the summary below. It gives the main ideas talked about in this chapter.

> After the Civil War, settlers began moving into the Last West in great numbers. Some went to farm the hard sod of the Great Plains. With the help of new farm machinery, they turned the area into the grain-producing center of the nation. Some went to produce cattle. They supplied the animals for the nation's growing meat-packing industry. Some went to mine gold and silver. They stayed to develop a great new mining industry. Piece by piece, these settlers took over Indian land and destroyed the Indian way of life. From then on, the only land left to the Indians was on reservations.

Look back over the chapter. Find the four major headings in it: "Farms from the Plains"; "Ranches from the Plains"; "Mining the Plains and Mountains"; and "People of the Buffalo."

Now read the above summary again. As you can see, it contains two or three sentences dealing with each of these headings. These two or three sentences give the main ideas in each of the four sections. Taken altogether, they give you a summary of the chapter.

Turn back to a chapter in this book that you have already read. Pick out the major chapter headings. Then reread the material under these headings, one section at a time. Write what you think are the major ideas of this section in a few sentences. Then move on to the next major section and do the same. When you have finished, you will have a summary of that chapter.

Words to Know

Use each of the words listed below in a sentence.

homesteader	reservation	summary
prospector	sod	thresher

Facts to Review

1. Who were the Boomers and the Sooners?
2. What problems did homesteaders face on the Great Plains?
3. Why did the Great Plains come to be called the "breadbasket of the nation"?
4. What was the Long Drive?
5. How did ranching become an important business?
6. Why did big companies take over mining?
7. Who was John Muir? What did he say to Americans?
8. Why did many people disagree with John Muir?
9. Why was the buffalo important to the Plains Indians?
10. How was Indian life in the Last West destroyed?

Things to Think About

1. Try to imagine that you were part of the land rush for Oklahoma that day in 1889. Write a paragraph or two in which you describe your experiences in the few hours after the bugle sounded and the rush was on.
2. How do you suppose Chief Joseph and his people felt as they were being forced to leave their land? Pretend that you are one of these people—a young brave, a young mother, or an old person. Then, in this role, tell what you think your people should do—fight, move to the reservation, or try to escape. Give your reasons for your opinion.

21 New Americans in a New America

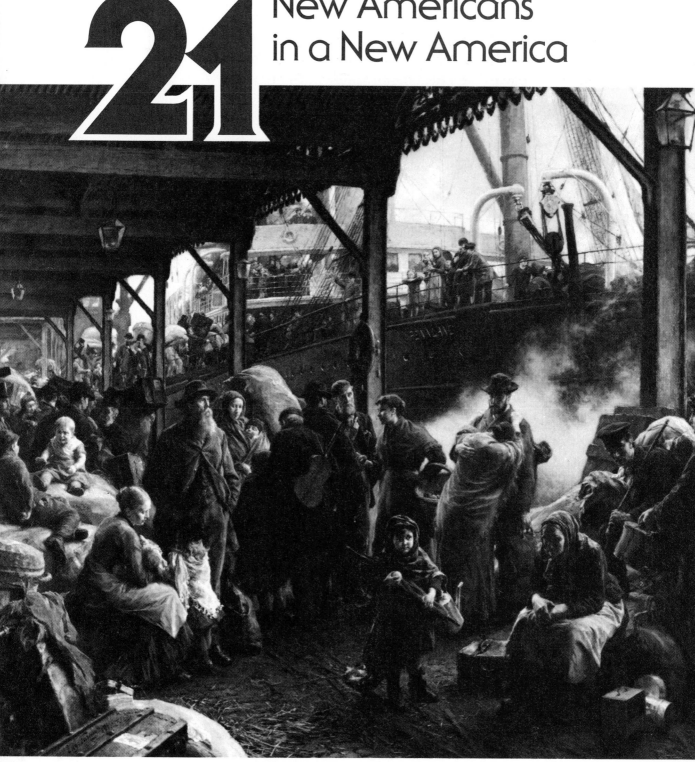

The United States was changing in many ways in the 50 years following the Civil War. It was changing from a nation based on farming to a nation based on industry. The last frontier was opened and then rapidly settled. Through it all, one thing remained the same: The U.S. was still a "nation of immigrants."

In fact, it was during this time that the number of immigrants coming here reached its peak—about 25 million over those 50 years. Immigrants continued coming to the U.S. from the countries of Northern Europe—Ireland, Germany, Scotland, England, Norway, and Sweden. Now, though, people from Southern and Eastern Europe began coming in great numbers. Millions of people came from countries such as Russia, Italy, Poland, Hungary, Turkey, and Greece. Millions more came from Asian countries such as China and Japan.

Why did they come? They had many reasons. Most came to escape being poor and hungry in their old countries. In Italy, famine and disease wiped out whole families. In Eastern Europe, there also was great poverty.

In Russia, many Jewish people were very poor. Poor or not, almost all Jews suffered from cruel laws that made it very hard for them to live. In Turkey and Greece, there was also poverty and violence. As one immigrant said: "When I found that the only way I could keep my family from starving was to steal, I decided it was time to go."

To these people, America was a land of hope. In America, there was the promise of a better life. There was cheap land. There was freedom to worship as one pleased.

So people packed what little they could take and said good-bye to friends and family. The immigrants crowded onto ships and made the long, hard trip across the ocean to the New World.

On page 314: European immigrants say their last good-byes before boarding the boat for a journey to a new life in America.

Ellis Island in New York harbor was called the "Gateway to the New World." Millions of immigrants landed here and filled out forms before moving on to New York City and other places.

LIVING IN A NEW AMERICA

Life in the new land was a struggle. The immigrants had to get used to strange sights and sounds. They had to learn a new language. They sometimes had to learn new skills in order to get jobs. Many people who had lived their entire lives on farms now found themselves living in cities and working in factories.

It was a hard life. The immigrants who went to the cities lived in the poorest parts. They had to live in dark and dirty tenements with little light or air. Garbage piled up in the streets.

Yet, with all their troubles, most immigrants never stopped believing in the United States. They believed that the United States was the land of opportunity. They believed that with their own hard work, they could make a better life for themselves and their families. They believed that in their old countries, they had no future. They believed that in the U.S. they had a future.

What was it like to be an immigrant? In the next few pages, you will read about three immigrants. The first two immigrants wrote about their first days in the United States. The third one wrote a letter to a newspaper asking for advice.

Coming to the City

Edward Corsi was born in Italy in 1887. His father died, and his mother had trouble supporting the family. Edward and his brothers and sisters often met Italian-American immigrants who had returned to Italy for a visit. The immigrants wore fancy clothes and bragged about the riches to be made in the U.S.

Young Edward dreamed of going to the U.S. and making his fortune. Unfortunately, his family did not have the money to make the long trip. Then Edward's mother married again, and the family decided to go to the U.S. Bursting with excitement, Corsi and his family boarded a ship for the trip to New York City in 1907.

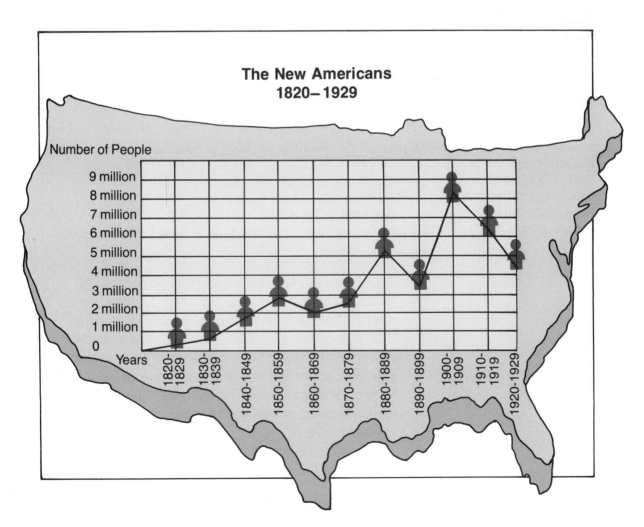

The New Americans
1820–1929

New York City's Lower East Side was home to many immigrants from Europe. This picture of its crowded streets was taken in 1905. Today the Lower East Side is still home to newcomers from Puerto Rico, South America, Europe, and Asia.

Two weeks later, they crowded at the rail of the ship in New York harbor. They were eager to catch their first glimpse of the U.S. Edward saw it first. "Mountains. Look at them," he shouted to his brother. Then they looked closer. The "mountains" were really the tall buildings of New York City.

Arriving at their first home in New York City, though, was not so exciting. Here is how Edward Corsi described their new life.

> Our new home was a sad disappointment. We found ourselves paying a high rent for four dirty rooms. There was only one outside window, and this looked down on a dark street. My mother was discouraged by the sight of the apartment the moment she stepped into it, and she never overcame that feeling. She was never happy here. Though she tried, she could not get used to the poverty in which we had to live.
>
> I am sure that our life was like the lives of thousands upon thousands of immigrant families. There

were many times when we had nothing to eat in the house. There was one period when my stepfather was out of work for 18 months.

When I was old enough for my first job, I went to work as a lamplighter. [In those days, most street lights were lit by gas, not electricity. Each light had to be lit by a lamplighter every evening and put out every morning.]

I rose at four in the morning to put out the lamps on my route. Then I would have breakfast and get to school by nine o'clock.

All through my boyhood, I worked at various jobs. This paid my way through school and at the same time added to our small family income. The few hours that remained to play, and they were few indeed, I spent on the streets. I had many friends my age in the neighborhood. Many of my friends rose from their poor beginnings to useful careers serving the community.

Coming to the Farm

O. E. Rolvaag was a young fisherman in a small town on the coast of Norway in the last years of the 1800's. Like others, Rolvaag dreamed of coming to the United States. He had almost no money, but he did have an uncle who lived in South Dakota. In 1893 Rolvaag wrote his uncle a letter, asking him to send a boat ticket to the U.S. Shortly afterward, the ticket arrived. Here is Rolvaag's story of what followed.

I went to a port down the coast and took a ship for the New World. I wasn't used to traveling. You'll have an idea of how poor I was when I tell you that I wore one shirt from Norway to South Dakota. It had its last washing the day before we arrived in New York.

When I landed in New York, I became very confused by the big harbor, the big city, and the strange language. I couldn't speak or understand a word of English. It wasn't until I got on board the train [for

A child takes a bath in a tenement apartment. Immigrants worked hard in hopes that their children would have a better life.

South Dakota] that I discovered meals weren't included in the railroad ticket. By that time, I was down to 10 cents in American money. I went without food for three days and three nights, all the way from New York to South Dakota.

I left the train at a little station on the Dakota plains. Looking around, I saw nothing but level land, like the sea. My uncle was to have met me, but had made a mistake in the day of my arrival. I tried to ask my way, but no one at the station spoke Norwegian.

At last a Swede who worked on the railroad came along. I was able to communicate with him. He thought he knew where my uncle lived and gave me some directions. I had a 12-mile walk ahead of me. When he found that I hadn't eaten for three days, he gave me what remained of his dinner—one sandwich and some coffee.

By this time, the sun was going down. I struck out on foot, soon lost my way, and walked far into the night. It was one of those quiet plains nights, hot and silent. I've learned to love them now, but then I was worn out and discouraged. I felt as if I had been dropped down in the darkness. Then out of the darkness a dark form appeared. It was a man driving a horse hitched to a wagon. The man was Norwegian, and he took me to the farm where my uncle worked. I stumbled into the house, feeling more dead than alive.

Looking Toward the Future

Often immigrant families had left practically everything they owned in the old country. Now they were poor, and making a living was often quite difficult. Sometimes it was difficult for a family to keep a child in school. The following letter was written by a girl in about 1910 to a New York City newspaper, the *Jewish Daily Forward*.

In it, she tells of a serious problem and asks the editor of the newspaper for some advice.

Dear Editor,

There are seven people in our family—my parents and five children. I am the oldest child, a 14-year-old girl. We have been in this country two years. My father, who is a frail man, is the only one working to support the whole family.

I go to school, where I do very well. But times are hard now. My father earned only five dollars this week. I have talked about giving up my studies and going to work in order to help my father as much as possible. But my mother didn't even want to hear of it. She wants me to continue my education.

I really love my parents. My mother is going to have another baby, but she still has to take care of the three boarders we have in the house. Mother and Father work very hard, and they want to keep me in school.

I am writing to you without their knowledge. I beg you to tell me how to act.

Your reader, S.

In school, immigrant children learned about their new country and how to speak English (above). Children found ways to play in the crowded slums. Below, children play stickball, a city version of baseball, in an alley.

Why do you think the girl's parents wanted her to stay in school? What would you have said to the girl if you had been the editor of the newspaper? In this case, the editor told the girl that she should obey her parents and stay in school. What reasons might the editor have had for giving her this advice?

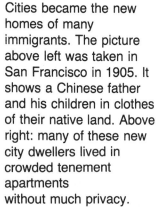

Cities became the new homes of many immigrants. The picture above left was taken in San Francisco in 1905. It shows a Chinese father and his children in clothes of their native land. Above right: many of these new city dwellers lived in crowded tenement apartments without much privacy.

Many Peoples, One America

Like millions of past and present immigrants, these three young people came to the U.S. with a dream. They had little in their pockets, but they had high hopes for a better life. For Edward Corsi, hard work did bring him a better life. He became U.S. Commissioner of Immigration in his later years. For O.E. Rolvaag, there was a future of fame as a writer. And one day, his grandson would be governor of Minnesota. We don't know what happened to "S." Perhaps she too made her dreams come true.

The stories of these three people show the promise of the U.S. They also show one of its greatest strengths—the mixture of the people who made our nation. They came from many different places and had many different beliefs. Yet over the years, they showed that they could live and work together in peace. They showed that differences among people can add to a nation's strength.

WORKING IN A NEW AMERICA

In the 1800's, a writer named Horatio Alger (*huh*-RAY-*shee-oe* AL-*jer*) wrote a series of books. His stories said that success was the sure result of hard work, honesty, a willingness to take a chance, and a little luck. In books such as *Luck and Pluck* and *Tattered Tom*, the hero always started out poor but worked hard and became rich.

These were storybook tales. They came true for some, but not for everyone. In some of the new industries, thousands of people worked hard under terrible conditions. Most of these people found it very hard to get ahead.

Hard Times for Industrial Workers

In some American industries, workers labored in **sweatshops.** These were factories where goods such as clothing were made. The factories were crowded, dark, and stuffy. Men, women, and children worked in them 12 to 14 hours a day, six days a week. These workers earned between $400 and $600 a year. No one received a paid vacation.

In many industries, machines were more important (and better cared for) than workers. New machines made old skills unwanted. New machines meant that **unskilled workers** could do jobs that **skilled workers** once held. Unskilled workers could be paid less.

Many children worked in factories. In 1906 as many as two million children worked for as little as 25 cents a day. They had little fresh air, food, playtime, or school. Said a poet, "We grind in our mills the bones of the little ones."

Safety measures were poor in most industries. Poisonous fumes, unwatched machines, never-ending noise, and germ-filled air were just some of the dangers. In coal mines, workers faced underground explosions, fires, fumes, and unsafe mine shafts. Many factories were built of wood and caught fire easily. Jobs on the railroad were especially dangerous. Between 16,000 and 17,000 workers were hurt every year.

Workers who got hurt or became ill—and many did—received no pay. They were likely to lose their jobs.

Said the workers: "We can't work any harder. We can't save money when we earn barely enough to buy food. How can our children be taught to try harder when they are worn out from work and never get to school at all?"

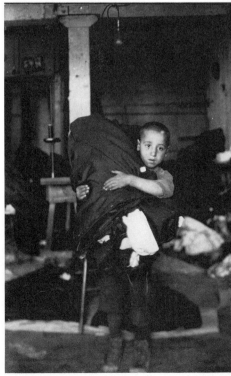

Many children worked long hours in sweatshops and factories. They had no time to play or go to school. Laws were later passed to prevent children from working this way.

LABOR UNIONS ARE FORMED

Many workers wanted to improve their way of life. They wanted better pay, shorter hours, and better working conditions. They decided to band together as a group and demand these things. Then maybe their employers (the people they worked for) would listen to them. So workers began to join together and form **unions.** One of the most important unions was called the American Federation of Labor (AFL). It was started by Samuel Gompers in 1886.

Gompers said the AFL should have "bread and butter" goals. It should try to win higher pay, a shorter working day, more safety measures, a better place to work, and an end to child labor.

Gompers helped the AFL grow strong. By 1911 it had more than two million members.

By 1918 labor unions had made some important progress. For one thing, they were now recognized by employers and the American public as a force that was here to stay. Working hours were shorter. Laws forbidding child labor were passed. In some states, there were laws that provided help for workers who became hurt or ill while on the job. Safety laws were being passed too.

For many Americans, it looked as though they would someday reach the goal of "a better tomorrow."

Most businesses did not want workers to form unions. When workers went on strike, business leaders brought in other workers to replace them. Do you think the artist of this painting sides with the workers or the boss? Why?

Learning from Cartoons

What does a cartoon mean to you? Charlie Brown? Snoopy? Or some other character in your favorite comic strip?

Yes, these are all cartoons. They were drawn to entertain and amuse you. But there are other kinds of cartoons that have another purpose. They too may make you laugh. But their purpose is to make you think about things. They are called **political cartoons.**

Symbols are often used in cartoons to make statements. You have to know what the symbols stand for to understand what the cartoon means. You also have to know something about the people, places, and events represented.

Look at the cartoon on this page. Find the symbols. What do the stars and stripes stand for? What does Uncle Sam stand for? What might the black clouds represent? Can you explain what the cartoonist is trying to say?

JANE ADDAMS OF HULL HOUSE

One person who saw how difficult life in the city could be for poor immigrants was Jane Addams. When she was six years old, Jane had her first glimpse of poor people. She was shocked. She had always taken her fine house and clothes for granted. Jane made a promise to herself to help poor people when she grew up.

Jane Addams kept her promise. With her friend Ellen Starr, she moved into Hull House on Halstead Street. Hull House was in Chicago's poorest section. The two finely dressed young ladies attracted attention. Why would they want to live in the midst of all of these "foreigners," people asked. Soon these people had their answer.

Jane Addams and Ellen Starr made friends with their neighbors. The two women set up a nursery school and kindergarten. They made Hull House a center to help the immigrants.

Other people came to Hull House to help out. They started drama programs, a music school, reading groups. A gym and playground were built. Doctors and nurses treated the sick. A summer camp in the country was started for poor youngsters who had never seen meadows and forests.

Soon there were other houses like Hull House in Chicago and in other big cities. They were called **settlement houses.** Settlement houses were centers devoted to improving community life.

People like Jane Addams also made millions of Americans aware of the suffering of poor people. New laws were passed which made poor people's lives easier.

Jane Addams

Words to Know

Use each of the words listed below in a sentence.

political cartoon   sweatshop
settlement house   union
skilled worker   unskilled worker

Facts to Review

1. How did immigration change after the Civil War?
2. What reasons did immigrants have for coming to the United States?
3. What problems did immigrants face when they got here?
4. Why did immigrants "believe in" the U.S.?
5. In the years after the Civil War, what were working conditions like for factory workers?
6. How did machines sometimes make workers' lives more difficult?
7. What were safety conditions like for workers in coal mines or on railroads?
8. Why did workers join unions?
9. Who was Samuel Gompers? What was the American Federation of Labor? What were its goals?
10. What improvements for workers did unions bring about?

Things to Think About

1. Pretend that you are a young person living in a poor village in Europe in the late 1800's. People who left your village to go to the United States have come back to visit. What questions would you ask them about their new home? How do you think they might answer your questions?
2. Horatio Alger's stories said that "luck and pluck" would help a person get ahead in America in the 1800's. Make a list of other traits you think a person needed then to go "from rags to riches."

Using New Words

On a piece of paper write the paragraph below. Fill in the blanks with the correct words from the list.

homesteaders   sod
prospectors   sweatshops
reservations   tenements
skyscrapers

The period after the Civil War brought growth in both agriculture and industry to the U.S. People called ＿＿ flocked to the Last West to claim free land. There, with new machinery, they broke through the ＿＿ and replaced it with fields of wheat. The mining industry began when ＿＿ began searching the hills and mountains for minerals. As these new settlers came west, the Indians were forced to move to ＿＿ to live. In the cities, beautiful tall ＿＿ were being built, but so were dark and stuffy apartment buildings called ＿＿. Some people who lived in these unpleasant buildings had to work in dark places called ＿＿.

Sharpening Your Skills

1. Suppose that your community has more classrooms than it needs. So, your school is going to be closed next month. What changes can you predict for your class? Where will you go to school then? What will probably happen to your teacher? How will the way you get to school change?
2. Look through your local newspaper and find a political cartoon. What is the subject of the cartoon? How do you know? Are any symbols used? What do you think the cartoonist is trying to say?

Expanding Your Knowledge

1. Make a time line to hang as a border across one wall of your classroom. Show some of the important events and people in the U.S. in the years from 1865 to 1890.

2. Suppose you are an immigrant to this country and cannot speak English. In your homeland, you worked as a tailor and would like to find a job now. Show how you would try to communicate. See if your classmates can figure out what you are saying.

3. Pretend you are a cowboy on the Long Drive. At night you often hum or sing softly to keep the cattle calm. Make up a song that you might sing when you are out on the range, alone in the dark. In your song, tell about your day in the saddle.

Your Own History

You have read about how some cities grew so fast that they had many problems. Find out how your community grew. Was it planned well? Or did it grow too quickly? What problems did it face as it grew? How were these problems solved?

Check with your local historical society or library. It may have old maps or drawings that show what your community was like in the early 1900's. See if you can find old pictures of buildings that still stand.

Which immigrant groups have come to your community? Find out about them. Find out about the contributions they have made to your community's growth.

What services does your community offer now? With your class, write a short skit or play about the history of your town or city.

Unit Seven
A World Power

22

America Moves Beyond Its Borders

July 1, 1898. A lone officer charges up a hillside on horseback. Bullets whiz around his head. He stops at a barbed wire fence and dismounts. He slashes at the fence with his sword. Then he turns to his men who are hiding in the tall grass. "If we must die," he shouts, "let's die moving instead of standing still." The officer climbs over the fence. The soldiers follow him, cheering.

Who was this man? What was going on? Colonel Theodore (Teddy) Roosevelt (ROE-*zuh-velt*) was the commander of a group of soldiers called the Rough Riders. They were in Cuba, an island in the Caribbean Sea. Cuba belonged to Spain, and the United States was at war with Spain. Roosevelt and the Rough Riders helped win a great victory that day. Within a few months the U.S. had won the war, and Cuba gained its independence from Spain. Teddy Roosevelt became an American hero. Soon he would become President of the U.S. He had changed a great deal since his childhood, when he was a weak, nearsighted boy with asthma. Roosevelt built up his body with exercise and became a great leader.

Going to war with Spain was the sign of a major change in the role of the United States in the world. For the past century, the U.S. had been concerned mainly with itself. During this time, the U.S. had stretched across the continent. It had built up its agriculture and its industry. Now it was a giant in both.

Its farm and factory production had made the U.S. important to the rest of the world. U.S. ships entered ports all over the world to find raw materials. These same ships brought U.S. goods to trade with other countries.

This growing world trade meant that the U.S. had many interests outside its borders. It was this world involvement that brought the U.S. to fight in Cuba.

On page 332: Colonel Teddy Roosevelt leads the Rough Riders into battle up San Juan Hill.

WAR WITH SPAIN

In 1898 Cuba was a colony that belonged to Spain. Some Cubans were fighting the Spanish to gain independence for their country. Many Americans wanted to help. Others said it was none of our business.

U.S. President William McKinley (*muh*-KIN-*lee*) wanted to keep the U.S. out of the war in Cuba. Some U.S. newspapers, though, began printing stories about Cuba. The stories told the American people that the Spanish were cruel rulers. Such stories made many Americans want to enter the war to help Cuba.

"I'll Furnish the War"

The battleship *Maine* blows up in Havana harbor. A total of 260 American sailors were killed. To this day, experts are not sure what caused the explosion.

Sometimes the newspapers made up these stories. William Randolph Hearst (*hurst*) owned the New York *Journal*. He sent an artist, Frederic Remington, to Cuba to make drawings of the fighting. (In those days newspapers printed drawings, not photographs.) When Remington got to Cuba, he sent Hearst a message: EVERYTHING IS QUIET HERE.

THERE IS NO TROUBLE. Hearst answered: YOU FURNISH THE PICTURES. I'LL FURNISH THE WAR. Hearst knew that papers with exciting war stories sold more copies.

President McKinley still did not want to go to war. He sent the battleship *Maine* to Cuba. McKinley hoped that this would keep things peaceful. Then, on the night of February 15, 1898, a tremendous explosion ripped through the *Maine*, which was at anchor in Havana, Cuba. The battleship burst into flames. In five minutes, the *Maine* and 260 American sailors sank to the bottom of the harbor.

At home people thought the Spanish had blown up the *Maine*. "Remember the *Maine*!" they said. Soon war was declared. (Even today, no one is sure what caused the *Maine* to blow up.)

An Easy Victory

One of the first to join the Army was Teddy Roosevelt. He helped form his own outfit. The Rough Riders were unlike any other outfit in the Army. There were cowboys and hunters from the West. There were gamblers, police officers, and rich people.

The war with Spain was short. The U.S. Navy destroyed the Spanish fleet. The Army won a series of victories. In a few months, the Spanish were defeated.

Americans were proud of their victory. In Europe people were surprised at how easily the U.S. had won the war. Most leaders saw that the United States had become an important force in the world. It was now a world power.

Cuba became an independent country in 1902. But before leaving Cuba, the U.S. Army won another victory. The biggest killer of Americans in the war had not been Spanish bullets. It was a disease called yellow fever.

Dr. Walter Reed guessed that yellow fever was spread by a mosquito. He did experiments which proved that certain mosquitoes carried yellow fever. Workers were sent out to drain swamps and cover water containers. Soon there were no cases of yellow fever in Cuba.

Back home, Teddy Roosevelt was elected governor of New York in 1898. Two years later, he was elected Vice President of the U.S. Then, in 1901, President McKinley was killed by an **assassin** (*uh-*SASS*-in*). At age 42, Teddy Roosevelt became the youngest U.S. President.

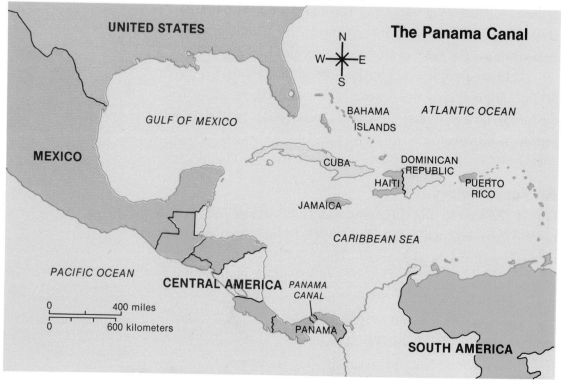

BUILDING THE PANAMA CANAL

The peace treaty with Spain after the war gave the U.S. new land. The treaty turned over Puerto Rico, an island in the Caribbean Sea, to the U.S. It also gave Guam (*gwom*), an island in the Pacific, to the U.S. The United States bought the Philippine (FILL-*uh-peen*) Islands from Spain. In the same year, the Hawaiian Islands also came under the control of the United States.

Roosevelt wanted to make it easier and faster for ships to reach these new American lands. At that time, a ship sailing from the Atlantic to the Pacific had to travel all the way south around the tip of South America. So, Roosevelt decided to cut a canal through Central America. This canal would join the Atlantic and the Pacific.

The narrowest part of Central America was part of the Republic of Colombia. The Colombians would not give the U.S. the right to build a canal there, though. Roosevelt wanted action. So he helped the people of an area, called Panama, revolt against Colombia. Panama became independent and gave the U.S. the land for the canal.

In 1903 Roosevelt sent engineers and workers to Panama. Their orders were to "make the dirt fly."

Once again Americans had to fight yellow fever. Now they knew how. Dr. William Gorgas (GOR-*gahs*) came to Panama. He had worked with Dr. Walter Reed in Cuba. In a year, Panama was safe from yellow fever.

Then it was the engineers' turn. Colonel George Goethals (GOE-*thulz*) was in charge of building the canal. It was a huge job. The jungle had to be cleared and mountains had to be knocked down. Then a ditch 50 miles (*nearly 80 kilometers*) long had to be dug.

Finally, in 1914, the Panama Canal was finished. It had taken 10 years to build. People called it "one of the marvels of the age."

Building the Panama Canal was a challenge for American know-how. Workers moved mountains and cleared the jungle to build the "Big Ditch."

For the children of rich families (above left) life was full of toys and fun. For many poor children life meant working from dawn to dusk at dangerous jobs (above right). These photographs were taken by Lewis Hine. He traveled around America taking pictures of how people worked and lived.

THE PROGRESSIVE ERA

Teddy Roosevelt had other challenges as President. The United States was a very rich country in the early 1900's. However, it had many problems.

One problem was that wealth was not spread evenly. There were some very rich people who lived in houses as big as palaces. These people seemed to be getting richer all the time. Millions of other Americans worked on farms or in factories. Many of them earned little money and had few conveniences.

Another problem was health and safety. Many factories were unsafe. Thousands of women and children worked long hours. Many children worked in coal mines from dawn to dusk and rarely saw the sunshine.

A group of Americans, called **Progressives,** were upset by these conditions. These people came from many different political groups. But Progressives all shared the belief that American life could be improved.

What was their answer? Progressives thought the government should pass laws to prevent the rich and powerful from hurting other people. Nowadays we have many such laws. In the early 1900's this was a new idea in American government. Before this time, most Americans had believed that people could take care of themselves. If there was something wrong with a job, a person should look for another one. When a person was sick or poor, his family or neighbors might help.

Now times were changing. Millions of people were crowding into cities. Often they had no choice of jobs. In big cities, people often did not have families to help them. They might not know their neighbors very well. This is why the Progressives said that it was time to make new laws. Industry was making the United States a very different country from what it had been.

Progressives Speak Out

Progressive writers and speakers tried to persuade Americans that new laws were necessary. They said that our laws were out-of-date. They said that these laws were all right for a young and small nation made up of country people. They were not all right, though, for a large and strong country like the U.S.

One writer was Upton Sinclair. In 1906 he wrote a book called *The Jungle*. In it he told about the terrible conditions in the meat-packing industry. Sinclair told about the unhealthy way meat was packed. Workers were not well protected. The meat was not well cleaned and checked.

Teddy Roosevelt read Sinclair's book and ordered a study of the meat-packing industry. When Roosevelt got the report, he said it made him "sick." Roosevelt then got Congress to pass laws about how meats and other foods were processed. The results were the country's first pure-food laws. These laws said that meat-packing plants must be inspected by government officials.

Lewis Hine found this young girl standing at her loom in a cotton mill. What sort of life do you think she lived?

Special Years

In these years, Progressives also worked for changes in state and local government. Soon laws were passed that made government more honest. Other laws made factories safer, and protected children and women workers.

Many new laws improving conditions were passed during this time. So many were passed that these years are often called the Progressive Era.

NEW WAR CLOUDS

The summer of 1914 was a good one for Americans. The warm weather brought people out to beaches. Americans also listened to bands playing on village greens and spent many hours riding their bicycles.

People were also still talking about a big auto race. It had been held on July 4 in Sioux City, Iowa. A man named Eddie Rickenbacker had won this race in a car called a Dusenberg. People were still buzzing about his speed—78 miles (*about 125 kilometers*) per hour. Imagine! A few years ago, cars had barely reached the speed of horses. And now this!

In 1914 Americans were just beginning to buy cars. Some people said that soon everyone would have one. Others thought that this was impossible—nothing could ever replace the horse and buggy.

For Americans, the year seemed full of promise.

In Europe it was another story. Europe was at war. Americans were well aware of the war, but Europe was 3,000 miles (*4,827 kilometers*) from the U.S. In the age before airplane travel, this was a long way. Steamships took six or seven days to cross the Atlantic Ocean. To many Americans, Europe was just a faraway place.

What caused the war? Many Americans in 1914 had little idea. Archduke Francis-Ferdinand had been murdered. He would have been the next king of a country in

Europe called Austria-Hungary. The experts said the arch-duke's murder started the war. Still, most Americans were surprised when war broke out in Europe.

Most of the countries in Europe were fighting. On one side were the Allies. Britain, France, and Russia were the most important Allies. On the other side were the Central powers. These included Germany and Austria-Hungary.

Not Our War

At first U.S. President Woodrow Wilson said the nation would remain **neutral**—not take sides in the war. Many Americans agreed with Wilson. "Let the Europeans fight," they said. "It's none of our business."

Then, as time went on, Americans began to be drawn into the war. German submarines, called U-boats, were sinking British ships. Americans frequently traveled on

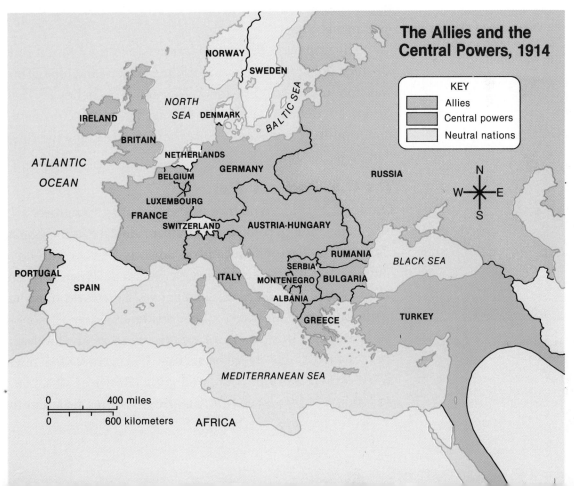

The Allies and the Central Powers, 1914

KEY
Allies
Central powers
Neutral nations

World War One was a "total war." Posters such as these urged citizens at home to pitch in and help the war effort.

these ships. In 1915 a German U-boat sank the British ocean liner *Lusitania (loo-suh-TAY-nyuh)*. Most of the passengers drowned with the ship. More than 100 of them were Americans.

In the U.S., people called it murder. They wanted the U.S. to declare war on Germany.

President Wilson held back. He sent German leaders an angry letter. The Germans answered with a promise not to sink unarmed ships without warning.

In 1916 Wilson was reelected President for a second term. His campaign slogan was: "He kept us out of war." However, pressure was growing for the U.S. to enter the war. More Americans were now opposed to Germany and for the Allies.

In Europe the fighting continued with neither side able to defeat the other. Only death was doing well. In one battle, the British army alone lost more than 60,000 men in just a single day!

Then, in early 1917, the Germans said they would sink all ships going to Britain—including American ships. This was too much for President Wilson. He believed that American democracy would be in danger if Germany, under military rule, could bully the U.S. He knew the time had come for the U.S. to act.

The U.S. Declares War

On April 2, 1917, Woodrow Wilson went to Congress. He asked the members of the Senate to declare war against Germany and the other Central powers. Wilson was very disturbed that war could not be avoided. However, he believed that now there was no choice. "The world must be made safe for democracy," the President said.

Although the American people were ready for war, their armed forces were not. The U.S. Army had only 375,000 men and some outdated guns. However, the U.S. was soon filled with activity. Congress set up a program to

Airplanes were used in battle for the first time in World War One. Daring pilots fought each other in one-on-one "dogfights."

get men into the Army and Navy. Training camps sprang up. Other Americans worked overtime in factories to make goods needed for the war. Farmers worked long hours to grow more food. Children were given time off from school to work on farms. All of the U.S.'s energy was used in the fight against Germany.

It took some time before American soldiers could get to Europe, where they were badly needed. The Allies were running out of men.

The first American troops landed in France in June 1917. The Allies were eager to see the Yanks, as they were called. There was a ceremony in Paris to welcome the Americans. It took place in front of a statue of General

Armies used a new way of fighting. They dug long trenches across battle-fields. The muddy trench became a soldier's home.

Lafayette. You have already read about Lafayette, the French general who helped Americans in the American Revolution. Now an American officer looked up at the statue and said, "Lafayette, we are here!" The crowd roared. The Yanks were in France.

Soon fresh American troops were in battle against the Germans. Now the Allies began to push the German armies back toward Germany. There were many bloody battles in which American troops played a leading part.

On November 11, 1918, World War One ended. On the battlefields of France, Allied and German soldiers embraced. In Paris people cheered. In the U.S., people danced in the streets.

The war changed the way Americans lived and worked. Many women went to work for the first time. They did jobs that only men had done before.

POSTWAR CHANGE

The war changed the United States. It changed the way people thought and it changed the way they lived.

Before the war, many women did not work outside their homes. The war created many new jobs, and women rushed to fill them. With factories working around the clock, and with many men in the Army, women stepped in. They proved they could do the same work as men.

Women were active in politics too. Many states did not allow women **suffrage** (SUFF-*rij*), the right to vote. Women called suffragettes (*suff-ruh*-JETS) worked to change this. They held marches and they paraded in front of the White House. Some of them were even arrested and went to jail. Finally, in 1920, women won the right to vote in all elections. (For more on women's suffrage, read "Votes for Women" on pages 346–347.)

The war changed life for many black people too. Blacks were often treated as if they were not full citizens. In the South, where most black people then lived, they often weren't allowed to vote. They were separated from whites in most public places. Black and white children went to

different schools, ate at different lunch counters, and drank from different water fountains. This was called **segregation** (*seg-ruh-*GAY-*shun*). In the North, many blacks lived in tenements in the poorest sections of the cities.

Soldiers in an all-black unit wave good-bye as they leave France. These men fought in many battles and won many honors.

During the war, more than half a million blacks moved to the North. There they took jobs in factories and hoped life in the North would be better for them.

Thousands of blacks also served in the Army. They fought in all-black regiments. Many black heroes came out of these regiments. Among them were Henry Johnson and Needham Roberts, the first Americans to win France's highest military honor.

Black soldiers were disappointed when they came home. They had fought to "make the world safe for democracy." Yet they found little democracy for black people in the United States.

Many Americans began to realize that racial equality was something for the whole nation to think about. They saw that the U.S. still had work to do at home.

VOTES FOR WOMEN

Although the work that American women did during World War One helped them to win the right to vote, the fight for this right had begun many years earlier.

On a hot July afternoon in 1848, five women met for tea near Seneca (SEN-*eh-kuh*) Falls, New York. Elizabeth Cady (KAY-*dee*) Stanton was happy to see her old friend Lucretia (*loo*-KREE-*shuh*) Mott. They talked of how women were treated unfairly in the U.S. They decided to hold a meeting.

On July 19, 1848, more than 300 people came to the Seneca Falls Methodist Church. Women, and men too, talked about how women were not full citizens in the U.S. They could not vote. A married woman had few rights under the law.

Elizabeth Cady Stanton poured out her feelings. She was the mother of seven children. "Motherhood," Mrs. Stanton told people, "takes more knowledge than any other branch of human affairs."

The Seneca Falls Convention was the beginning of an organized fight for women's rights. A few years after the convention, Elizabeth Cady Stanton met Susan B. Anthony. She was interested in women's rights. Together the two women began a long struggle to win the vote for women.

Many women were also active in the fight against slavery. They fought for abolition, and they fought to give blacks the right to vote. They felt that if both blacks and women could vote, they could elect people who would make the laws more fair.

In 1870 the 15th Amendment of the U.S. Constitution was passed. The amendment gave the vote to black men—but not to women of any color.

Elizabeth Cady Stanton and Susan B. Anthony were angry. They promised never to rest until women could vote too.

The first victories in their fight came in the West. Even before Wyoming became a state, women there had the right to vote. Then Wyoming applied to be admitted to the Union as a state. Congressmen asked Wyoming to change the law that allowed women to vote. Wyoming leaders wired back. "We will remain out of the Union a hundred years rather than come in without the women." In 1890 Wyoming joined the Union, becoming the first state that gave the vote to women.

Elizabeth Cady Stanton died in 1902. Susan B. Anthony died four years later. A new generation of leaders took over the women's rights movement. They promised to finish the work of Mrs. Stanton and Miss Anthony.

One leader was Carrie Chapman Catt. She put together the final push for victory. Every year an amendment giving the vote to women was voted down in Congress, Mrs. Catt organized parades in front of the White House.

In 1919 Congress finally passed the 19th Amendment. It gave women the right to vote. Now 36 states had to approve the amendment for it to become law. In 1920 Tennessee became the 36th state to approve the amendment. It was now the law of the land.

A suffragette parade

SKILL BUILDER

Separating Fact from Opinion

If you had been around on the morning of February 17, 1899, you might have seen this headline stretched across the top of the front page of the New York *Journal:*

> ### THE WARSHIP *MAINE* WAS SPLIT IN TWO BY AN ENEMY'S SECRET BOMB

From what you have read about the explosion of the battle-ship *Maine,* do you think this headline was true to the facts?

Big headlines get people's attention, but the headline can be misleading. This headline gave the writer's opinion, not the facts. How the *Maine* blew up was a mystery. Although many people guessed that Spain was responsible for the explosion, no one knew for sure. There was no way to prove it. Can you think of a headline that would have been closer to the facts?

When reading **news stories,** it is important to separate the facts from the opinions. Good reporters try to keep their opinions out of news stories. However, they often report the opinions of others. It is the reader's job to decide whether the facts support the opinions.

Here are some statements that could have been in your morning's newspaper. Which ones are facts?

- "These people will not listen to reason," said Mayor Wu.
- Three new sand trucks have been ordered for the city.
- TAXPAYERS CALL NEW TRUCKS WASTE OF MONEY.
- A crowd of 2,000 people gathered before the town hall.

Pick up a copy of your local newspaper and examine one or two news stories. Put a line under the statements that are facts. Put two lines under the statements that are opinions.

Now turn to the editorial page of the newspaper. An **editorial** is different from a news story. It gives the opinion of the writer. Compare the editorials to the news stories. In what ways are they alike? In what ways are they different?

Words to Know

Use each of the words listed below in a sentence.

assassin	neutral	Progressive	segregation
editorial	news story	suffrage	

Facts to Review

1. What are some changes that took place in the U.S. between 1800 and 1900?
2. Why did the U.S. go to war with Spain?
3. Why did Teddy Roosevelt want to build a canal across Central America?
4. What kinds of new laws did the Progressives help pass?
5. Why did many Americans want to stay out of World War One at first?
6. Why did President Wilson finally decide to go to war?
7. How did World War One affect women's chance to work?
8. What important right did U.S. women win just after World War One?
9. What is segregation?
10. In what ways did World War One change the United States?

Things to Think About

1. Imagine that you are a soldier in the war against Spain. You are one of the Rough Riders. Write to a friend back home telling about something you saw in Cuba.
2. Pretend it is 1917. The United States has just entered World War One. You want the people at home to help win the war. Make up a poster in which you tell something you think they should do.

CHAPTER

23 From Boom to Bust

The U.S. was filled with hope when World War One ended. The country had just helped win a war and the soldiers were coming home. A new decade was beginning—the 1920's. Business had never been better. It seemed that now was the time to have a good time.

The high hopes would continue for awhile. The U.S. was booming. However, real problems were growing. When people finally saw these problems, the good times ended with a bang. Many people lost their jobs. Good times had turned to hard times.

How had this happened? What had gone wrong? How could everything change so quickly? In this chapter, you will read about how it happened.

GOOD TIMES

Young people set the style for the new times. In the 1920's, more young people were going to school than ever before. These young people had more leisure time and more money than ever before.

Young women took the lead in making a new style for the time. They were called "flappers." Flappers and their young men did not like anything old-fashioned. They danced new fast dances such as the Charleston. They listened to new music called jazz, often played or sung by black musicians. It was loud and fast—just the way young people liked it.

All young women in the 1920's weren't flappers. But times were changing for many American women.

Before the 1920's, most women worked long hours keeping house and raising their families. This was more than a full-time job, so these women had little free time.

On page 350: The good times are over. A farmer looks at his ruined crops. The newspaper in his lap tells how his fertile farmland has turned to dust.

The 1920's was a time of fads. Flappers dance the Charleston at a party.

The 1920's brought many improvements. For the first time, many Americans had refrigerators, washing machines, radios, and vacuum cleaners.

Cooking was also made easier. Canned goods and frozen foods cut down on the hours it took people to prepare a meal.

Some women took jobs in offices. Others spent more years in school learning professions.

Henry Ford and His Tin Lizzie

By the 1920's, there were millions of cars in the U.S. A man named Henry Ford, more than any other person, made this happen.

Henry Ford had a great vision: He wanted to build a simple, cheap car that many people could afford. He called his car the Model T.

Henry Ford built his first Model T in 1908. He offered it "in any color, as long as it's black." People looked at the Model T and laughed. They said it was ugly. "Just a black box on wheels," some said. Still the Tin Lizzie, as people called it, caught on. It was king of the road for 20 years.

To produce his cheap car, Ford used an **assembly line.** Here's how the assembly line worked. The carriage of the car was carried on a moving belt past many workers, who had piles of parts next to them. As the car came by, a worker added a part. The car then went on to a new station

The Sunday drive became an American favorite. Families piled into their cars and went for a drive. The result? Traffic jams.

where another worker added another part. By 1925 one Model T rolled off the assembly line every 10 seconds! And Ford could sell the car for less than $900.

The automobile was now big business. It gave birth to other big businesses too. Gasoline, tire, and road-building businesses all grew tremendously. With a car, people could now go to more places. So, restaurants, theaters, and motels sprang up. The car helped link a large nation of separate towns.

Music and News

The 1920's saw the birth of another part of modern life— the radio. The first radio station, KDKA, was in Pittsburgh, Pennsylvania. In 1920 it broadcast the results of the Presidential election. About 500 people listened that night and learned that Warren G. Harding was the new President. Soon radio sets were selling faster than they could be made. Everyone wanted one.

By 1924 there were about 580 radio stations in the U.S. There was more than news on the air. Stations hired bands to play music. There were comedy and mystery shows and dramas. Radio brought people closer together. Millions of people listened to the same show at the same time. With cars and radios, Americans were getting to know one another better.

Swinging Harlem

In the Roaring Twenties, no place roared like Harlem. Harlem is part of New York City. In the 1920's, it was the center of black arts and entertainment. Many blacks who had left the South during World War One and the years after it came to the cities of the North. They brought their energy, their talent, and their dreams.

Soon Harlem was alive with activity. Black writers, black painters, black actors, and black musicians were

Bessie Smith was one of the great stars of jazz. Her records, made in the 1920's, are still listened to today.

everywhere. Jazz was originally black music. It had started as Dixieland in New Orleans. Then musicians like Louis "Satchmo" Armstrong and Bessie Smith came North and spread their music over the whole country.

However, the 1920's did not bring justice for blacks in the U.S. Most blacks were too poor to go to the fancy places where their music was played. They still had trouble getting the same jobs that white people had. They were not always welcome in the same apartment buildings or neighborhoods. Often the schools their children went to were not as good as those of white people.

A Hero in the News

The 1920's was a great age for heroes. There were many people whose names filled the newspapers. One man, Charles A. Lindbergh, became one of the greatest heroes of the age.

Lindbergh was a young pilot in 1927. No one had ever flown across the Atlantic Ocean without stopping. Lindbergh decided to try.

His plane was called *The Spirit of St. Louis*. It was a small plane, with only one engine and no fancy instruments. Lindy, as he was called, loaded it up with extra gasoline for the long trip.

He took off from Long Island, New York, on May 20, 1927. People prayed for his safety. There were many, though, who didn't think he would make it.

Lindy himself had no thought of failure, though he did have some serious problems. At one point, ice began to form on the wings. Ice was dangerous because its weight could drag his plane down into the ocean. Lindy pointed the nose of the plane upward. At first the plane wouldn't climb. Then gradually, the little plane fought its way to the open sky.

Then, about 1,000 miles *(1,609 kilometers)* from France, Lindy began to get sleepy. He knew that if he fell

Charles A. Lindbergh in front of his plane, *The Spirit of St. Louis.*

Thousands of people watched Lindy take off from Long Island. Most people did not think he would make it safely across the Atlantic.

asleep, the plane would crash. He slapped his face and stamped his feet. That did not help. Then Lindy stuck his head out of the open cockpit. The cold air tore into his lungs and forced him wide awake.

At Paris a huge crowd waited for Lindy. People cheered wildly when they heard the sound of a plane overhead. More than 33 hours after leaving New York, *The Spirit of St. Louis* landed. The crowd mobbed Lindy. He had done it!

At home there was a big parade to welcome him back to the U.S. Millions cheered "Lucky Lindy," the hero of the age!

THE BUBBLE BURSTS

However, it was not all cheering in the 1920's. Some people were worried about money. Farmers were worried. They were growing more than they could sell. This caused farm prices to drop sharply. Sometimes farmers could not even get back their costs after selling their crops.

Many factory workers were also left out of the good times. Like the farms, factories began making more goods than people could buy. So, these goods stopped selling. Soon the factories that made them closed. This threw the

During the Depression, many people could not repay money they had borrowed to buy homes. These women and children traveled to Washington, D.C., to ask government leaders for help.

workers out of their jobs. Now they could not buy things. More factories closed, and more people were out of work.

On it went until millions of people were out of work. Banks and businesses closed. Millions went hungry. Children grew weak and sick from not having enough food. Many people had no money for new clothes. They wore old clothes, and some children went barefoot. The U.S. had entered the Great Depression.

The Great Depression Spreads

By 1932 the **Depression** (a period when a nation's economy is in very bad shape) had reached its worst point. One out of every four American workers was without a job. Every week thousands of people lost their homes because they could not pay the money they owed on the homes. Families were sometimes put out on the street with their belongings. Many people had to eat at places called "soup kitchens." There they would line up to get free food.

The Depression was very hard on children. Teachers noticed that their students seemed sleepy and lifeless. One teacher asked a sick boy what was the matter. "I'm tired and hungry," the boy answered.

"You can go home and eat, if you want to," answered the teacher.

"No," said the boy. "Today's my sister's turn to eat."

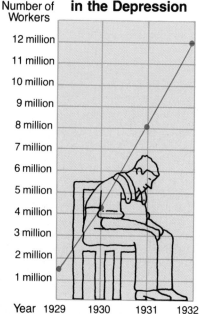

Out of Work in the Depression

Number of Workers

12 million
11 million
10 million
9 million
8 million
7 million
6 million
5 million
4 million
3 million
2 million
1 million

Year 1929   1930   1931   1932

Forgotten People

Some groups of people suffered special hardships. Blacks were often fired before whites. In the hard times of the Depression, the slogan was "Last hired, first fired." Since blacks were often the last people hired, they were the first ones fired.

Farmers also had a hard time. For many of them, the Depression had begun in the 1920's. Farm prices dropped sharply. Sometimes the farmers staged angry protests.

Rather than sell at low prices, they dumped milk into rivers. They burned fields of corn. This made many other people angry because thousands of Americans were hungry. Others just shook their heads and wondered how things had gotten so bad.

The farmers of the Great Plains really suffered. In the early 1930's, little rain fell in this large area and top soil began blowing away. Soon all that was left was dust. Now huge dust storms blew across the plains. The dust was so thick it sometimes blotted out the sun. It got through cracks in houses and got into people's food. People now called the Great Plains by another name—the Dust Bowl.

Many farmers gave up and decided to find other jobs. The problem was that there were few new jobs for these farmers to take.

Dust blowing across the prairie has just about buried this shack on an Oklahoma farm.

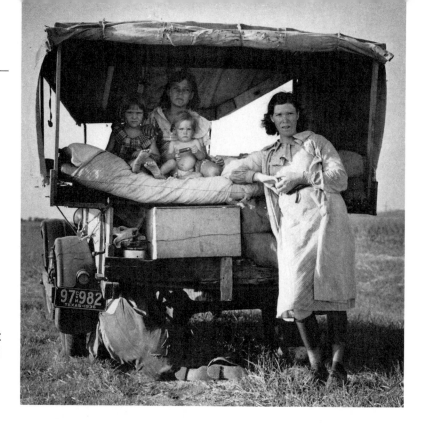

Many Dust Bowl families gave up and headed west to California. People used their old cars as earlier westward travelers had used covered wagons.

THE NEW DEAL COMES IN

The worst time of the Depression came in the fall of 1932. A popular song then told the story. It was called "Brother, Can You Spare a Dime?"

That fall there was an election for President. The current President, Herbert Hoover, was running for a second term. Franklin Delano (DELL-*uh-noe*) Roosevelt was his opponent.

Roosevelt promised to do something to end the Depression. He promised the American people a "new deal." Some people weren't sure about FDR, as he liked to be called. Others remembered that he was a distant cousin of a popular President—Teddy Roosevelt.

Most Americans were sure of one thing, though—they wanted some changes. FDR won the election easily.

FDR knew that people were worried. He told them that "the only thing we have to fear is fear itself." Millions of Americans listened to him on radio. They heard the new President say that the U.S. was as strong as its people. They believed that he cared about them. People began to trust their new President.

Putting the New Deal into Action

FDR knew how terrible the Depression was. New ways of doing things—a New Deal—had to be found.

FDR began by bringing new people into government. A reporter named them FDR's "brain trust."

The President wanted action. He told the brain trust: "Take a method and try it. If it doesn't work, admit it and try something else. But above all, try something."

What did the New Deal do? FDR strengthened the banks. He got Congress to pass laws that helped workers and farmers. He put millions of people to work building schools, parks, hospitals, and bridges.

Although the hard times did not go away, many people were working again. Then FDR got Congress to pass laws to protect people in hard times. He got Congress to pass laws to help those who were out of work. He set up a system called **Social Security** to help retired workers.

The Depression did not end overnight. Hard times lasted through the 1930's, but FDR gave people hope.

FDR

Who was the man behind the New Deal? Franklin Delano Roosevelt was born in Hyde Park, New York, in 1882. The Roosevelts were a wealthy family who lived in a large house near the Hudson River.

After college, Franklin went into politics. In 1913 he and his wife, Eleanor, moved to Washington. He was named Assistant Secretary of the Navy by President Wilson. In 1920 Franklin ran for Vice President of the U.S. He lost but impressed many people.

Life was easy for Franklin Roosevelt. Many people thought he had a great future. Then, in 1921, it all nearly came to an end. Franklin got very sick after swimming at his summer house in Canada. For a few days, doctors weren't sure he would live. His fever finally broke, but the

Franklin D. Roosevelt talks to a voter after delivering a campaign speech. FDR's legs were paralyzed by polio when he was a young man.

illness had done its damage. FDR could not move his legs. He had polio, a disease which often crippled its victims. Usually it struck children.

Franklin did not know the meaning of the word *defeat*. He learned to use braces so he could stand up. He made his chest and arms powerful so he could pull himself up.

With Eleanor's help, Franklin went back into politics. In 1928 he was elected governor of New York. Then he became U.S. President. FDR served as President longer than any other person. Four times Americans voted to make him their President. He led the nation through its difficult times—the Great Depression and World War Two. He died in 1945, just before World War Two ended. Millions wept when they heard the news.

LIFE IN THE THIRTIES

The 1930's were hard times for most Americans. This didn't mean they didn't have fun, however. Many went to the movies—often two or three times a week. Movies had been popular for the last 20 years. Until the late 1920's, though, movies had no sound. The beginning of the "talkies" made movies even more popular. Voices and sound effects made them seem real.

Almost everyone loved movie stars. Some of the stars weren't even people. One was Mickey Mouse, the first cartoon character of artist Walt Disney. In the thirties, the movies were a place to escape to—to forget hard times.

Still, even as people were trying to forget one set of problems, more were popping up. The news from Europe was bad. Some said there would be another war. A man named Adolf Hitler had taken over Germany. Hitler and his Nazi party ruled with an iron hand. He talked of conquering the world.

Americans did not want to think about war. However, the shadow of war grew over the U.S.

Mickey Mouse won the hearts of people all over the world.

WALT DISNEY'S MICKEY MOUSE iN STEAMBOAT WILLIE

SOIL SOLDIERS

One of the best known programs of the New Deal was the Civilian Conservation Corps (CCC). It helped more than three million young men during the Depression. For a dollar a day, they planted trees and did other conservation work. To these "soil soldiers," this was a good deal. Here is a letter one soil soldier sent to his girl friend.

December 13, 1935

Dear Karen,

I am tired. There is so much to tell you. We live in camp, army style. Life in the country is very different from the city. I am getting strong from the fresh air and three square meals a day.

The army guys say their job is to make us strong. We do exercises and run around the camp every morning. Some days we listen to talks by conservation people. They teach us about planting trees and irrigation.

Other days we work—hard. The last couple of weeks, we have been planting trees. The trucks drop us at these bare fields. We plant the trees all day. If he works hard, a guy can plant about 100 trees an hour. I sometimes wonder what these fields will look like in 40 or 50 years.

Next week we're going to start building a dam. Some of the other guys in camp are building trails in the national park. Other guys are building roads. Imagine me working on the land! Before I got here, I didn't trust anything that didn't have pavement. Now I'm a soil soldier.

Well, it's bedtime now. Tomorrow we're up at dawn!

Love, Larry

"Soil soldiers" pose in front of their tents at a CCC camp.

SKILL BUILDER

Organizing Information

If you were going on a camping trip, you would first organize, or plan it. You might make a list of everything you would need on the trip.

In much the same way, you have to organize information when you are writing a report.

Suppose you are writing a report on what happened to farmers during the Great Depression. You have read several books on the subject and have taken notes.

You are now ready to arrange your notes for use. You put all the cards on the same subject together. Then you organize the subjects under main topics or ideas. You can now make an outline. You arrange the main ideas in an order that makes sense. Place your supporting ideas below the main ideas.

This is how you might begin your outline. Note that it is not finished. Copy this outline on a piece of paper. Then finish the outline by putting the items in the right column in the correct places in the outline.

Farmers in the Great Depression

  I. Farmers go broke
    A.
       1.
       2. Hogs are 3¢ apiece.
    B. Drought destroys crops.
    C. Farmers can't pay
       back loans.
 II. Farmers leave land.
    A. Some go to cities.
    B.
III. Life in cities is hard.
    A. There are no jobs.
    B.
    C.

Corn is 15¢ a bushel.

Apartments are scarce.

People are cold and hungry.

Some go to California.

Prices for farm products fall.

Words to Know

Use each of the words listed below in a sentence.
    assembly line
    Depression
    Social Security

Facts to Review

1. How did young people enjoy themselves in the 1920's?
2. What improvements during this time made housekeeping easier?
3. How did Henry Ford's assembly line work?
4. Why was Harlem the center of black America?
5. What made Charles A. Lindbergh one of the greatest heroes of the age?
6. What were some of the causes of the Great Depression?
7. Why were the Great Plains called the Dust Bowl?
8. What kinds of help did the New Deal offer the American people?
9. Why was FDR popular in the 1930's?
10. What kinds of changes in American life took place during the 1930's?

Things to Think About

1. Amelia Earhart was the first woman to fly the Atlantic Ocean alone. Learn something about her life and compare her trip with Charles Lindbergh's.
2. Get a firsthand account of life during the Great Depression. Interview someone who lived through it. Find out what life was like for this person during the Depression.

24 World War Two

December 7, 1941, was a peaceful Sunday morning. The giant U.S. Navy base at Pearl Harbor, Hawaii, was quiet. Many sailors were off their ships for the weekend. Others were still in their bunks.

At 7 A.M., a soldier looked at his radar screen at a nearby air field. He was surprised to see "blips" on the screen. These meant a lot of planes were flying in the area. It seemed early for planes to be arriving from the mainland U.S. The soldier was new at the job and did not notice that the planes were coming from the wrong direction.

A little later, a sailor on the battleship *Arizona* came out on the main deck. The morning sun shone brightly in his eyes. It was going to be a beautiful day, the sailor thought. The sound of airplanes made him look up. In the distance, he could just make out a large group of planes nearing Pearl Harbor.

The planes came closer. Then they began diving toward the Navy base. "What are those wise guys up to?" asked the sailor as he reached for his binoculars. He couldn't believe what he saw. These weren't U.S. planes. On the wings, he could make out a rising sun, the symbol of Japan. Before the sailor could do anything, the first plane released its bombs.

The next hour was very confused. Sailors stumbled out of their bunks, thinking it was some kind of practice, or drill. Finally a voice called out: *"Battle stations! This is no drill!"* Bombs exploded on the American ships. The *Arizona* took a direct hit and quickly sank.

In hours, the U.S. Navy in the Pacific was almost destroyed. Thousands of sailors and soldiers were dead. Hundreds of planes were knocked out too.

The Japanese had attacked Pearl Harbor. The U.S. would soon go to war.

On page 364: U.S. Marines under enemy fire raise the American flag on a mountain top on the island of Iwo Jima.

BACKGROUND OF THE WAR

In the 1930's, Japan needed oil, rubber, and other resources. Japan's neighbors had these resources. So, Japan began building an army and a navy. Japan began to invade its neighbors and take these resources by force.

American leaders were very upset by Japan's actions. The U.S. had long been interested in the Pacific. The U.S. had close relations with China. The U.S. also still controlled the Philippine Islands and other places in the Pacific. U.S. leaders did not like Japan breaking the peace. However, few Americans ever expected the Japanese to attack the U.S. They thought the U.S. was too strong.

The Rise of Adolf Hitler

Nazis salute their dictator, Adolf Hitler.

In Europe Germans had been listening to a man named Adolf Hitler. Hitler was a good public speaker. He said things that many Germans liked to hear.

What did Hitler tell the Germans? He said that Germany had not lost World War One in 1918. Hitler claimed that Germany was "stabbed in the back" by **traitors.** He said that Jews living in Germany had acted against their country.

Adolf Hitler was full of hate. Most of all, he hated the Jewish people. Hitler blamed the Jews of Germany for all of that country's problems.

This was all untrue. The Jews did not have much power in Germany. However, the German people had been through hard times after World War One. The Depression had hit Germany just as hard as it had hit the U.S. Many Germans were ready to listen to Hitler.

In 1933 Hitler won an election and took over the German government. Hitler said he would make Germany strong. He immediately started building up the army. He turned German factories to producing tanks, planes, guns, and submarines.

Preparing Germany for War

Hitler also destroyed democracy and ended all elections. He rounded up people who spoke against him and had them shot. He arrested Jews and sent them to **concentration camps,** or large prisons.

Other countries in Europe began to worry about Hitler. Some people feared he was preparing for war. However, Hitler said that he was not. He told European leaders that he only wanted peace and was just getting Germany back on its feet again. Many of the leaders believed him.

One man in Britain—Winston Churchill—did not believe Hitler. Churchill was an important member of the British Parliament. He tried to warn his people that Hitler was dangerous, but they wouldn't listen. Still Churchill continued to speak out against Hitler and the Nazis.

Hitler then signed a treaty with Japan. Italy also signed the treaty. Italy's leader, Benito Mussolini (*buh-*NEE-*toe moo-suh-*LEE-*nee*) wanted to win glory and new land for his country. The three countries—Germany, Italy, and Japan—joined together as the Axis powers.

Jewish families are marching to their deaths in this picture of Nazi terror in Poland. The Nazis rounded up Jews in every country they conquered. Most of the Jews were killed in concentration camps.

Winston Churchill walks down a London street to inspect the damage done by German bombs.

THE WAR BEGINS

With his new friends, Hitler grew bolder. On September 1, 1939, the German army invaded Poland. France and Britain declared war on Germany. World War Two had begun.

The Germans crushed the French army and took over France. Now Hitler turned his attention to Britain. German planes pounded British cities. In London, people hid in the subway tunnels.

Winston Churchill was now the leader of Britain. In a ringing speech, Churchill kept up the spirits of his brave people. He said: "We shall fight in the seas and oceans. We shall fight on the beaches. We shall fight on the landing grounds. We shall fight in the fields and on the streets. We shall fight in the hills. We shall never surrender."

Other countries later joined France and Britain as Allies to fight the Axis. (See the map below.)

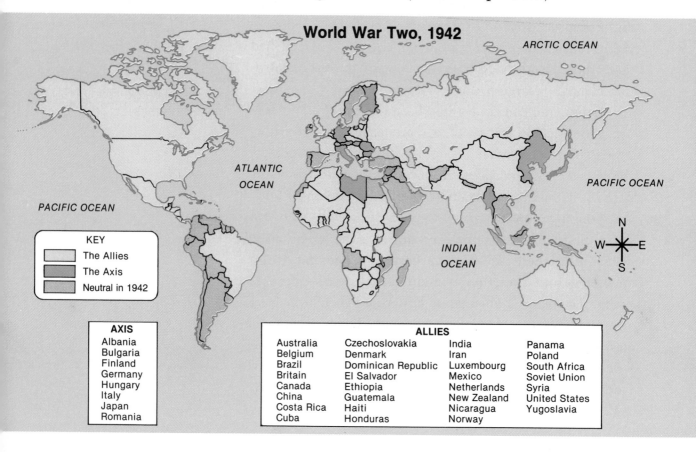

World War Two, 1942

ARCTIC OCEAN

ATLANTIC OCEAN

PACIFIC OCEAN

PACIFIC OCEAN

INDIAN OCEAN

KEY
The Allies
The Axis
Neutral in 1942

AXIS
Albania
Bulgaria
Finland
Germany
Hungary
Italy
Japan
Romania

ALLIES			
Australia	Czechoslovakia	India	Panama
Belgium	Denmark	Iran	Poland
Brazil	Dominican Republic	Luxembourg	South Africa
Britain	El Salvador	Mexico	Soviet Union
Canada	Ethiopia	Netherlands	Syria
China	Guatemala	New Zealand	United States
Costa Rica	Haiti	Nicaragua	Yugoslavia
Cuba	Honduras	Norway	

Americans Join the Fight

As the war went on, the U.S. lent ships and guns to Britain. Once again, Americans argued about getting involved in world affairs. President Franklin Roosevelt thought that the U.S. soon would have to fight Hitler. Like President Wilson before him, Roosevelt did not think democracy could survive an Axis victory.

Still the attack on Pearl Harbor surprised most Americans. Most people had been so worried about Hitler, they hadn't really thought too much about the Japanese. Suddenly the U.S. was in a war on two fronts. It had to fight the Japanese in the Pacific. It had to fight Hitler in Europe.

War in the Pacific

The U.S. quickly rebuilt its Navy after Pearl Harbor. Then the fleet steamed out after the Japanese. The war in the Pacific was a new kind of war. Each side had battleships and aircraft carriers. These huge "flattops" were like floating airports. They carried planes that bombed the enemy.

At first the U.S. Navy suffered some defeats. Then the U.S. won an important victory at Midway Island in the Pacific. The U.S. fleet began to push the Japanese back toward Japan.

Near the end of the war, the Japanese fought desperately to stop the Americans. Here a Japanese plane is shot down as it flies low over an American aircraft carrier.

Americans worked to win the war at home as well as on the battlefield. As in World War One, women took over factory jobs that were previously done by men.

The Home Front

Life in the U.S. during the war was busy. Factories worked round the clock making tanks, planes, ships, and guns.

Few people were out of work now. In fact, there was a shortage of workers. Since millions of men had joined the armed forces, women again took their places in the factories. Many women did such heavy jobs as welding.

Children also helped. Many families grew "victory gardens" in their backyards. These gardens turned out about half of the nation's supply of fresh vegetables.

The War in Europe

In 1942 American soldiers began fighting the Germans in North Africa. The next year, the U.S. Army landed in Italy. In heavy fighting, the U.S. began to push the Axis troops back toward Germany.

The quickest way to Germany led through France. As long as the Nazis held France, Germany was safe. So, the Allies prepared to invade France. Millions of soldiers gathered in Britain under the command of U.S. General Dwight D. Eisenhower (*dwite* IZE-*en-how-er*). Everyone called Eisenhower "Ike." He was a popular general with the soldiers and knew how to keep the Allies from many different nations working together.

The Nazis knew the invasion was coming, but they did not know when or where the Allies would land. The Nazis turned all the beaches in France into death traps. They planted mines in the sand. They built machine-gun nests into the cliffs above the beaches.

On the night before the invasion, the Allied army boarded a large fleet of ships. In the darkness, they crossed the English Channel to France. At dawn on June 6, 1944, Allied troops landed on the shore. The fighting was heavy. In a few days, the Allies had taken over the beaches.

The Germans fought hard, but more and more Allied troops were coming into France each day. The Allies began to push the Germans back. In August, the Allies reached Paris, the capital of France. Millions of French people lined the streets to cheer the Allied army.

THE WAR DRAWS TO A CLOSE

Soon the Allies were in Germany. There the Allied soldiers found something that made them sick and angry.

American soldiers came upon the concentration camps Hitler had filled with the people he hated. There the soldiers learned that he had used these camps to kill more

General Dwight Eisenhower talks to the troops before the invasion of Europe. Ike told the men "You are marching to victory."

than six million people. Most of the Jews of Europe died in these camps and many other people were also killed.

By May 1945, the Allies were closing in on Germany. Adolf Hitler refused to surrender. He killed himself instead. In a few days, the war in Europe was over.

The Atomic Bomb

Now the U.S. turned its full attention to Japan. While Americans were happy to have defeated Germany, they were also sad. In April 1945, FDR died. He had been President for more than 12 years. This was longer than any other President in our history.

Harry Truman became the new President. He had been Vice President under FDR.

His first job was to defeat the Japanese. Soon after he became President, Truman made an important decision. He told American military leaders to use a new weapon against Japan. It was the **atomic bomb,** the most powerful weapon that any nation had ever had.

The first atomic bomb was dropped on the Japanese city of Hiroshima (*hir*-OH-*shee-muh*) on August 6, 1945. It killed almost 80,000 people and destroyed much of the city. Three days later, another atomic bomb was dropped—this time on the city of Nagasaki (*nah-guh*-SAH-*kee*). After this, Japan surrendered. The war was finally over.

The United Nations

As World War Two neared its end, the American people generally agreed that the U.S. must play a leading role in keeping world peace. Shortly before the war ended, a **conference** was held in San Francisco. People from 50 nations came to form the United Nations. Its goal was to work for world peace.

The U.N. built its headquarters in New York City. Today almost every nation in the world is a member of the United Nations.

Flags of the United Nations fly at U.N. headquarters in New York City.

THE "FIGHTING 442ND"

America's sad mistake. This is what people now call the roundup of Japanese Americans during World War Two. Thousands of people were taken from their homes and put in detention camps. Why did this happen? Because some frightened Americans thought Japanese Americans might be spies.

Japanese Americans were not allowed to serve in the armed forces at first. Then the government changed its mind. Hundreds of Japanese Americans joined the Army. They were eager to prove their loyalty to their country.

An Army unit was formed, made up entirely of Japanese Americans. It was called the 442nd Regimental Combat Team. From the beginning, the 442nd was different. Every officer in training camp saw this. The members of the 442nd wanted to prove something to their fellow Americans.

The 442nd was sent to Italy where the U.S. Army was then fighting the Germans and the Italians. The enemy soldiers were dug in and well protected. The Americans were taking heavy losses.

The 442nd went into the heart of battle. Right away, the soldiers showed great courage and ability. Many soldiers were killed and wounded. Still the 442nd knew how to travel in only one direction—forward.

The 442nd had many heroes. A young soldier named Daniel Inouye (in-NOE-ay), who lost an arm from battle wounds, won a number of medals. Years later, he was elected to the U.S. Senate from the state of Hawaii.

The 442nd Regimental Combat Team displays the American flag.

SKILL BUILDER

Collecting Information for an Oral Report

Suppose you live in Old Town. You are going to make an oral report to your class about the history of your town. Obviously you can't cover the whole history of the town. Your first job is to find one thing about your town that really interests you.

Perhaps your town has a volunteer fire department. You decide to report on it. Or perhaps there's an interesting story to be told about your town hall. If something doesn't come to mind, you might read some books written about your town. Perhaps you will find an interesting bit of history that would be fun to report on.

Now that you have a topic, how will you do the research? Naturally, your library is the first place to go. Later you might interview some people to get some firsthand information.

In which of these places might you find information about your town? Books about your state? Travel books? Books by local writers? Local newspapers?

From whom might you get some interesting firsthand information about your town? Parents and grandparents? Town officials? "Old-timers"?

Unless your report is to be a written speech, you can write your notes on 3 × 5 cards. You need not write every paragraph. A sentence or two to remind you of each subject should be enough. Be sure to give special attention to your opening and closing remarks.

What interests you about your town? Find out more about it and prepare a report for your class. Perhaps you might pick one of these topics.

The Oldest House in Town	The Public Library
Downtown Architecture	A Walk in the Park
The First School	The Athletes on My Block
Mayors of Our Town	My Neighborhood
Early Settlers	Before We Had Cars

Words to Know

Use each of the words listed below in a sentence.

atomic bomb   conference
concentration camp   traitor

Facts to Review

1. What event got the U.S. into World War Two?
2. Why did the German people listen to Adolf Hitler?
3. Who were the Axis powers?
4. In what two areas did the U.S. fight in World War Two?
5. Why were some Japanese Americans treated poorly during the war?
6. Who was the commander of the Allied forces in Europe?
7. What happened in Hitler's concentration camps?
8. What important decision did President Truman make soon after he became President?
9. What reasons did Americans have for wanting to fight World War Two?
10. What is the goal of the United Nations?

Things to Think About

Think back to what you have learned about World Wars One and Two. Make a list of the following for each:

a. What caused the U.S. to enter each war?
b. Who was on each side in each war?
c. Where did American troops fight in each war?
d. How did each war end? Who won and who lost?

Using New Words

On a piece of paper, write the paragraph below. Fill in the blanks with the correct words from the list.

atomic bomb	segregation	Depression
concentration camps	suffrage	neutral

At the start of World War One, the U.S. wanted to stay ____. However, events elsewhere in the world brought the nation to war. The work of many women during World War One helped them to win the right of ____. Blacks' work during the war didn't win an end of ____ for them, though. The loss of business activity after World War One led the nation into the ____, and many people were out of work. But World War Two got most Americans working again. Before this war ended, Europe would know the horror of ____ and Japan would know the horror of the ____.

Thinking About the Unit

1. Compare Teddy Roosevelt and Franklin Roosevelt. What important events happened when each was President? What problems did each face? How did each man meet the challenges of his time? What progress was made? Which period do you think would have been more interesting to live in? Explain your opinion.

2. Suppose you were old enough to own a car in 1910. You want a car but your parents say: "No, cars will never amount to anything. The horse and buggy will always be the way to get around." What arguments would you use to convince them to try this new machine?

3. Which victory do you think was more important—the U.S. defeat of Spain in Cuba, or the defeat of yellow fever? Give reasons for your answer.

4. Make a list of changes that came about after World War One. Do you think they were all good? Why or why not?

Sharpening Your Skills

1. Read your daily newspaper or look at the TV news. Pick a big story, one of interest and concern to you. Then handle this story in two ways. First write a brief newspaper account. Write this story in such a way that your own feelings and opinions do not creep into it. Then pretend that your job is to write a newspaper editorial about the same set of facts. Here your job is to express your own opinions as clearly as you can.

2. Imagine that you have to explain to someone how to do something. Choose something that you know how to do.

    Now organize your information and make your explanations to someone in class.

Expanding Your Knowledge

1. Pretend you are a radio announcer in the 1920's. Find out about 10 news items to include on your news program. "Broadcast" your radio show to the class.

2. In this unit and earlier ones, you have read about different ways people are persuaded to change their minds, to join a group, or to work for a cause. Make a list of ways people can be persuaded.

Your Own History

What was life like in your community during the Great Depression and during World War Two? A good way to find out is to interview people who lived there then. Before you start, prepare a list of questions. Then, if possible, start talking with your grandparents or other older relatives. Talk to people who have lived or worked in your neighborhood for a long time. Take notes or use a tape recorder during your interviews. Then write up your material as a report. Add it to your history scrapbook or files.

Unit Eight
Today and Tomorrow

CHAPTER 25 New Problems, New Dreams

Berlin, Germany, 1948. Snow blows across an icy airport runway. A giant plane lands. Trucks hurry out. There are no passengers on this plane. Instead it carries tons of coal and food.

Quickly, people work to unload the plane. In minutes the job is done, and the plane refuels. Soon it is back up in the air. Another plane arrives, and the scene is repeated.

In the winter of 1948, this happened around the clock in Berlin. Airplanes filled the sky and the Berlin airport became the center of life. What was going on?

After World War Two, Germany was divided into four parts—one each governed by the U.S., Britain, France, and the Soviet (SOVE-*ee-et*) Union. Berlin, the old capital of Germany, was divided the same way. Berlin, however, was deep inside the Soviet part of Germany.

The U.S. and the Soviet Union had been allies against the Nazis. Soon after the war ended, however, they began to quarrel. The Soviet Union wanted to spread its form of government—**communism**—to other countries around it. The U.S. tried to keep this from happening.

In 1948 the Soviets tried to take over Berlin. The Soviets blocked all roads leading to Berlin. This meant that no supplies could get into the big city.

The U.S. decided not to give in. American pilots flew supplies in around the clock. In all sorts of weather, they landed their planes at Berlin's airport. For 11 months, the Berlin Airlift supported the people of Berlin. Then the Soviets gave in and took down the road blocks. The Berlin Airlift was over.

The Berlin Airlift was part of a "Cold War" between the U.S. and the Soviet Union. In this war, soldiers did not shoot at each other. Instead the two nations exchanged threats. Each nation built up its army and tried to win the

On page 380: The people of Berlin watch an American plane prepare to land. Berlin was still in ruins from World War Two.

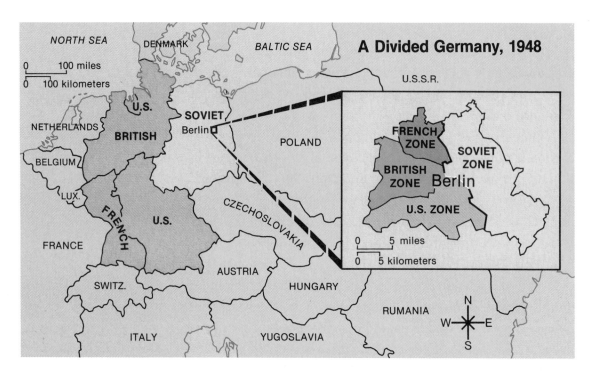

support of other countries. All over the world, the U.S. and the Soviet Union became rivals.

The Cold War changed life in the U.S. The U.S. was now leader of the free world. Before 1945 many Americans did not think much about the rest of the world. Americans now realized that their country had to play a role if there was to be a peaceful world. Americans could no longer mind their business and let the rest of the world fight. Americans were learning that the world was very small.

THE GOOD LIFE

What was life like in the U.S. after World War Two? People worried about the Cold War. In some ways, however, these were very good years. American business was growing quickly. Many people found jobs that paid well.

In 1952 the U.S. elected a new President—Dwight Eisenhower, the hero of World War Two. He was a popular President. "Ike" wanted the U.S. to grow. He believed in helping business to grow.

Disabled veterans (left) returning from World War II had to learn new skills, such as driving a car with hand controls. Elvis Presley (below) became the favorite singer of many young people.

Boom Time

Business wasn't the only thing to grow in those days. The whole country was in a building boom. Houses, factories, and office buildings were going up everywhere. New houses were built outside big cities. These communities were known as **suburbs.** Shopping centers with big parking lots were built in the suburbs. Large highways connected suburbs with cities. The highways also connected one city with another city across the country.

There were a lot more people too. Soldiers came home from the war, got married, and had children. Soon there was a "baby boom." Millions of children were born in these years. New schools had to be built for them.

There were more young people in the 1950's than ever before. These teenagers had their own heroes. They had their own music too. "Rock 'n roll" first became popular in the 1950's. A young singer named Elvis Presley was the first great rock star. Elvis was from Memphis, Tennessee. When he sang, his fans screamed with delight. His records sold millions of copies.

Television Arrives

Teenagers enjoyed their music. There was something else they enjoyed too—television.

TV sets were first sold after World War Two. In the 1950's, however, TV became a smash hit. Soon almost

A family watches TV in the evening. Television changed family life. Some said having the TV on was like having a constant visitor in the house.

everyone wanted a TV set. By 1960 almost all American homes had at least one TV.

Television changed American life in many ways. Children grew up watching hours of TV programs. This caused many experts to worry that too much television might harm children. (For more on the role of TV, see page 389.)

EQUAL JUSTICE FOR ALL

The U.S. was busy growing in these years and some people thought that things had never been better. The good times, however, had not come to all people. The U.S. had fought two world wars to defend freedom. At home, however, black Americans did not enjoy the same rights as white Americans.

In the South, there were still laws to keep blacks and whites apart. Blacks still could not go to the same schools, restaurants, or beaches as whites.

In the North, the problems were different. There were no laws in the Northern states to segregate the races (keep them apart). Still, most blacks lived in neighborhoods that were separated from whites. It was hard for black people to get good educations. It was also hard for them to get good jobs.

After World War Two, many people—both black and white—tried to change this. They started a movement for civil rights. Civil rights are the rights all citizens have to be treated equally under our laws. Black leaders went to law courts to try to get laws changed. They held protests to make known their points of view. More and more Americans came to believe that the time had come to make sure that all Americans were treated alike under our laws.

The Brown Case

In 1954 an important case reached the Supreme Court of the United States. The case started when a black girl named Linda Brown was kept from going to a school near her home. The school was for whites only. The girl's father then took the case to court. He argued that it was wrong for states to have laws allowing schools to admit whites only.

The Supreme Court agreed with the father. It ruled that Linda Brown should be able to go to the school closer to her home. The Court went on to say that all laws allowing separate schools for blacks and whites were wrong. The Court said that these laws did not live up to the Constitution of the United States.

This was an important victory for civil rights. It meant that there could be no laws allowing segregated schools— separate schools for blacks and whites.

No More Segregated Buses

Another important victory took place in Montgomery, Alabama, in 1956. In Montgomery and in many other cities, there were often separate sections on the buses for whites and blacks.

In December 1956, a black woman named Rosa Parks left her job in a department store. Mrs. Parks was tired. It was near Christmas and the store had been filled with shoppers. She got on a public bus and sat down. Soon the bus began to fill up. When it was full, the driver called out, "All colored [black] people move to the back of the bus."

Rosa Parks sits in a seat of her choice after the bus protest. The Montgomery bus boycott was the start of a movement for full equality for black Americans.

Mrs. Parks decided she would not move. The driver stopped the bus and called the police. An officer came, arrested Mrs. Parks and took her off to jail.

The story did not end here. Black people in Montgomery decided to protest. A meeting was called by a young minister named Martin Luther King, Jr. Dr. King told the meeting if blacks could not sit where they wanted, they should not use the buses at all. They should **boycott** (refuse to use) the buses.

The Montgomery bus boycott lasted more than a year. Blacks walked to work, rode bicycles, or drove in car pools. The bus companies lost money. In time the bus company gave in. The blacks of Montgomery won the same rights as whites on the city's buses.

Martin Luther King, Jr.

After Montgomery, Americans everywhere began to learn of Martin Luther King. Dr. King taught Americans a new way to fight for their rights. He did not believe in using violence to gain rights. Instead he preached **nonviolence.**

Black and white Americans marched for full equality in the 1960's. In 1963, more than 250,000 people came to Washington, D.C. They heard Martin Luther King, Jr., speak about his dream for America—a dream of brotherhood. Later, King led a march across Alabama. Dr. King preached nonviolence. Sometimes, nonviolent protests were met with violence.

Martin Luther King, Jr., was loved and admired by millions of Americans, black and white.

He thought that people should band together peacefully to work for their rights. If they were attacked, they should not fight back. Their nonviolence in the face of violence would win them support, he believed.

There were other blacks who did not agree with Dr. King. Many blacks were growing angry because they thought change was too slow. Some black leaders called for "black power." Some called for violence.

Violence did break out in some Northern cities in the 1960's. In some cities, whole blocks or neighborhoods were burned out.

Still, Martin Luther King refused to call for violence. He went on working peacefully for justice. Then, on April 4, 1968, Dr. King was shot and killed by a man named James Earl Ray.

Some people were very angry after Dr. King's death. These people said it proved that nonviolence did not work. Others believed in Dr. King's ideas, however. They tried to make sure that his work would go on. They worked for better conditions for all people. They worked for a time when all Americans would live together in peace.

THE WORLD OF TELEVISION

The U.S. changed quickly in the years after World War Two. One reason for this change was the invention of television.

Television was a big hit from the beginning. Soon the movie business, the restaurant business, and even the jukebox business went down. Americans stayed home to watch television.

And why not? Even though a TV set cost a lot of money, the shows were free. Comedy, Western, and detective shows were the most popular.

Television also changed the way Americans elect their Presidents. Candidates could reach millions of voters on television. How a candidate looked on TV became very important. In 1960 John F. Kennedy and Richard Nixon ran for President. They held a series of debates on television. Many experts felt that neither man won the debates. Yet many voters who watched liked Kennedy because of his good looks. Kennedy went on to win the election by a very close vote.

Some people worried that television was bad for children. They knew that many children spent a lot of time each day watching TV shows. These people said that most TV shows were stupid and that children should be encouraged to do other things with their time.

People still argue about television. Yet almost everyone agrees that TV has been an important force in our lives. TV news shows tell us of things happening around the world. Sports fans watch games from across the country. People running for election use TV to get their messages across to voters.

Whether they are rich or poor, live in the city or the country, Americans share the same world they see through TV. It brings them close to what is happening across town, across the U.S., and around the world.

Making a Flow Chart

A **flow chart** is a drawing that shows how something happens. It shows the order in which it happens. A flow chart might show the steps in keeping the Berlin Airlift going.

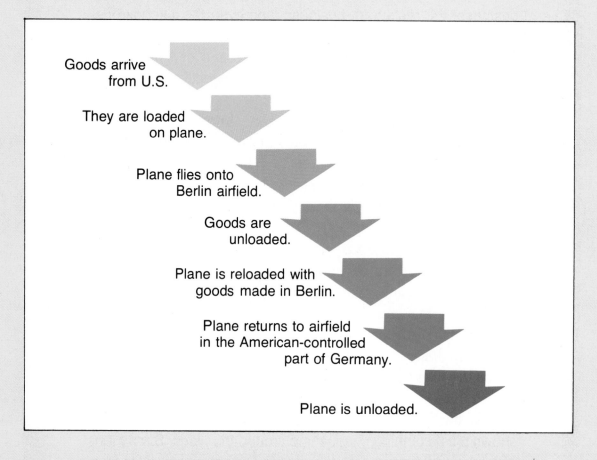

A flow chart might show the steps you go through to wash dishes. It might show the steps you need to fix a flat tire on a bicycle. A business flow chart might show what happens to cotton as it is made into cloth. Another could show all the steps it takes to turn a pile of typed pages into this book. What other kinds of flow charts can you think of?

Look back at the information you were asked to organize on page 362. Make a flow chart that shows the steps you took in order to finish that assignment.

Words to Know

Use each of the words listed below in a sentence.

boycott	communism	nonviolence
civil rights	flow chart	suburb

Facts to Review

1. What was the Berlin Airlift?
2. Who were enemies in the Cold War?
3. What war hero became President in the 1950's?
4. In what ways did the U.S. grow after World War Two?
5. Name three ways that television changed American life.
6. What was the aim of the civil rights movement?
7. What important ruling did the U.S. Supreme Court make about segregated schools?
8. Who was Rosa Parks, and what did she do?
9. Describe the means Martin Luther King, Jr., used to fight for what he believed in.
10. How would you say the civil rights movement changed American life?

Things to Think About

1. Choose a TV show that is a favorite of yours. Think about the last time you watched it. Do you think experts would think it is harmful to you? Why or why not?
2. Look back to the Declaration of Independence quote on page 157. Think back to what you decided the U.S.'s founders meant by this statement. Do you think the civil rights movement agreed with this statement? Explain your answer.

26 New Directions

Washington, D.C., January 20, 1961. The temperature was well below freezing. Snow covered the ground. Yet thousands of people gathered outside the U.S. Capitol building. On this day, John F. Kennedy was being sworn in as the 35th President of the United States.

Millions of Americans watched on television at home as Kennedy spoke. He told them what he thought the U.S. should do at home and around the world. Then he said: "Ask not what your country can do for you. Ask what you can do for your country."

Many young people in the U.S. liked Kennedy. He was younger than most Presidents. He was full of energy and liked action. He got the U.S. moving faster into its space program. He set up the Peace Corps (*kor*). Young Americans who joined the Peace Corps were sent all over the world to help other people.

Some people said that Kennedy made the U.S. an exciting place. JFK was not President for long, however. On November 22, 1963, he was killed by an assassin.

John F. Kennedy's days as President showed what the 1960's would be like. These years were full of new beginnings. Out of these years came new directions for our country to follow in the 1970's and 1980's.

TWO WARS

Lyndon (LIN-*dun*) Baines Johnson was Vice President in 1963. When Kennedy died, LBJ became President.

LBJ had been an important U.S. Senator from Texas before becoming Vice President. He knew how to work with Congress. He was able to get Congress to pass a law protecting many civil rights. He also started what he called a "war on poverty." This "war" aimed to help the poor people of the U.S. get better jobs and schooling.

On page 392: A U.S. astronaut puts up the flag on the moon.

The war on poverty was not the only war the U.S. was fighting. U.S. soldiers were fighting another war in the Asian country of Vietnam (*vee-et*-NAHM). At first U.S. soldiers were just training South Vietnamese soldiers. Then Communist North Vietnam began winning the war. So, U.S. soldiers began doing more and more fighting.

By the time the Vietnam war ended, more than 50,000 Americans had been killed in it. The Vietnam war divided Americans as no other war had since the Civil War.

A President Resigns

In 1968 Americans elected a new President, Richard M. Nixon. In 1972 he was elected for a second term. Just before the election, however, police in Washington, D.C., arrested some men who had broken into the headquarters of the Democratic party in a building called "Watergate."

After the election, it was shown that people close to the President had planned the break-in. Then it was shown that Nixon himself had tried to cover up the crime. Covering up a crime is a crime itself.

Nixon then decided to **resign,** or give up his office, as President. He was the first President ever to resign. He was succeeded as President by Gerald Ford, who had been Vice President. In 1976 a new President, Jimmy Carter, was elected.

American soldiers on patrol in Vietnam meet a farmer in his rice field.

EQUALITY FOR ALL

In the last chapter, you read how blacks fought **discrimination**—unfair treatment of a group of people. In the 1960's and 1970's, other groups of Americans stepped forward to demand their rights. Some of these groups were Spanish-speaking Americans (Hispanics), Asian Americans, Indians, and disabled people. Still another group of Americans were also demanding equal treatment under our laws. In this group were American women.

A New Call for Equal Rights

There are about 12 million Americans whose native language is Spanish. Within this group, there are many differences. The roots of some of these Americans are in Mexico. Some have their roots in Puerto Rico, and some have their roots in other parts of Latin America.

There are many things that unite this group of Americans. One, of course, is the Spanish language. Another is the feeling that they have not been allowed to share the same rights as other Americans. They have organized their own groups to fight for better housing, better schools, and better jobs.

The same can be said about Asian Americans and Indians. They also come from many different backgrounds. For example, Asian Americans include people whose roots are

Many Americans today work for equal rights for all, under our laws.

in China, Japan, the Philippines, Korea, Vietnam, and other countries of Asia. In each of these countries, people speak a different language and have a different culture. In the United States, however, Asian Americans are often faced with the same problems. In many cases, they must work at low-paying jobs. Some live in poor housing and have a hard time getting a good education.

Some of these Asian-American groups have been a part of U.S. history for a long time. The Chinese started coming to the U.S. in the days of the California Gold Rush (see page 213). Chinese workers helped build the great railroad that spanned the United States (see page 287). Many Chinese have become successful in business, science, and the arts. I.M. Pei is an architect who has designed many tall, beautiful buildings. Maxine Hong Kingston is a writer who has written books about how it feels to grow up as a Chinese American.

The Japanese began arriving in the U.S. in the 1880's. They were excellent farmers. Soon after their arrival, they were farming land in California and other western states that no one else could farm. During World War Two, many Japanese Americans were treated poorly (see page 373). But today many Japanese Americans have done well in such fields as business, medicine, engineering, and the arts. Isamu Noguchi is a famous sculptor who makes beautiful objects out of marble, clay, and metal. Daniel Inouye and S.I. Hayakawa have served as U.S. Senators.

In the 1900's, immigrants from the Philippines began coming to the U.S. Lately many immigrants have come from Korea and Vietnam. Many Vietnamese came after the war in their country (see page 394). They too have worked hard and become part of American life.

Maxine Hong Kingston writes books about Chinese Americans.

Women's Rights

In Unit Seven, you read how some women demanded equal rights in the 1800's. In 1920 women won the right to vote in all elections. As the years passed, more women went to college and got good jobs. But many women felt that they were not being treated as equals.

Feminists is the name given to people who want equal rights for women. In the 1960's, many feminists began arguing that men were still being paid more for doing the same jobs as women. Men were more likely to be hired for the top jobs in business. Men had an easier time getting bank loans.

Things began to improve in the 1970's. New laws were passed giving women the same legal rights as men. And some people's ideas about the role of women outside the home began to change. More and more women began moving into new careers.

At the same time, there were many women who didn't want careers outside the home. They believed that there were important things for women to do at home. They believed that women had a special role in bringing up children. "If all women went to work," they said, "who would keep families together?"

There is no "right" answer to which kind of life American women should lead. Women are individuals—people with different backgrounds, likes and dislikes, and hopes. The important thing is that all Americans should have the freedom to decide what they want to do with their lives.

Women do many jobs today that once were done only by men.

AMERICA'S FUTURE

Americans could be proud of how this country had grown. However, this growth had brought us new problems.

One of these problems was harm to our environment (*en-*VIE*-run-ment*). The wastes from American factories had caused air and water **pollution.** Americans now have started to clean up dirty air and waterways. In the future, we will have to find new ways to protect the environment. We will also have to learn to **conserve** (protect by using carefully) our great natural resources.

President Ronald Reagan (left) and Vice President George Bush listen to a reporter's question at a news conference.

One of those resources, oil, presents another important problem. Americans use more oil than we produce. Oil is the most important fuel used for **energy.** Now we must **import** (buy and bring from other countries) part of the oil we use. The price of imported oil has become very high. In the 1970's, Americans talked of an **energy crisis.** Now we know that energy must be conserved. Meanwhile we are developing new sources of energy such as **solar energy** (energy from the sun).

At the beginning of the 1980's, many Americans felt there was another great problem. People said that the United States was losing its leading role as a great industrial nation. Prices and taxes seemed to be very high. The costs of borrowing money to run businesses or to buy homes were too high for many people. **Inflation** (rapidly rising prices) seemed to be everywhere. People were out of work. Some of the larger American companies were losing billions of dollars.

In 1980 Americans elected a new President, Ronald Reagan. President Reagan moved quickly with a bold new approach to the problems faced by the nation. Although Americans were not sure if this approach would work, many wanted to try it.

By the early 1980's, a new mood of confidence seemed to return to the U.S. The problems had not gone away. But Americans began realizing that this nation had faced many challenges in the past and always met them head-on. Long ago, Americans settled the land and built strong communities out of the wilderness. They fought a war and won their independence from Britain. They created a new kind of government, a democracy, that had lasted for more than 200 years.

The future will surely hold many more challenges for the United States. How will these challenges be met? They will be faced and overcome by the Americans who are young today.

RACE TO THE MOON

In the 1960's, the U.S. began another age of discovery. Americans began going into outer space.

At that time, the Soviet Union had a head start in the "space race." Soviet astronauts (space pilots) had made a number of space flights around Earth. In 1961 President John F. Kennedy promised that the U.S. would put an astronaut on the moon before 1970.

By the next year, 1962, an astronaut named John Glenn became the first American to orbit (circle) Earth. After this, U.S. astronauts made many other flights.

Apollo 11 blasted off from Florida on July 16, 1969. Four days later, hundreds of millions of people watched on TV as Neil Armstrong took his first step on the moon.

After Apollo 11, the U.S. sent five more flights to the moon. Scientists learned a great deal about our world from these flights.

There were many Americans who thought that the U.S. should not explore outer space. They thought it was wrong to spend so much money on space when the money could have been used to solve other problems right here on Earth.

Michael Collins, one of the astronauts of Apollo 11, did not agree. Collins wrote a book about his trip to the moon. In it, he agreed that the U.S. must keep working to solve our problems on Earth. However, Collins said, it would be wrong to wait until all our problems on Earth are solved before exploring outer space. He wrote:

> The American people are explorers. They have always gone where they have been able to go. It's that simple. They will continue pushing back their frontier, no matter how far it might carry them from their homes.

Americans today are still pushing back their frontier.

SKILL BUILDER

Being a Good Citizen

On January 20, 1961, President John Kennedy gave a plan to the American people. He talked about some problems the nation faced—at home and in the world outside. He urged Americans to try to solve these problems. Then he said:

In the long history of the world, only a few generations have been given the role of defender of freedom in time of great danger. I do not shrink from this responsibility. I welcome it. . . . The energy, the faith, the devotion which we bring to this task will light our country and all who serve it. The glow from that fire can truly light the world.

And so, my fellow Americans, ask not what your country can do for you. Ask what you can do for your country.

Students paint trash containers, so that people will not litter.

With these words, President Kennedy told the American people what he thought they should be willing to do as citizens. He told them how valuable their freedom as Americans was. He told them that they must work to defend this freedom and to make sacrifices to keep it. They must work for their country, not expect their country to work for them.

President Kennedy thought that being a good citizen called for giving something to one's country. How does a person give something? There are several ways. Obeying the law is one. Voting for leaders is another. So is joining in community activities that make life better. Can you think of anything else people should do to be a good citizen?

Words to Know

Use each of the words listed below in a sentence.

conserve	energy crisis	inflation	resign
discrimination	feminist	pollution	solar energy
energy	import		

Facts to Review

1. Name two programs that John F. Kennedy worked on as President.
2. What was the "war on poverty"?
3. In what way was the war in Vietnam like the Civil War?
4. What other groups besides blacks stepped forward to demand their rights in the 1960's and 1970's?
5. What are some different views people have about the "space race?"
6. What was Watergate? What effect did Watergate have on President Nixon?
7. How did the women's rights movement grow in the 1970's?
8. How did the growth of the United States create new problems? How have Americans dealt with these problems?
9. Do you agree with this statement? "There is no 'right' answer to which kind of life American women should lead." Why or why not?
10. What would you say are the most important challenges the U.S. faces in the future?

Things to Think About

1. Choose an event since 1976 that Americans can look on with pride. Pretend it is 2076 and the people running the 300th birthday celebration of the U.S. have asked you to make a poster showing this event. Draw the poster.
2. Think about how much energy you use every day. Make a list of ways you could conserve energy.

UNIT REVIEW

Using New Words

On a piece of paper write the paragraph below. Fill in the blanks with the correct word from the list.

boycott   demonstration   nonviolence
civil rights   feminists

The ___ movement began in the U.S. because some groups of people were receiving unfair treatment. In one such group were blacks in Montgomery, Alabama. They staged a ___ of the buses to stop having to sit in separate sections. Their leader was Martin Luther King, Jr., who preached using ___ in fighting for one's rights. In another group demanding equal rights were the ___, who wanted full equality for women in our society. They often gathered in large numbers to hold a ___ where they would make their demands.

Thinking About the Unit

1. Compare the Cold War to World War Two. Who were our enemies in each? How was each war fought? How did each war change life for Americans?
2. You have probably watched many hours of television already in your lifetime. What is your opinion of TV? Is it helpful? Harmful? Both? Make a list of reasons to support your opinion. Discuss these reasons with your classmates, parents, and teachers. Does everyone agree? Why or why not?
3. Martin Luther King, Jr., had a dream of a United States without discrimination. What dreams, hopes, and plans do you have? Are there changes or improvements that you would like to see made? What things would you like to do? How do you think the heritage of America will help you have the future you want?

Sharpening Your Skills

1. Special charts are used to give us certain kinds of information. What kinds of information can we get from a flow chart?

For which item below might a flow chart be helpful?
a. The sizes of cities.
b. The steps in preparing a report.
c. How steel is made.

2. Write a paragraph in which you answer this question: How would you describe a good citizen?

Expanding Your Knowledge

1. Make a collage to show what life was like in the 1950's. Include items that tell us about world problems, the building boom, the music, the coming of television, and the civil rights movement.

2. Pretend you are a television reporter. You are interviewing people on the street about one of the civil rights movements in the U.S. Make up a list of questions to ask. Remember, you want to get both sides of the story.

3. Make a list of things that you think Americans can be proud of. Cut out or draw pictures to illustrate each item.

4. In the 1940's, people laughed at the idea of going to the moon. In the 1960's, the first humans set foot there. What discovery, exploration, or invention seems impossible today? Think of something that you believe could happen in the next 20 years. With your classmates, write a skit about this event.

Your Own History

Plan a tour of your town or neighborhood. Include some places that tell about the past—historic buildings, memorials listing military people who gave their lives in a war, places made famous by the people who used them. Include some places that make your town special—a pretty park, a famous view, a neighborhood where Americans have strong roots in another culture. Include a place that shows something about the future of your community—a new building, a clean-up program, a preservation project.

Write a script that a guide could use when taking visitors on the tour you have planned. Invite another class to go on your tour.

27 Neighbors to the North and South

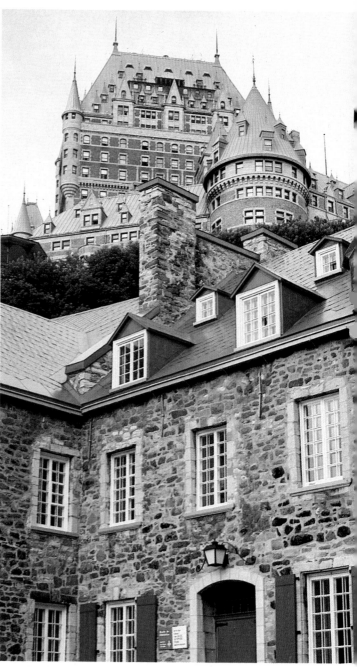

A long canoe floats down a wilderness river. It is paddled by several weary men. Suddenly the men let out a great cheer. They have reached their goal—the mighty Pacific Ocean. Their leader, Alexander Mackenzie, is the first out of the canoe on the shore. The men talk happily in both English and French. Then Mackenzie writes these words on a rock:

Alexander Mackenzie
From Canada by land
22 July 1793

Mackenzie and his men were the first whites to cross North America by land. Their journey took place 12 years before Lewis and Clark reached the Pacific in 1805 (see pages 203–206).

Alexander Mackenzie explored the Canadian wilderness. He was one of many explorers to discover the vast beauty of the United States' neighbor to the north—Canada.

CANADA

What sort of country is Canada? In size it is the second largest nation in the world. Only the Soviet Union is larger.

Like the U.S., Canada extends from the Atlantic to the Pacific. But Canada extends more than 600 miles (966 *kilometers*) farther east than Maine, the easternmost part of the U.S. To the north, Canada borders on yet a third ocean, the Arctic. At its most northerly point, it is only 500 miles (*805 kilometers*) from the North Pole.

On page 404: Tourists visit Mexico today to see buildings made more than a thousand years ago by the Maya Indians (left).
In Canada, buildings put up by French settlers 300 years ago are used today as hotels and restaurants (right).

Like the U.S., Canada is a fairly young country. Since Canada was once a colony of Britain, many of its residents speak English.

But unlike the U.S., Canada has another official language—French. The French were the first Europeans to settle Canada (see pages 106–111). Many Canadians today still speak French and have their own customs.

In government Canada kept its ties to Britain for many years. Unlike the American colonists, Canadians did not fight a revolution to win their independence.

Being farther north, Canada also has a much harsher climate than the U.S. This harsh climate discouraged many people from settling in Canada. Most of the immigrants from Europe who came to North America in the 1800's chose the milder climate of the U.S. Though Canada is larger than the U.S., it has only one tenth as many people. Most Canadians live in the southern part of their country, near the U.S. border. Today vast parts of Canada are still wilderness.

Despite these differences, the two countries have grown in similar patterns. In both countries, pioneers settled the frontiers. Cities with factories and industry grew up around pioneer settlements. Today the two neighbors are close friends.

Let's look at the history of this good neighbor.

Explorers and First People

As you read in Chapter 3, the first people in North America were Indian groups who thousands of years ago crossed a land bridge from Asia to Alaska. Another group of people called the Eskimo, or Inuit, came as recently as 5,000 years ago. The Inuit people live in the cold northern parts of Canada and Alaska.

The first Europeans to visit Canada were Viking sailors who came about the year 1000 A.D. (see pages 53–55). These hardy explorers did not stay in the New World.

You have also read about the explorers from Britain, France, and the Netherlands who came to Canada in the 1500's and 1600's (see pages 76–79). John Cabot sailed for the British. Henry Hudson sailed first for the Dutch and then for the British. Jacques Cartier and Samuel de Champlain sailed from France.

New France

Champlain founded the colony of the New France in 1608 (see pages 106–108). New France did not attract many people looking for land. The main business of the colony was the fur trade.

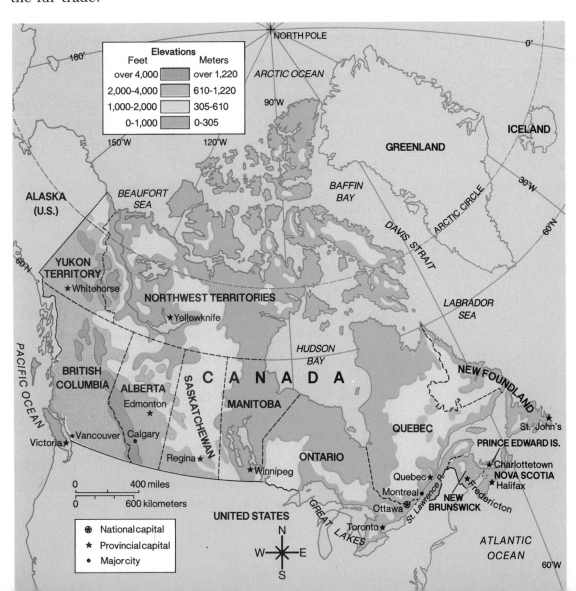

The furs were trapped by Indians deep in the Canadian wilderness. French traders traveled up the rivers to trade for the furs. The traders depended on men called *voyageurs (voy-ah-*ZHER*)* to get them up the rivers.

Voyageurs were the river men of early Canada. With their powerful arms and chests, voyageurs could paddle all day and never get tired. They loved to sing their French songs as they paddled through the wilderness.

The voyageurs' canoes were much larger than present-day canoes. They were 30 feet *(about 10 meters)* long and six feet *(about two meters)* wide. One canoe could carry several tons of furs and took eight or 10 men to paddle up the rivers. The canoe was light enough, though, to be carried by two or three men around waterfalls or other river obstacles. This canoe-carrying was called *portage*, a word still used in canoeing today.

The voyageurs made their canoes out of a wood frame covered with birchbark. If a rock made a hole in the canoe, the voyageurs would simply cut some bark from a birch tree and sew it over the hole.

Canoes were the best way to get around Canada in the early days. As in the U.S., the rivers and lakes were the first highways.

Most settlements in New France were built next to rivers. Farmers called *habitants (ah-bee-*TAN*)* cleared the land in long narrow strips from the riverbank into the woods. Today the land is still farmed this way in Quebec.

The two main towns of New France were Quebec and Montreal. Both cities are on the St. Lawrence River. French settlers built houses and churches similar to the ones they had left behind in France. The city of Quebec sits high on a bluff above the river. It has a wall around it, as do the old cities of Europe.

Life in New France was hard. The winters were long and bitterly cold, but the settlers worked to make life as comfortable as possible.

One such settler who deserves to be remembered was Mother Marie of the Incarnation, a nun in Quebec. She came from France to run a school for Indian children. Mother Marie learned Indian languages so she could talk to the children. Then she wrote books for them to read in their own languages.

Mother Marie came from a famous family of weavers in France. In Quebec she taught her skills to other nuns and Indians. They used furs and leather to make clothes and moccasins.

This painting of Quebec was made in 1688. It shows ships carrying goods in and out of New France on the St. Lawrence River.

France and Britain

About 1670, British fur traders set up a company called the Hudson's Bay Company. The company claimed vast amounts of land in the north. Much of this land was also claimed by the French.

Over the years, the French and British quarreled over Canada and other matters. Finally the quarrels led to war.

You read about the war, called the French and Indian War, on pages 141–142.

The most important battle of the war took place in 1759 at Quebec. The British, led by General Wolfe, had the city cut off from the river. Still the French, led by General Montcalm, believed they were safe inside the walled city.

One night the British set out to sneak up the steep cliff from the river. They were stopped by a French guard who called out, "Who goes there?" One of the British soldiers answered the guard in perfect French. Then the British surprised the guard.

In the morning, the French found the British army camped in the fields outside the city. The French marched out to meet them. In the furious battle, both generals, Wolfe and Montcalm, were killed. But the British won. It was the most important battle in Canadian history. Four years later, in 1763, Canada became part of Britain.

British soldiers surprised the French at the Battle of Quebec. This print shows how British troops sneaked up a steep cliff behind the city.

A British Colony

The British changed the name of New France to the **province** of Quebec. (A province is like a state.) Most of the people in Quebec were Catholics. In 1774 the British passed a law called the Quebec Act, which granted freedom of religion and other rights to the French Canadians.

Soon after this, the American Revolution began. Thousands of American colonists called Loyalists did not want to be free from Britain. Many of them fled north to Canada where the British government gave them land. But this bothered the French Canadians. They were afraid Canada would become a mostly English-speaking country.

The conflict between French- and English-speaking people has been a part of Canadian history for many years. It continues to this day. More than anything else, it is what makes Canada so different from the United States.

In 1791 the British tried a new plan for governing Canada. They divided it into two parts. The English-speaking area around Lake Ontario was called Upper Canada. The area around Montreal and Quebec, which was mostly French-speaking, was called Lower Canada.

The English- and French-speaking Canadians did not get along very well. Both groups were frightened, though, by the War of 1812 between Britain and the U.S. (see pages 220–223). American troops invaded Canada, and for years most Canadians were afraid of their growing neighbor to the south.

Becoming a Nation

Around 1840, people in Canada began talking about governing themselves. British leaders favored this idea too.

But several things stood in the way of Canada's becoming a country. Unlike the U.S., Canada was still sparsely settled. People lived far apart from each other. Those in the east felt they had little in common with settlers on the western frontier.

French Canadians were also against the idea. The English-speaking settlers were spread all over Canada. French Canadians, who lived in Quebec, thought they would be better off as one part of a British colony, than as one part of an English-speaking country.

The Civil War in the United States helped Canadians make up their minds (see Chapter 17). Great Britain clearly favored the South. British textile mills depended on cotton from the South. Britain and the United States nearly got into a war over British support of the Confederacy.

This made Canadians fearful. They did not want to get involved in war with their closest neighbor. They were afraid that the U.S. might win the war and take over Canada. This made the different areas of Canada realize that they needed to strengthen themselves by uniting into one country.

In 1867 Canada won self-government, though it still kept many close ties with Britain. Today Queen Elizabeth the Second of Great Britain is also the Queen of Canada, but she has no power in the government.

Like the U.S., Canada has a federal government (see pages 177–178). The central government meets in Ottawa, the capital. The leader of the government is called the prime minister. Each province has its own government, whose leader is called the premier.

Modern Canada

In 1867 Canada was made up of four provinces: Quebec, Ontario, Nova Scotia, and New Brunswick. In the next 50 years, the nation grew to just about its present size of 10 provinces and two enormous wilderness territories (see the map on page 407).

As with the U.S., railroads have been very important to Canada's growth. The Canadian Pacific Railroad, which stretched across the continent, was finished in 1885. The new railroad opened Canada's plains to settlers.

Thousands of settlers came to the plains to farm the rich earth. Like the settlers to the south, whom you read about in Chapter 20, they worked hard, breaking the ground and building their first houses out of sod.

During this period, thousands of settlers came to Canada from Europe. Many settled in the east where there were jobs in the factories of growing cities like Toronto, Hamilton, and London. Ontario became an industrial center much like the nearby North Central region of the U.S.

In the 20th century, the U.S. and Canada have become close friends. The two nations share a border that is more than 3,000 miles *(4,830 kilometers)* long. Many nations have soldiers and barbed wire along their borders. The U.S. and Canada have none. Theirs is the longest border in the world that is not guarded by soldiers.

The first railroad to run across Canada was finished in 1885. It helped bring settlers to farm acres of untouched land in the center of the country.

The wealth of resources along Canada's West Coast have made Vancouver one of the fastest-growing cities in North America.

In the 1950's, the two nations built a project called the St. Lawrence Seaway. Before the seaway was built, big ocean-going ships could not go up the St. Lawrence River very far. The seaway makes it possible for ocean-going vessels to travel up the St. Lawrence, through the Great Lakes to inland ports such as Toronto, Detroit, Chicago, and Duluth, Minnesota.

Today Canada is a thriving and prosperous nation. Oil has been discovered in Alberta and other western provinces. The plains provinces of Alberta, Manitoba, and Saskatchewan produce huge amounts of wheat and other grains. Vast amounts of lumber and paper products come from the Canadian north and west.

Canada is also challenged by some problems that cloud its future. Many French Canadians of Quebec want to form their own separate country. Many people in the western provinces think they should keep more of the money from their oil than they do.

Still Canadians can face the future with hope. They are a people who have carved a nation out of the wilderness. Much like their American neighbors, they are confident that they can meet the challenges that face them.

LATIN AMERICA

Long ago there was a place of beautiful cities and fertile farms. A powerful empire was connected by thousands of miles of roads. There were beautiful temples and buildings covered with gold. A wise government made laws that were obeyed.

Where was this land? On the west coast of South America where an Indian group called the Incas lived for hundreds of years. Long before Columbus landed in the Americas, the Incas lived in an advanced civilization.

The Incas were expert farmers and builders. They built terraced fields on the sides of the steep Andes Mountains. They built irrigation projects, bringing water from far away. They also built roads that went up and down the steep cliffs of the Andes. The Inca roads made up the longest road system ever built in the world until longer ones were built in the 1800's.

Like the Aztec civilization of Mexico (see pages 71–72), the world of the Incas was changed forever by the coming of Europeans to the New World. But out of this mixing of European and Indian have grown the modern nations of a part of the world known as Latin America.

These ruins of an ancient Inca city are high in the Andes Mountains. The city was built hundreds of years before Columbus came to the Americas.

The Conquistadores

In the years after Columbus' voyages, the Spanish king sent soldiers to the New World. The soldiers were called *conquistadores (kahn-*KEES-*tah-doh-rayz),* which means conquerors. Hernan Cortes, who conquered the Aztecs in Mexico, was perhaps the most able of these soldiers. But there were others.

In the 1530's, conquistadores led by Francisco Pizarro conquered the Incas. Pizarro's men shipped tons of gold and silver back to Spain. But the conquistadores were greedy for more. They quarreled among themselves. Pizarro himself was killed by other soldiers in a fight for power and gold.

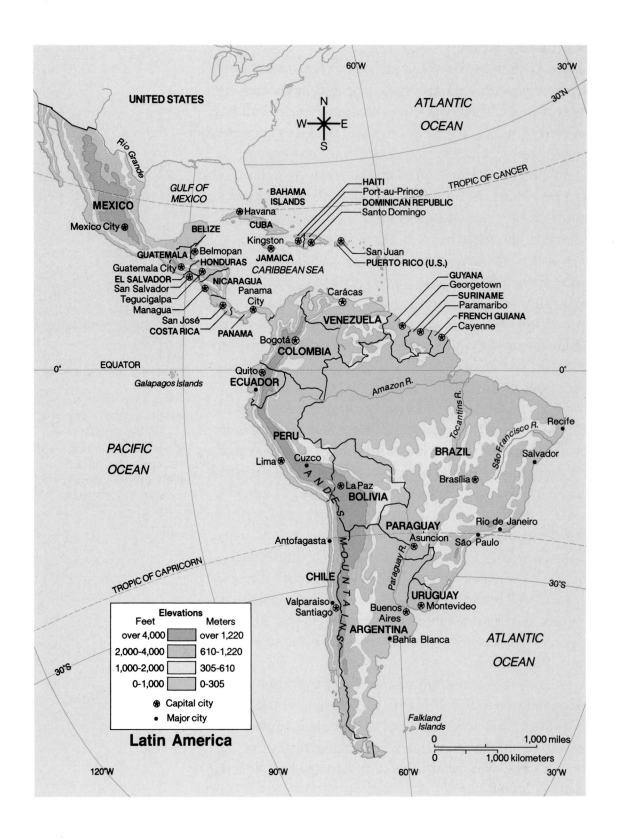

Latin America

UNITED STATES

ATLANTIC OCEAN

N
W — E
S

30°N

TROPIC OF CANCER

GULF OF MEXICO

BAHAMA ISLANDS

HAITI
Port-au-Prince
DOMINICAN REPUBLIC
Santo Domingo

MEXICO

⊛ Havana

Mexico City ⊛

CUBA

Kingston ⊛

San Juan
PUERTO RICO (U.S.)

BELIZE

Belmopan ⊛

GUATEMALA

Guatemala City ⊛

HONDURAS

JAMAICA

CARIBBEAN SEA

EL SALVADOR
San Salvador
Tegucigalpa
Managua

NICARAGUA

Panama City

San José
COSTA RICA

PANAMA

Carácas

VENEZUELA

GUYANA
Georgetown
SURINAME
Paramaribo
FRENCH GUIANA
Cayenne

Bogotá ⊛

COLOMBIA

EQUATOR

0°

Quito ⊛

ECUADOR

Galapagos Islands

Amazon R.

Tocantins R.

São Francisco R.

Recife

PERU

PACIFIC OCEAN

Lima ⊛

Cuzco

A N D E S

BRAZIL

Salvador

La Paz ⊛

Brasília ⊛

BOLIVIA

PARAGUAY

Rio de Janeiro

Antofagasta

Asuncion ⊛

São Paulo

Paraguay R.

TROPIC OF CAPRICORN

CHILE

M O U N T A I N S

URUGUAY

Montevideo ⊛

30°S

Valparaiso ⊛
Santiago ⊛

Buenos Aires ⊛

ARGENTINA

Bahía Blanca

ATLANTIC OCEAN

30°S

Rio Grande

Elevations

Feet		Meters
over 4,000		over 1,220
2,000-4,000		610-1,220
1,000-2,000		305-610
0-1,000		0-305

⊛ Capital city
• Major city

Falkland Islands

1,000 miles

0

0

1,000 kilometers

120°W

90°W

60°W

30°W

60°W

30°W

The soldiers stayed in the New World, and soon other settlers came too. One part of South America, Brazil, was claimed by the king of Portugal. Portuguese soldiers conquered the Indians and settled Brazil in these years.

The Spanish and Portuguese settlers brought their languages and customs. Both the Spanish and Portuguese languages come originally from Latin, the language of ancient Rome and the Roman Catholic Church. Spain and Portugal also took most of their laws from the laws of Rome and the Roman Catholic Church. Because of this Latin influence, the part of the New World settled by Spain and Portugal is known as Latin America.

Colonial Life

Most of the people from Spain and Portugal who settled in the New World lived in cities. They built beautiful, spacious homes like those they left behind. Mexico City and Lima, Peru, were both large cities before there were towns of any size in the British colonies in North America.

The settlers also started ranches called *haciendas (ahs-ee-*EN*-duhs)*. A hacienda was like a small village. The owner lived in a great house that was built around a patio or courtyard. Servants lived in small houses nearby and worked in the fields, shops, and mills.

Since both Spain and Portugal were Catholic countries, the Catholic Church was very important in colonial life. The Church was in charge of education.

In government there was no democracy in the colonies of Latin America. A representative of the king made all the laws. In addition, people were not considered equal.

There were four groups or classes of people in the Spanish colonies. The upper class was made up of people born in Spain. Just beneath them were people called *Creoles (*KREE*-ohlz)*, who were born of Spanish parents, but in the New World. People in the third group were called *mestizos (meh-*STEE*-zohs)*. They were people of mixed Spanish and Indian background. The last group was made up of Indians and black slaves who were brought over from Africa.

The Spanish colonies of Latin America were different from the 13 British colonies in several ways. First, the British colonies had some democracy. Second, while the British colonies had slavery, they had nothing like the class system of Latin America. Third, in North America, the settlers and Indians were enemies and lived apart. In Latin America, the settlers and Indians lived closer together.

Wherever they lived, the Spanish settlers and the Indians created a new culture. Each group made important contributions. The Spanish brought horses, cows, and sheep to the New World, where none of these animals existed. They brought crops like sugarcane and bananas. They brought their culture and their Catholic religion.

The Indians contributed important crops like corn, potatoes, tomatoes, and avocados. They were advanced farmers whose crops are grown all over the world today.

Many of the fruits and vegetables sold in this Mexican market were first grown by Indians hundreds of years ago.

Toward Independence

Spain and Portugal ruled Latin America for almost 300 years. Then, in the beginning of the 1800's, the people of Latin America started a series of revolutions that led to independence.

Laws made by the Spanish king were a cause of the revolutions. The king had very strict rules about trade with other countries. People in the Spanish colonies believed these laws were unfair and hurt trade.

Latin Americans also followed closely the revolt of the 13 colonies in North America against Britain. The independence of the United States started people in Latin America thinking about freedom from Spain. But there were still many people in Latin America who supported the Spanish king.

Then, at the beginning of the 1800's, a powerful general named Napoleon Bonaparte came to power in France. He soon conquered Spain and other countries in Europe. Napoleon made his brother king of Spain. Latin Americans felt no loyalty to this new king.

Toussaint L'Ouverture was a general who helped Haiti win freedom from France.

The Liberators

The first successful revolution in Latin America was not against Spain. It took place in the island nation of Haiti in the West Indies. There black slaves revolted and defeated the French who ruled the colony.

The leader of the Haitians was a former slave named Toussaint L'Ouverture (TOO-*san* LOO-*vair*-TOOR). Toussaint was one of the great generals of his time. After one battle, a French general said in amazement, "Toussaint can find an opening in our lines wherever he chooses." That's how Toussaint got his nickname "L'Ouverture," which means "The Opener."

Toussaint did not live to see his country win its freedom. But soon after his death in 1803, Haiti became the first independent country in Latin America.

General José San Martín leads his troops across the icy Andes Mountains. He helped win freedom for Argentina in 1817.

Simón Bolívar, "The Liberator"

The great hero of the war against Spain was Simón Bolívar (*see*-MOHN *boe*-LEE-*var*). This brilliant general is called "The Liberator" because he liberated (freed) several countries from Spanish rule.

Bolívar knew the advantage of surprise in fighting the Spanish. In 1819 the Spanish army held the city of Bogotá (*boe-go*-TAH) in Colombia. Bolívar decided he could surprise the Spanish by crossing the Andes in the dead of winter. When people told him this was impossible to do, the general replied, "Where goats go, my army can go!"

Bolívar and his army set out on the long march to Bogotá. First they walked through a swamp in the rainy season. For a week, the soldiers waded through water and mud that was often waist deep.

Then they got to the Andes. In the dead of winter, the army marched up the icy trails. They scaled steep cliffs and walked through fierce blizzards. Many died on the way. But finally Bolívar's army reached Bogotá. He easily defeated the surprised and disorganized Spanish army.

In Argentina and Chile, two other heroic generals also lead a march across the Andes. José San Martín (*ho*-SAY *san mar*-TEEN) freed Argentina from Spanish rule. San Martín then helped Bernardo O'Higgins free Chile. Later the people of Brazil won their independence from Portugal.

Spain's last colonies in Latin America were Cuba and Puerto Rico. In 1898 the U.S. defeated Spain in the Spanish-American War. Cuba became an independent country, and Puerto Rico became a possession of the U.S. (see pages 333–336).

Mexico

Mexico's revolution began in 1810. A Catholic priest named Father Miguel Hidalgo (*mee*-GEL *ee*-DAHL-*go*) led a revolt of poor farmers and Indians against the Spanish. Father Hidalgo was captured and killed, but others took his place and the revolt spread. Finally, in 1821, Mexico won its independence.

In its early years as a nation, Mexico was a very large country. It included Texas, California, and the rest of the U.S. Southwest. But in two wars, Mexico lost all of that land to the United States (see pages 208–209, 211–213).

This painting honors the poor people of Mexico who fought for independence in 1910.

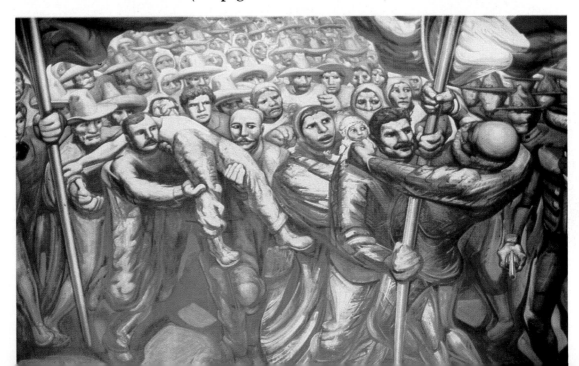

In 1910 another revolution broke out. For years Mexico had been ruled by a dictator whose government was dishonest. (A **dictator** is a ruler who has the power to say how everything will be run in a country.)

Many poor farmers had no land because most of the land was owned by a few rich people. This revolution lasted 10 years and left more than one million Mexicans dead. But out of it came the constitution of 1917 that made Mexico a democratic nation. In the years that followed, thousands of poor farmers received land to farm. Thousands of workers received the rights to bargain and to strike.

Today Mexico is a strong, growing country. Oil has recently been discovered and promises to bring great wealth to the Mexican people. Mexico has a strong, stable government, and the Mexican people take great pride in their democratic traditions.

The discovery of oil in Mexico has brought new wealth to the country.

Dictators

In the years following independence, many Latin American countries had trouble making democracy work. Often governments were controlled by a few rich people. These people made laws that helped themselves, but did not always help the rest of the people. Sometimes a powerful general would take over the government and rule with a strong hand. Many dictators ruled in Latin America in these years.

Latin America and the United States

The United States welcomed the new, independent countries of Latin America in the 1820's. But American leaders were afraid that other European countries would try to take over Spain's former colonies.

In 1823 President James Monroe told the Europeans to stay out of the entire Western Hemisphere. This statement was called the Monroe Doctrine. (A **doctrine** is a rule or a teaching.) In his statement, President Monroe said that no European nation could start a new colony in the Americas. In return, American armies would stay out of Europe. The Monroe Doctrine has been a part of U.S. dealings with other countries ever since.

The United States has had close ties with its southern neighbors for many years. In the 1880's, the U.S. and Latin American nations met in the Pan-American Union (*pan* means "all"). This group works to help the nations of the Americas work closely together. Later another group called the Organization of American States was formed. The OAS works like a United Nations for the Americas.

Sometimes the U.S. has been closely involved with Latin America. The United States sent soldiers and ships to Latin America to bring order in troubled times. This stirred a great deal of anger in Latin America. Many Latin Americans thought it was wrong for the U.S. to send soldiers into their country.

In the last 50 years, the U.S. has tried to be a good neighbor. In the 1930's, President Franklin D. Roosevelt promised that the U.S. would stay out of Latin America. Later President John F. Kennedy started the Alliance for Progress. This program sent tools, medicine, and money to Latin American nations to help improve life there.

Latin America today mixes the old and the new. The top picture shows Colombian farmers using an ox-drawn plow. In the bottom picture, a Mexican farmer tests new equipment at an experimental farm.

Buenos Aires, in Argentina, has modern skyscrapers and green parks. But, like many Latin American cities, it also has large slums.

One Latin American nation, Cuba, has been a problem for the U.S. In 1959 Fidel Castro became the ruler of Cuba. Castro was a Communist who made a close alliance with the Soviet Union. In 1962 the U.S. and the Soviet Union almost went to war over Cuba. Today the U.S. and Cuba are still not friendly. Many Cubans who oppose Castro have left Cuba and come to live in the United States.

Latin America Today

In some ways, the nations of Latin America are rich lands. Some have oil and other valuable natural resources. Most have modern cities with booming factories.

But in other ways, Latin America is faced with many challenges. Many people there are still very poor. Some do not get enough to eat and do not have decent homes. Democracy is still not widespread in Latin America. Violence is too often a part of government.

Some nations, like Mexico, have made more progress than others. With the help of its neighbors and organizations like the United Nations, many Latin American countries are working to meet the challenges they face. The goals of peace and progress are ones that all the people of the Americas—North and South—can work for.

INDIAN PRESIDENT OF MEXICO

Benito Juarez (beh-NEE-toh WAHR-*ehs*) was born in a poor Indian village, but he grew up to become the first Indian president of Mexico. Young Benito learned to read and write in a church school. He proved to be an excellent student and, after years of study, became a lawyer.

Juarez went into politics and quickly made a name for himself. Many people in politics in Mexico's early days spoke loudly and made great promises. Juarez was quiet, and impressed people with his honesty and respect for the law.

In the 1850's, he was elected governor of the state of Oxaca (*wha*-HA-*ka*). Indians came from miles away to see one of their own take over this important office. Though they were very poor, many brought gifts for Juarez. Since the Indians had no place to stay in the capital, Juarez asked them to stay in the governor's palace.

In 1858 Juarez became president of Mexico. These were troubled times in Mexican politics. A civil war took place. Foreign soldiers invaded Mexico. Several times Juarez had to hide out in remote areas. But he promised the Mexican people he would never leave his country to seek safety, and he never did.

With great courage and effort, Juarez held the government of Mexico together in these years. He upheld the law, improved the country's finances, and built many roads and schools.

When he died in 1872, Mexicans mourned his loss. Today he is still honored as a great patriot of Mexico. The city of Juarez, which lies across the border from El Paso, Texas, is named for this hero of Mexico.

Benito Juarez

Reviewing Maps

In other Skill Builders in this book, you have learned how to "read" maps. You have learned how to use a map scale, a compass rose, and a map key. You have learned to use lines of latitude and longitude to locate a spot. You have learned to use different kinds of maps, such as political and climate maps.

Here is a map of Canada, which is made up of 10 provinces, the Yukon Territory, and the Northwest Territories. This map combines geographical and political features.

Use the map to answer the questions below. If you have trouble, turn back to the Skill Builders on pages 27 and 80.

1. In which provinces does the elevation climb above 4,000 feet *(1,220 meters)*?

2. What is the national capital of Canada? What province is it in?

3. About how many miles is Ottawa (45°N, 76°W) from Winnipeg (50°N, 97°W)? About how many kilometers?

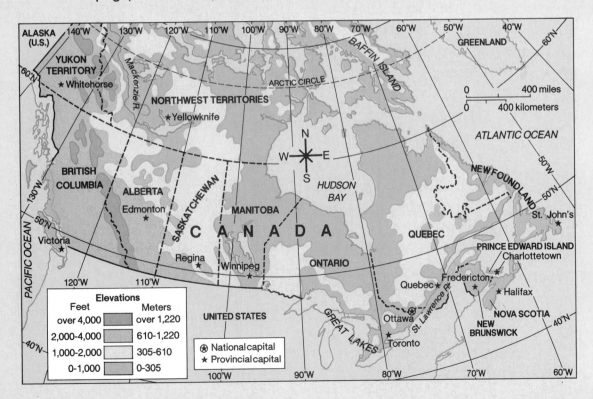

Words to Know

Use each of the words listed below in a sentence.

dictator   doctrine   province

Facts to Review

1. Who was Alexander Mackenzie?
2. How does Canada compare with other nations in size?
3. What are the two languages of Canada?
4. Who were the *voyageurs*? Who were the *habitants*?
5. What was the result of the important 1759 battle of the French and Indian War?
6. What is unusual about the U.S.-Canada border?
7. Why is the part of the New World settled by Spain and Portugal called Latin America?
8. What did Spanish settlers and Indians each contribute to a new culture?
9. Where did the first successful revolution in Latin America take place? Who led the revolutionaries?
10. How did Simón Bolívar surprise the Spanish?

Things to Think About

1. Think about the three neighbors—Canada, the U.S., and Mexico. Can you name three things they have in common and tell how these things might encourage them to be good neighbors?
2. During colonial times, the U.S., Canada, and Mexico were ruled by European nations. Tell how you think one of the three countries might be different today if it had not become independent.
3. You have read about many different explorers in this book. What kinds of skills do you think an explorer should have? What kind of person should he or she be? List the qualifications you think an explorer must have.

THE PRESIDENTS OF THE UNITED STATES

President	**George Washington**	**John Adams**	**Thomas Jefferson**
Born-Died	1732-1799	1735-1826	1743-1826
Years in Office	1789-1797	1797-1801	1801-1809
Party	None	Federalist	Democratic-Republican
Home State	Virginia	Massachusetts	Virginia
Vice President	John Adams	Thomas Jefferson	Aaron Burr
			George Clinton

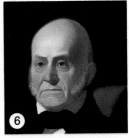

President	**James Madison**	**James Monroe**	**John Quincy Adams**
Born-Died	1751-1836	1758-1831	1767-1848
Years in Office	1809-1817	1817-1825	1825-1829
Party	Democratic-Republican	Democratic-Republican	Democratic-Republican
Home State	Virginia	Virginia	Massachusetts
Vice President	George Clinton	Daniel D. Tompkins	John C. Calhoun
	Elbridge Gerry		

President	**Andrew Jackson**	**Martin Van Buren**	**William H. Harrison**
Born-Died	1767-1845	1782-1862	1773-1841
Years in Office	1829-1837	1837-1841	1841*
Party	Democratic	Democratic	Whig
Home State	Tennessee	New York	Ohio
Vice President	John C. Calhoun	Richard M. Johnson	John Tyler
	Martin Van Buren		

*Died in office.

President	**John Tyler**	**James K. Polk**	**Zachary Taylor**
Born-Died	1790-1862	1795-1849	1784-1850
Years in Office	1841-1845	1845-1849	1849-1850*
Party	Whig	Democratic	Whig
Home State	Virginia	Tennessee	Louisiana
Vice President	None**	George M. Dallas	Millard Fillmore

President	**Andrew Johnson**	**Ulysses S. Grant**	**Rutherford B. Hayes**
Born-Died	1808-1875	1822-1885	1822-1893
Years in Office	1865-1869	1869-1877	1877-1881
Party	Republican	Republican	Republican
Home State	Tennessee	Illinois	Ohio
Vice President	None**	Schuyler Colfax Henry Wilson	William A. Wheeler

President	**William McKinley**	**Theodore Roosevelt**	**William H. Taft**
Born-Died	1843-1901	1858-1919	1857-1930
Years in Office	1897-1901*	1901-1909	1909-1913
Party	Republican	Republican	Republican
Home State	Ohio	New York	Ohio
Vice President	Garret A. Hobart Theodore Roosevelt	None first term** Charles W. Fairbanks	James S. Sherman

*Died in office.
**None because Vice President filled post of former President.

Millard Fillmore
1800-1874
1850-1853
Whig
New York
None**

Franklin Pierce
1804-1869
1853-1857
Democratic
New Hampshire
William R. King

James Buchanan
1791-1868
1857-1861
Democratic
Pennsylvania
John C. Breckinridge

Abraham Lincoln
1809-1865
1861-1865*
Republican
Illinois
Hannibal Hamlin
Andrew Johnson

James A. Garfield
1831-1881
1881*
Republican
Ohio
Chester A. Arthur

Chester A. Arthur
1829-1886
1881-1885
Republican
New York
None**

Grover Cleveland
1837-1908
1885-1889, 1893-1897
Democratic
New York
Thomas A. Hendricks
Adlai E. Stevenson

Benjamin Harrison
1833-1901
1889-1893
Republican
Indiana
Levi P. Morton

Woodrow Wilson
1856-1924
1913-1921
Democratic
New Jersey
Thomas R. Marshall

Warren G. Harding
1865-1923
1921-1923*
Republican
Ohio
Calvin Coolidge

Calvin Coolidge
1872-1933
1923-1929
Republican
Massachusetts
None first term**
Charles G. Dawes

Herbert C. Hoover
1874-1964
1929-1933
Republican
California
Charles Curtis

*Died in office.
**None because Vice President filled post of former President.

President	Franklin D. Roosevelt	Harry S. Truman	Dwight D. Eisenhower
Born-Died	1882-1945	1884-1972	1890-1969
Years in Office	1933-1945*	1945-1953	1953-1961
Party	Democratic	Democratic	Republican
Home State	New York	Missouri	New York
Vice President	John N. Garner	None first term**	Richard M. Nixon
	Henry A. Wallace	Alben W. Barkley	
	Harry S. Truman		

President	John F. Kennedy	Lyndon B. Johnson	Richard M. Nixon
Born-Died	1917-1963	1908-1973	1913-
Years in Office	1961-1963*	1963-1969	1969-1974***
Party	Democratic	Democratic	Republican
Home State	Massachusetts	Texas	New York
Vice President	Lyndon B. Johnson	None first term**	Spiro T. Agnew***
		Hubert H. Humphrey	Gerald R. Ford

President	Gerald R. Ford	James E. Carter, Jr.	Ronald Reagan
Born-Died	1913-	1924-	1911-
Years in Office	1974-1977	1977-1981	1981-
Party	Republican	Democratic	Republican
Home State	Michigan	Georgia	California
Vice President	Nelson R. Rockefeller	Walter F. Mondale	George Bush

*Died in office.
**None because Vice President filled post of former President.
***Resigned from office.

abolitionist *(ab-uh-LISH-uh-nist)* a person who opposed slavery

A.D. an abbreviation of *Anno Domini,* a Latin phrase meaning "in the year of our Lord"; used to indicate dates following the birth of Jesus Christ

amendment a change in or addition to a law or document such as a constitution

anthem *(AN-thum)* the national song of a country; "The Star-Spangled Banner" is the national anthem of the United States

apprentice *(uh-PRENT-iss)* a person who learns a trade or business by working under another; a beginner or assistant

archaeologist *(ahr-kee-AHL-uh-jist)* a person who studies the cultures of ancient people by digging up and examining their tools, pottery, and other relics

artifact *(AHRT-uh-fakt)* an object made by humans who lived long ago

assassin *(uh-SASS-uhn)* a person who murders someone of special importance

assembly line a special way of producing goods in which work passes from one person or machine to another until the product is completed

atomic bomb an extremely powerful bomb first used in World War Two

B.C. an abbreviation of *Before Christ;* used to indicate dates before the birth of Jesus Christ

bill of rights a list of basic rights and freedoms every person should have; the first 10 amendments to the U.S. Constitution are called the Bill of Rights

blockade to seal off an area to prevent supplies and people from getting through

boycott to refuse to buy, use, or deal with

burgess *(BURR-jess)* during colonial times, a representative in the lawmaking body in Virginia or Maryland

charter a document issued by a king or government giving colonists the right to settle an area

checks and balances the power of the three branches of the federal government to limit, or check, the activities of the other branches

civil rights the rights of a citizen guaranteed by law

civil war a war between different groups of people in the same country

colony *(KAHL-uh-nee)* a settlement ruled by another country

compact an agreement or contract

compromise *(KAHM-pruh-mize)* an agreement reached by sides giving in a little

concentration camp *(kahn-sen-TRAY-shun kamp)* large prison for political enemies, prisoners of war, or others

culture the way of life of a particular group of people; includes their customs, language, religion, science, tools, etc.

customs officers people who collect taxes on goods brought into a country

delegate *(DELL-ih-gut)* a person chosen to represent a group at a meeting

depression *(dih-PRESH-un)* a time when a nation's economy is not working well; usually, there is high unemployment

descendant *(di-SEN-duhnt)* a person who is related to someone who lived long ago

diplomat *(DIP-luh-mat)* a representative from one nation to another

discrimination *(dis-krim-uh-NAY-shun)* unfair treatment of people because they may be different in some way

document *(DAHK-ya-ment)* a written or printed paper that serves as a record or proof of something

elevation *(el-uh-VAY-shun)* the height of the land above sea level

emancipate *(ih-MAN-si-pate)* to set free from slavery

empire   a group of lands under the control of one ruler or country

energy (EN-*er-jee*)   the ability to do work or supply power; energy comes from many sources, including the sun, coal, oil, etc.

Executive Branch (*ig-*ZEK-*yet-iv branch*) the branch of the federal government which sees that laws are carried out; consists of the President and staff

explorer   a person who explores an unknown or little-known place

federal system   the system of government in which states and local governments share powers with a central government

feminist (FEM-*ih-nizt*)   a person who believes women should have the same rights as men

forty-niners   people who traveled to California during the Gold Rush days of 1849

free states   the states in which slavery was not allowed before the Civil War

frontier (*frun-*TEER)   the unsettled part of a country

geographer (*jee-*AHG-*rah-fur*)   someone who studies Earth's natural features and how people use them

heritage (HAIR-*uht-ij*)   traditions and beliefs passed on from one's ancestors

historian (*hiss-*TOR-*ee-uhn*)   a person who studies human events of the past

homesteader (HOME-*stedd-ur*)   a settler who made use of the Homestead Act of 1862, which gave government land to people who promised to work the land

House of Representatives (*house of rep-rih-*ZENT-*uht-ivz*)   the part of Congress in which the number of elected members is determined by the states' populations

immigrant (IM-*ih-grant*)   a person who moves to a new country to live

import   to bring goods into a country from another country

indenture (*in-*DEN-*chur*)   a contract under which a person agreed to work for someone for a set period of time

Industrial Revolution (*in-*DUSS-*tree-uhl rehv-uh-*LOO-*shun*)   the period in history when people began making most things by machine

Judicial Branch (*ju-*DISH-*uhl branch*)   the branch of the federal government that interprets laws and punishes criminals; the Supreme Court and lesser courts

landform   the shape or feature of the land; mountain, plateau, plain

latitude (LAT-*uh-tood*)   the distance north and south of the equator measured in degrees; lines of latitudes are called *parallels*

Legislative Branch (LEJ-*uh-slate-iv branch*) the branch of the federal government that makes laws; includes the House of Representatives and Senate

legislature (LEJ-*uh-slay-chur*)   a body of government that makes laws

line graph   a graph that uses lines to compare amounts

longitude (LAHN-*ji-tood*)   the distance east and west of the Prime Meridian measured in degrees; lines of longitude are called *meridians*

Loyalist (LOY-*uh-lust*)   at the time of the American Revolution, a person who opposed independence and wanted to remain loyal to Britain

majority (*mah-*JOR-*it-ee*)   more than half of those voting; the greater number

manor   in the Middle Ages, a lord's estate; a large house on a large piece of land

meridians (*muh-*RID-*ee-unz*)   the imaginary lines running from the North Pole to the South Pole used to locate places on Earth; lines of longitude

minority (*muh-*NOR-*it-ee*)   less than half of those voting; the lesser number

natural resource (NACH-*uh-ruhl REE-sors*) something found in nature of value to people; forests, wildlife, water, minerals, etc.

navigation (*nav-uh*-GAY-*shun*) planning and charting a ship's course

neutral (NOO-*trul*) not taking sides

nonviolence (*nahn*-VIE-*uh-lenz*) without violence; method of working peacefully

parallels (PAIR-*uh-lelz*) the imaginary east-west lines circling Earth used to locate places; lines of latitude

patriot (PAY-*tree-uht*) a person fiercely loyal to his or her country; at the time of the American Revolution, people who favored independence from Britain

pie graph a graph that uses portions of a circle to compare amounts

pioneer (*pie-uh*-NEER) an early settler

plantation (*plan*-TAY-*shun*) a large farm in the South

plateau (*plah*-TOE) a high flatland

pollution (*puh*-LU-*shun*) wastes that foul or poison the environment

primary source (PRY-*mair-ee sors*) a spoken or written account of an event by a person who witnessed the event

Progressives (*pruh*-GRESS-*ivz*) at the beginning of the 20th century, a group of people who worked for reforms in government and for laws improving safety and health conditions

representatives (*rep-rih*-ZENT-*uht-ivz*) people who are elected in order to act in place of the voters who elect them

reservation (*rez-er*-VAY-*shun*) an area set aside for a special purpose; an area of land set aside for American Indians

revolution (*rehv-uh*-LOO-*shun*) the overthrow of a government by force

secede (*si*-SEED) to withdraw from a group

secondary source (SEK-*uhn-dair-ee sors*) an account of an event by a person who was not present but learned about it secondhand

segregation (*seg-rih*-GAY-*shun*) keeping a group separate from the main group

separation of powers a term referring to the division of power among the three branches of the federal government

settlement house center devoted to improving community life

sharecropper a tenant farmer who pays a share of his or her produce as rent

skilled workers workers with special skills or experience in a trade

slave states the states in which slavery was allowed before the Civil War

social security (SO-*shul si*-KYUR-*uht-ee*) a system established by the federal government to provide retirement benefits

sod a layer of earth containing grass and its matted roots

solar energy (SOW-*luhr* EN-*er-jee*) the energy from the sun

strike to walk off the job until wage and other demands are met

suburbs residential communities near cities

suffrage (SUHF-*rij*) the right to vote

sweatshop a dark, crowded factory where people work long hours for little pay

traitor (TRAYT-*uhr*) a person who betrays his or her country

treaty an agreement between countries

unconstitutional (*uhn-kahn-stuh*-TOOSH-*nuhl*) not in agreement with the Constitution

union (YOO-*nyun*) a group of workers joined together to work for better wages, benefits, and working conditions

unskilled workers workers without special skills

veto (VEET-*oh*) to refuse to agree to

ATLAS

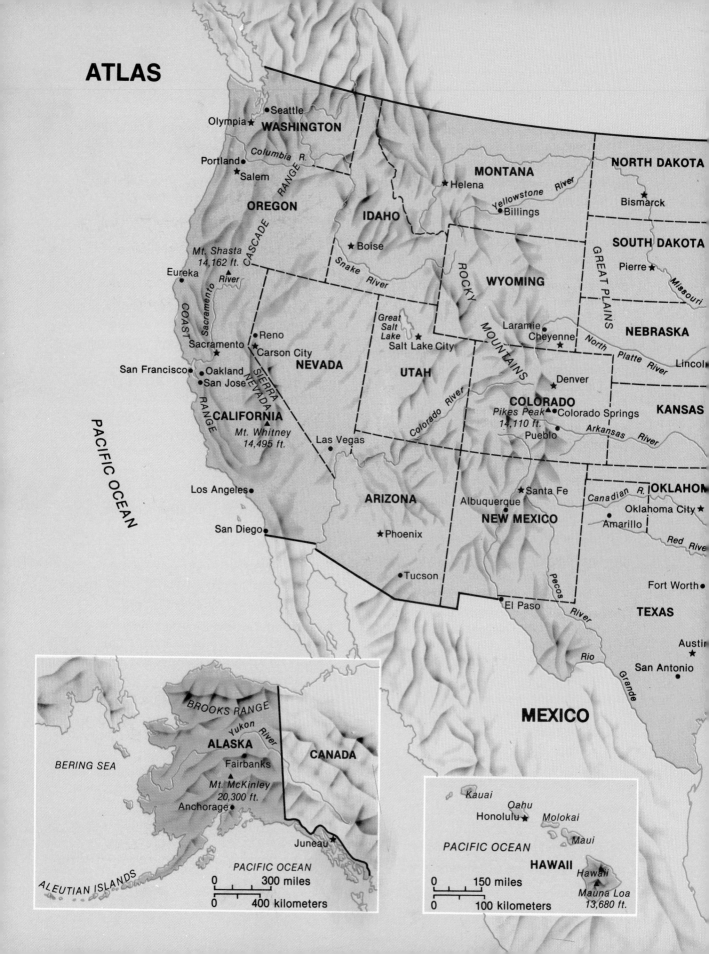

WASHINGTON
• Seattle
Olympia ★
Portland •
★ Salem
OREGON
Columbia R.

MONTANA
★ Helena
Yellowstone River
Billings •

NORTH DAKOTA
Bismarck ★

IDAHO
★ Boise
Snake River

Mt. Shasta
14,162 ft. ▲
Eureka •
Sacramento River

CASCADE RANGE

SOUTH DAKOTA
Pierre ★
Missouri

WYOMING
Great Salt Lake
Salt Lake City ★
Laramie •
Cheyenne ★
North Platte River

GREAT PLAINS

NEBRASKA
Lincoln

Reno •
Sacramento •
★ Carson City
San Francisco •
Oakland •
San Jose •
NEVADA
CALIFORNIA
Mt. Whitney
14,495 ft. ▲
Las Vegas •

UTAH
Colorado River

COLORADO
Denver ★
Pikes Peak ▲
14,110 ft.
Colorado Springs •
Pueblo •
Arkansas River

KANSAS

COAST RANGE
SIERRA NEVADA RANGE
ROCKY MOUNTAINS

PACIFIC OCEAN

Los Angeles •

San Diego •

ARIZONA
Albuquerque •
Phoenix ★
Tucson •

Santa Fe ★
NEW MEXICO

Canadian R.
OKLAHOMA
Oklahoma City •
Amarillo •
Red River

El Paso •
Pecos River
TEXAS
Fort Worth •

MEXICO

Rio Grande

Austin ★
San Antonio •

ALASKA
BROOKS RANGE
Yukon River
CANADA
BERING SEA
Fairbanks •
Mt. McKinley
20,300 ft. ▲
Anchorage •
Juneau ★
ALEUTIAN ISLANDS
PACIFIC OCEAN

0   300 miles
0   400 kilometers

Kauai
Oahu
Honolulu ★   Molokai
Maui
PACIFIC OCEAN
HAWAII
Hawaii
Mauna Loa
13,680 ft.

0   150 miles
0   100 kilometers

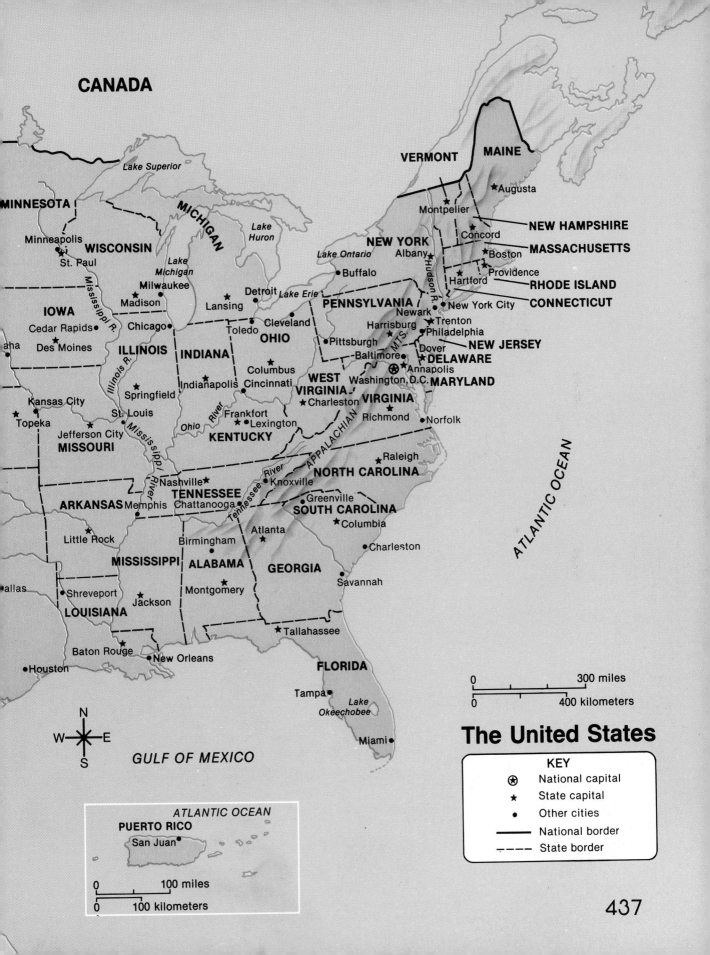

CANADA

Lake Superior

MICHIGAN

MINNESOTA

Minneapolis
⚹✶
St. Paul

WISCONSIN

Lake
Huron

Lake
Michigan

Milwaukee

Madison

Lansing

IOWA

Cedar Rapids

Chicago

Detroit
Lake Erie

Toledo

Cleveland

Lake Ontario

VERMONT   MAINE

★ Augusta

Montpelier
★

NEW HAMPSHIRE

NEW YORK
Albany ★

Buffalo

Concord ★

★ Boston   MASSACHUSETTS

Providence
Hartford ★ RHODE ISLAND

CONNECTICUT

New York City

PENNSYLVANIA

Newark

aha

Des Moines

ILLINOIS   INDIANA

OHIO

Columbus

Springfield

Kansas City

St. Louis

Topeka

Jefferson City

MISSOURI

Indianapolis
Cincinnati

Frankfort ★
Lexington

KENTUCKY

Ohio   River

Mississippi River

WEST
VIRGINIA
★ Charleston

Harrisburg
Pittsburgh

Trenton
★ Philadelphia

Baltimore
Dover
Annapolis
Washington, D.C.

NEW JERSEY

DELAWARE

MARYLAND

VIRGINIA

Richmond ★   Norfolk

Nashville ★

TENNESSEE

ARKANSAS   Memphis Chattanooga

Little Rock ★

MISSISSIPPI   ALABAMA

Jackson ★

Knoxville

Tennessee   River

APPALACHIAN

★ Raleigh

NORTH CAROLINA

Greenville

SOUTH CAROLINA

Atlanta
★

★ Columbia

Charleston

ATLANTIC OCEAN

Birmingham

GEORGIA

Montgomery ★

LOUISIANA

Baton Rouge ★
New Orleans

Houston

Shreveport

allas

Tallahassee ★

Savannah

FLORIDA

Tampa
Lake
Okeechobee

GULF OF MEXICO

N
W ✦ E
S

Miami

0   300 miles

0   400 kilometers

The United States

KEY	
⊛	National capital
★	State capital
•	Other cities
——	National border
- - -	State border

ATLANTIC OCEAN

PUERTO RICO

San Juan

0   100 miles

0   100 kilometers

437

The World

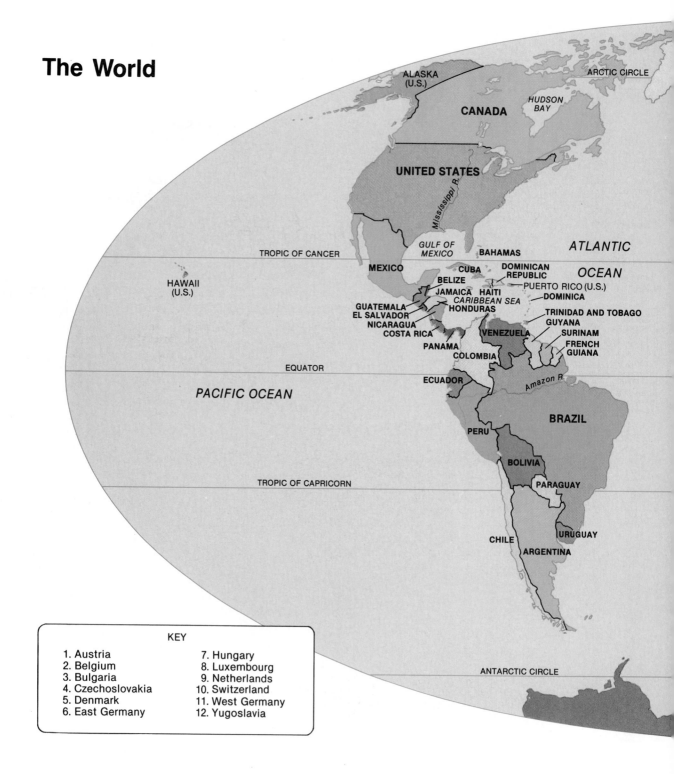

ALASKA (U.S.)

ARCTIC CIRCLE

CANADA

HUDSON BAY

UNITED STATES

Mississippi R.

GULF OF MEXICO

BAHAMAS

ATLANTIC

TROPIC OF CANCER

MEXICO

CUBA

DOMINICAN REPUBLIC

OCEAN

HAWAII (U.S.)

BELIZE

PUERTO RICO (U.S.)

JAMAICA HAITI

DOMINICA

CARIBBEAN SEA

GUATEMALA

TRINIDAD AND TOBAGO

EL SALVADOR HONDURAS

GUYANA

NICARAGUA

SURINAM

COSTA RICA

VENEZUELA

FRENCH GUIANA

PANAMA

COLOMBIA

EQUATOR

ECUADOR

Amazon R.

PACIFIC OCEAN

BRAZIL

PERU

BOLIVIA

TROPIC OF CAPRICORN

PARAGUAY

URUGUAY

CHILE

ARGENTINA

ANTARCTIC CIRCLE

KEY

1. Austria
2. Belgium
3. Bulgaria
4. Czechoslovakia
5. Denmark
6. East Germany

7. Hungary
8. Luxembourg
9. Netherlands
10. Switzerland
11. West Germany
12. Yugoslavia

438

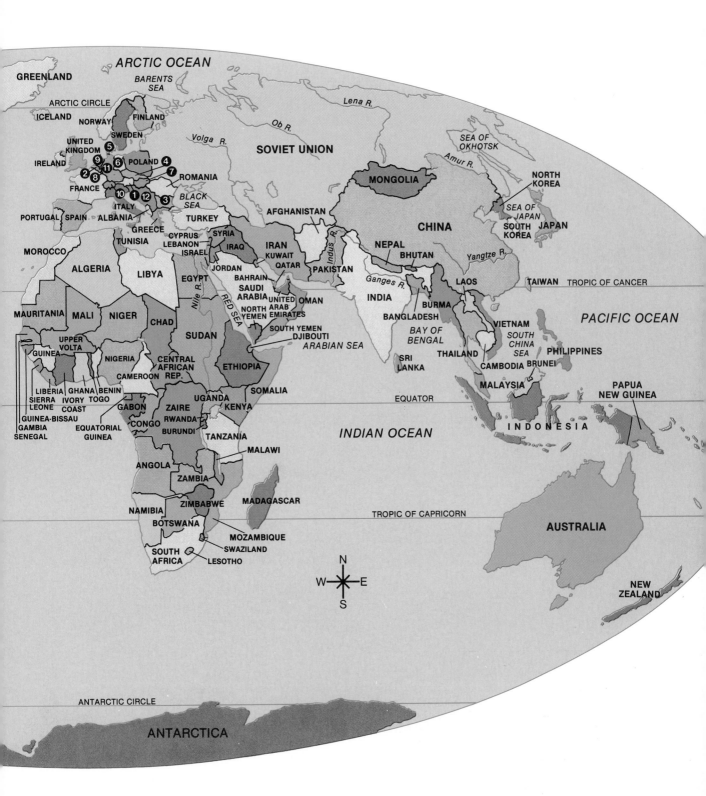

ARCTIC OCEAN

GREENLAND

BARENTS SEA

ARCTIC CIRCLE

ICELAND

NORWAY   FINLAND

SWEDEN

Lena R.

Ob R.

Volga R.

SOVIET UNION

UNITED KINGDOM

IRELAND

5

9

2

8

11

6

POLAND

4

7

ROMANIA

SEA OF OKHOTSK

Amur R.

NORTH KOREA

MONGOLIA

FRANCE

10

1

12

3

BLACK SEA

SEA OF JAPAN

JAPAN

ITALY   ALBANIA

PORTUGAL   SPAIN

GREECE

TURKEY

SOUTH KOREA

CHINA

TUNISIA

CYPRUS

LEBANON

ISRAEL

SYRIA

IRAQ

IRAN

KUWAIT

QATAR

PAKISTAN

NEPAL

BHUTAN

Yangtze R.

MOROCCO

JORDAN

BAHRAIN

Indus R.

LAOS

TAIWAN

TROPIC OF CANCER

ALGERIA

LIBYA

EGYPT

SAUDI ARABIA

UNITED ARAB EMIRATES

OMAN

Ganges R.

INDIA

BURMA

PACIFIC OCEAN

MAURITANIA

MALI

NIGER

CHAD

Nile R.

RED SEA

NORTH YEMEN

SOUTH YEMEN

DJIBOUTI

ARABIAN SEA

BANGLADESH

BAY OF BENGAL

VIETNAM

SOUTH CHINA SEA

PHILIPPINES

UPPER VOLTA

SUDAN

THAILAND

CAMBODIA

BRUNEI

GUINEA

NIGERIA

CENTRAL AFRICAN REP.

ETHIOPIA

SRI LANKA

MALAYSIA

PAPUA NEW GUINEA

CAMEROON

LIBERIA

SIERRA LEONE

GHANA

IVORY COAST

BENIN

TOGO

GABON

ZAIRE

UGANDA

KENYA

SOMALIA

EQUATOR

GUINEA-BISSAU

GAMBIA

SENEGAL

EQUATORIAL GUINEA

CONGO

RWANDA

BURUNDI

TANZANIA

INDONESIA

INDIAN OCEAN

MALAWI

ANGOLA

ZAMBIA

NAMIBIA

ZIMBABWE

BOTSWANA

MADAGASCAR

TROPIC OF CAPRICORN

AUSTRALIA

SOUTH AFRICA

MOZAMBIQUE

SWAZILAND

LESOTHO

N

W   E

S

NEW ZEALAND

ANTARCTIC CIRCLE

ANTARCTICA

439

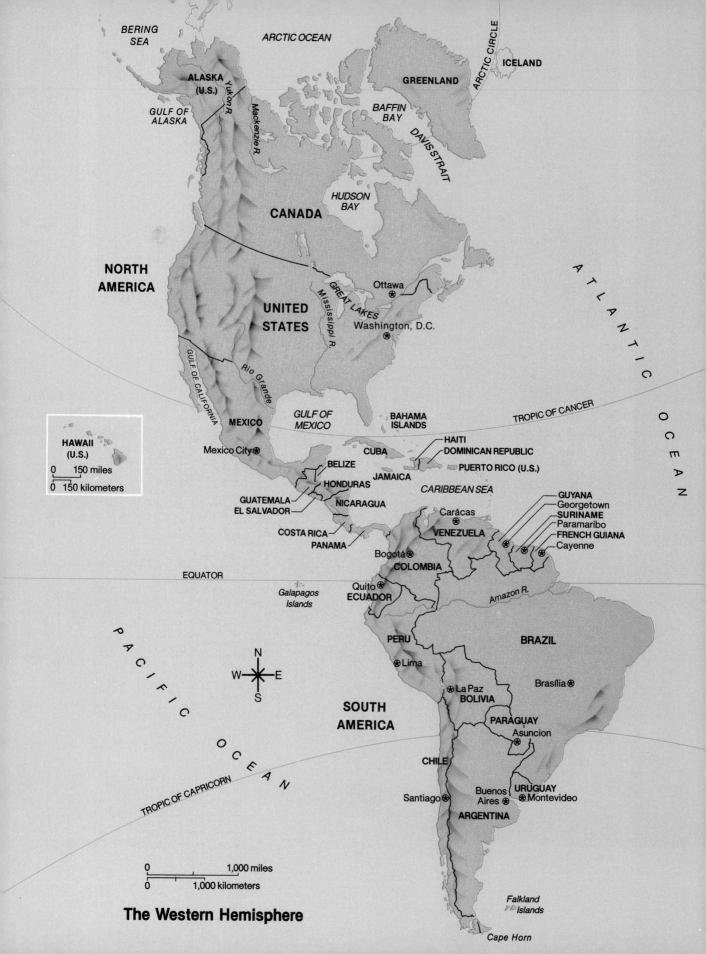

The Western Hemisphere

ACKNOWLEDGEMENTS

Photo Credits: 2–3: SCALA/Editorial Photocolor Archives. **10:** Norman Owen Tomalin (Bruce Coleman). **12:** *t* Michal Heron; *bl* Hella Hammid (Rapho/Photo Researchers); *bc, br* Joan Menschenfreund. **13:** Joan Menschenfreund. **15:** Bruce Roberts (Rapho/Photo Researchers). **17:** Michael Davidson. **20:** L. Foster (Bruce Coleman). **23:** *tl* (detail) William Stanton; *tr* The Houston Center for Amputee Services at The Institute for Rehabilitation and Research; *cr* Fred J. Maroon (Photo Researchers); *b* Russ Kinne (Photo Researchers). **24:** *t* (detail) Jim Balog (Photo Researchers); *b* M.W. Grosnick (Bruce Coleman). **26:** Joan Menschenfreund. **36–37:** Sante Fe Industries Collection. **38, 42:** Philbrook Art Center. **44:** (detail) The Royal Ontario Museum, Toronto, Canada. **45:** American Museum of Natural History, photo by G.F. Ramsey. **47:** *t, bl* (detail) National Collection of Fine Arts, Smithsonian Institution, gift of Mrs. Sarah Harrison; *br* (detail) Thomas Gilcrease Institute of American History and Art, Tulsa, Oklahoma. **49:** American Museum of Natural History. **52:** (detail) "The Vikings" by Frederic Ray, courtesy of the artist and "American History Illustrated." **56:** The Bettmann Archive. **57:** SCALA/Editorial Photocolor Archives. **58:** BBC Hulton Picture Library. **62:** (detail) National Gallery of Art. **63:** Bibliothèque Nationale, France. **66:** The Bettmann Archive. **68:** M.L.A. Strickland, Department of Environment, London; photo courtesy of Aldus Books, Ltd. **72:** *t* American Museum of Natural History, photo by Junius Bird; *b* National Museum of Denmark, Department of Ethnography. **73:** *l* (detail), *r* (detail) Ampliaciones y Reproducciones—MAS, Spain. **75:** *t* Andreas Feininger, Life Magazine, Time Inc.; *b* (detail) Remington Art Museum, Ogdensburg, New York. **78:** The Tate Gallery, London, photo by John Webb. **84:** George Holton (Photo Researchers). **88–89:** The Society of California Pioneers. **90:** Wide World Photos. **93** (detail), **96:** American Heritage Publishing Co. **97:** The John Hancock Mutual Life Insurance Co. **98:** (detail) Museum of Fine Arts, Boston. **99:** The Rhode Island Historical Society. **102:** (detail) The Society of California Pioneers. **105:** State Library of the Czech Socialist Republic. **107:** The Bettmann Archive. **109** (detail), **110:** Glenbow Museum, Calgary, Alberta. **112:** (detail) Museum of the City of New York. **116:** Prints Division, New York Public Library; Astor, Lenox & Tilden Foundations. **119:** Council of the Dorset Natural History & Archaeological Society, Dorset County Museum, Dorchester, Dorset. **120:** Bolton Metropolitan Borough Arts Department. **121:** (detail) Shelburne Museum, Shelburne, Vermont. **122:** (detail) Metropolitan Museum of Art, gift of Edgar William and Bernice Chrysler Garbisch, 1963. **123:** American Antiquarian Society. **124:** Library of Congress. **126:** (detail) Library Company of Philadelphia. **127:** Museum of the City of New York. **128:** (detail) The Henry Francis du Pont Winterthur Museum. **131:** (detail) Rare Books Division, New York Public Library; Astor, Lenox & Tilden Foundations. **136–137:** George F. Mobley, National Geographic, courtesy U.S. Capitol Historical Society. **138:** New York Historical Society. **140:** The Granger Collection, New York. **142:** *t* (detail) Washington/Custis/Lee Collection, Washington & Lee University, Virginia; *b* (detail) Colonial Williamsburg Foundation. **143:** New York Historical Society. **144:** *t* (detail) John Carter Brown Library, Brown University; *b* (detail) Museum of Fine Arts, Boston. **145:** Metropolitan Museum of Art, gift of Mrs. Russell Sage, 1910. **152:** The Bettmann Archive. **155:** (detail) Yale University Art Gallery, Mabel Brady Garvan Collection. **156:** *t, b* Anne S.K. Brown Military Collection, Brown University Library. **157:** (detail) Collection of Iowa State University, photo courtesy of Brandywine River Museum. **159:** Historical Society of Pennsylvania. **160:** Valley Forge Historical Society. **162:** *tl* (detail) New York State Historical Association, Cooperstown; *tr* (detail) Kennedy Galleries, Inc., New York; *b* courtesy of Embassy of Polish People's Republic. **163:** Virginia State Library. **167:** The Bettmann Archive. **172:** Photo by Jack Zehrt, courtesy of the U.S. Capitol. **174:** Historical Society of Pennsylvania. **175:** (detail) Bowdoin College Museum of Art, Brunswick, Maine. **180:** The Old Corner House. **182:** (detail) National Gallery of Art, gift of Edgar William and Bernice Chrysler Garbisch. **183:** (detail) Library of Congress. **188–189:** (detail) Thomas C. Ruckle, Maryland Historical Society. **190:** Washington University Gallery of Art, St. Louis. **194:** (detail) National Gallery of Art, collection of the Honorable Claiborne Pell. **195:** Collection of Carl S. Dentzel. **196:** Museum of the City of New York. **197:** Abby Aldrich Rockefeller Folk Art Center, Williamsburg, Virginia. **198:** National Gallery of Art. **199, 202:** The Bettmann Archive. **205:** Montana Historical Society. **206:** (detail) Woolaroc Museum, Bartlesville, Oklahoma. **207:** Photo courtesy of Native American Painting Reference Library, private collection. **209:** Texana Collection, University of Texas. **211:** Stanford University Museum of Art, Stanford Family Collection. **212:** Daughters of the Republic of Texas Library. **215:** (detail) Thomas Gilcrease Institute of American History and Art, Tulsa, Oklahoma. **218:** The St. Louis Art Museum. **220:** Collection of Irving S. Olds. **221:** The Granger Collection. **222:** (detail) The Peale Museum. **223:** (detail) Collection of the Corcoran Gallery of Art, gift of William Wilson Corcoran. **227:** Russ Kinne (Photo Researchers). **232–233:** Historical Society of Pennsylvania. **234:** Collection of J.B. Speed Art Museum, Louisville, Kentucky. **236:** Courtesy of J.P. Altmayer. **237:** Collection of Edgar William and Bernice Chrysler Garbisch. **239:** (detail) Chicago Historical Society. **241:** *t* The Brooklyn Museum, gift of Miss Gwendolyn O.L. Conkling; *b* National Portrait Gallery, Smithsonian Institution. **242:** *b* Culver Pictures; *b* Metropolitan Museum of Art, gift of I.N. Phelps Stokes, Edward S. Hawes, Alice Mary Hawes, Marion Augusta Hawes, 1937. **243:** (detail) I.N. Phelps Stokes Collection, New York Public Library; Astor, Lenox & Tilden Foundations. **246:** "The Gun Foundry" by John Ferguson Weir, Putnam County Historical Society, Cold Spring, New York. **248:** (detail) Merrimack Valley Textile Museum. **249:** Metropolitan Museum of Art, Edward W.C. Arnold Collection of New York Prints, Maps and Pictures, Bequest of Edward W.C. Arnold, 1954. **250:** Yale University Art Gallery, Mabel Brady Garvan Collection. **253:** Chicago Historical Society. **258:** The Bettmann Archive. **262:** *t* Culver Pictures; *b* Library of Congress. **263:** The Century Association. **264:** The Bettmann Archive. **266:** *t* (detail) National Archives; *b* Library of Congress. **267:** The Bettmann Archive. **270:** Culver Pictures. **272:** Courtesy of J. Cornelius Rathborne. **274–275, 276:** Library of Congress. **277:** *t* The Granger Collection, New York; *b* Culver Pictures. **278:** The Bettmann Archive. **279:** The Granger Collection, New York. **284–285:** John Stobart, Kennedy Galleries, Inc., New York. **286:** Museum of the City of New York. **289:** Nelson Gallery, Atkins Museum, Kansas City, Missouri (Nelson Fund). **290:** *t* The Bettmann Archive; *b* photo by Fred A. Schell, courtesy American Petroleum Institute Photographic & Film Services. **291:** The Bettmann Archive. **293:** Smithsonian Institution. **294–295:** Library of Congress. **296:** National Portrait Gallery, Smithsonian Institution. **300:** Photograph Archives, Division of Library Resources, Oklahoma Historical Society. **302:** (detail) Solomon D. Butcher Collection, Nebraska State Historical Society. **303:** The Bettmann Archive. **304:** *t* (detail) Denver Public Library, Western History Department; *b* David R. Phillips Collection. **305:** "The Homesteader's Wife" by Harvey Dunn, 1916, South Dakota Memorial Art Center Collection, Brookings. **306:** Buffalo Bill Historical Center, Cody, Wyoming. **308:** The Bettmann Archive. **309:** The Granger Collection. **310:** *t* National Anthropological Archives, Smithsonian Institution; *b* The Bettmann Archive. **316:** From the collection of Mr. August A. Busch, Jr., St. Louis, Missouri. **316:** Culver Pictures. **318:** Library of Congress. **320:** International Museum of Photography at George Eastman House. **321:** *t* (detail) Photograph by Jacob A. Riis, Jacob A. Riis Collection, Museum of the City of New York; *b* (detail) George Eastman House Collection. **322:** *l* (detail) California Historical Society Library; *r* (detail) Photograph by Jacob A. Riis, Jacob A. Riis Collection, Museum of the City of New York. **323:** International Museum of Photography at George Eastman House. **324:** Courtesy of Lee Baxandall/District 1199, National Union of Hospital & Health Care Employees RWDSU/AFL-CIO. **325:** Culver Pictures. **326:** Sophia Smith Collection, Smith College. **330–331:** (detail) Fred Pansing, courtesy Museum of the City of New York. **332:** Library of Congress. **334:** Chicago Historical Society. **337:** The Bettmann Archive. **338:** *l* Culver Pictures; *r* (detail) International Museum of Photography at George Eastman House. **339:** (detail) International Museum of Photography at George Eastman House. **342:** National Archives. **343:** *t* John T. McCoy; *b* Imperial War Museum. **344, 345:** National Archives. **347:** The Bettmann Archive. **350:** Estate of Ben Shahn. **352:** *t* The Bettmann Archive.; *b* Brown Brothers, Sterling, Pennsylvania. **353:** (detail) Rudi Blesh Collection, courtesy of Columbia Records. **354:** Brown Brothers, Pennsylvania. **355, 356:** The Bettmann Archive. **357:** Library of Congress. **358:** The Bettmann Archive. **359:** United Press International Photo. **360:** © Walt Disney Productions. **361:** The Bettmann Archive. **364:** National Archives. **366:** Photo by Underwood & Underwood, Inc. **367:** Associated Press Photo. **368:** Pictorial Parade. **369:** Courtesy of Navy Combat Art Collection. **370:** Margaret Bourke-White. **371:** U.S. Military Academy Library. **372:** Arthur Tress (Photo Researchers). **373:** U.S. Army Photo. **378–379:** NASA. **380:** Walter Sanders. **383:** *t* Wide World Photos; *b* Springer/Bettmann Film Archive. **384:** RCA. **385:** (detail) United Press International Photo. **386–387:** *b* Bruce Davidson (Magnum Photos). **387:** *t* Francis Kelley, Life Magazine, Time Inc. **388:** James H. Karales (Magnum Photos). **392:** NASA. **394:** Magnum Photos. **395:** *l* Lee Foster (Globe Photos); *r* Arthur Grace-Sygma. **396:** Thomas Victor. **397:** Hiroyuki Matsumoto (Black Star). **398:** C.L. Chryslin (The Image Bank). **400:** McAllister of Denver (Black Star). **404:** *l* Porterfield-Chickering (Photo Researchers); *r* Burt Glinn (Magnum Photos). **409:** The Granger Collection. **410, 413:** The Public Archives of Canada. **414:** George Hall (Woodfin Camp & Assoc.). **415:** N.H. Cheatham (Photo Researchers). **418:** Porterfield-Chickering (Photo Researchers). **419:** The Bettmann Archive. **420:** *t* The Bettmann Archive.; *b* The Granger Collection. **421, 422:** Robert Frerck (Woodfin Camp & Assoc.). **424:** *t* Carl Frank (Photo Researchers); *b* Robert Frerck (Woodfin Camp & Assoc.). **425:** Lisl Steiner (Photo Researchers). **426:** The Granger Collection. **429:** #1, 2, 4, 5, 6, 7, 8, 10, 12, 13, 14, 15, 18, 20, 21, 22, 24, 26, 27, 28, 29, 30, 32: The National Portrait Gallery, Smithsonian Institution; #3, 9, 17, 19, 25, 31, 38: The Granger Collection; #11: The Bettmann Archive; #16, 36: Tom McHugh (Photo Researchers); #23: Roloc Color Slides; #33: SCALA/Editorial Photocolor Archives; #34: Joseph Martin (SCALA/Editorial Photocolor Archives); #35: United Press International Photo; #37: Don Carl Steffen (Photo Researchers); #39: Dennis Brack (Black Star); #40: Michael Evans (Sygma). **Photo Research:** Joan Scafarello. **Illustration Credits: 48, 64, 65, 71, 254, 292:** Michael Hampshire. **Maps:** General Cartography, Inc. **Charts and Graphs:** Kirchoff/Wohlberg, Inc.